150 *of the* WORLD'S GREATEST
HYMN STORIES

THEN
SINGS
MY SOUL

BOOK TWO

THOMAS NELSON
Since 1798

NASHVILLE   DALLAS   MEXICO CITY   RIO DE JANEIRO   BEIJING

Copyright © 2004 Robert J. Morgan

All rights reserved. No portion of this book may be reproduced, stored in a retrieval system, or transmitted in any form by any means—electronic, mechanical, photocopy, recording, scanning, or other—except for brief quotations in critical reviews or articles, without the prior written permission of the publisher.

Published in Nashville, Tennessee by Thomas Nelson, Inc.

Thomas Nelson, Inc. titles may be purchased in bulk for educational, business, fundraising, or sales promotional use. For information, please email SpecialMarkets@ThomasNelson. com.

Scripture taken from *The Holy Bible*, New King James Version (NKJV). Copyright © 1979, 1980, 1982 by Thomas Nelson, Inc. Used by permission. All rights reserved.

New International Version (NIV) © 1973, 1978, 1984 by International Bible Society. Used by permission of Zondervan Publishing House. All rights reserved.

Contemporary English Version (CEV) of the Bible © 1991 by the American Bible Society. Used by permission.

American Standard Version (ASV). Public domain.

Library of Congress Cataloging-in-Publication Data is available.

ISBN-13: 978-0-78525-168-2
Printed in Canada

08 09 10 11 — 27 26 25 24

TO
Hannah

Table of Contents

Foreword
By Gloria Gaither

I am a child, probably four or five years old. It is Wednesday night, and we are having what we call prayer meeting. But at our little church in the tiny farming village where my father pastors, it is really an informal hour of singing, testimonies, and a short study of a passage of Scripture.

The person "leading the singing" is not a "minister of music" or even a "musician." He is a farmer who has finished his chores, taken a shower, put on a clean cotton shirt and "work pants," and eaten a simple supper with his family before heading off into town to the service.

His wife plays the piano as those gathered in the little white church by Michigan state road M-60 begin to sing.

I am singing, too. I know the familiar words by heart to the first song, "When We All Get to Heaven." But I have my finger in page 444, marking my favorite just in case the song leader says at the end of this song, "Does anyone have a request?"

When he issues his invitation, I am ready. "Page 444!" I say, before anyone else even has time to thumb through the hymnal.

"Turn to page 444," the song leader says with a twinkle in his eye and a smile in my direction. I am suddenly bathed in the warm embrace of acceptance, love, and confirmation. And I sing—do I ever sing!—at the top of my voice.

I love to tell the story of unseen things above,
Of Jesus and His glory, of Jesus and His love;
I love to tell the story because I know 'tis true;
It satisfies my longing as nothing else can do.

Now I am a songwriter myself. I have written my life's journey into nearly a thousand lyrics to the wonderfully accessible tunes my husband has heard in his head. I've watched amazed as my words of praise, discovery, question, and revelation have found their way into other persons' lives, words that at the time seemed so personal to our pilgrimage that I couldn't imagine them helping anyone else.

And I have come to believe that we as a body of struggling, growing, emerging believers need a shared history with God to stockpile against the winters of our lives and the dark nights of the soul. Like the Israelites who carried stones from the bed of the parted Jordan River, we need to have resources with which we can stoop to build an altar in celebration of those times when God "showed up" in our distress. We need to be able to point to these altars—these Ebenezers along our path—when "Satan would buffet," and say to each other and our children, "I know God is with us! He met us *there*, and *there* and *there*. I know He will be faithful in this hour, too."

The words I learned as a child flowed over me like a warm shower. I loved the sound of them, and the embrace of the voices around me singing them. But decades have passed since then. The words and the tune that glued them to my memory have been investigated and scrutinized under the glaring eye of reality. What have I discovered? A resource of truth richer and deeper and broader than I ever could have imagined. As the years have passed, life experiences have spotlighted the validity of different verses for me.

At this juncture of my journey, this is currently my favorite:

> *I love to tell the story for those who know it best*
> *Seem hungering and thirsting to hear it like the rest;*
> *And when in scenes of glory I sing a new, new song,*
> *'Twill be its old, old story that I have loved so long.*

When we tell the eternal story, let's tell more than the punch line. We need the whole song, all the verses and the choruses to serve us as our own story unfolds because—trust me—life is hard, but God is good.

THEN SINGS MY SOUL

BOOK TWO

O Sacred Head, Now Wounded

Based on Medieval Latin poem
Ascribed to Bernard of Clairvaux

Hans Leo Hassler
Harm. by J.S. Bach

1. O sa - cred Head now wound - ed, With grief and shame weighed down,
2. What Thou, my Lord hast suf - fered Was all for sin - ners' gain:
3. What lan - guage shall I bor - row To thank thee, dear - est Friend,

Now scorn - ful - ly sur - round - ed With thorns, Thine on - ly crown;
Mine, mine was the trans - gres - sion, But Thine the dead - ly pain;
For this thy dy - ing sor - row, Thy pit - y with - out end?

How pale thou art with an - guish, with sore a - buse and scorn!
Lo, here I fall, my Sav - ior! 'Tis I de - serve Thy place;
O make me thine for - ev - er, And should I faint - ing be,

How does that vis - age lan - guish Which once was bright as morn!
Look on me with Thy fa - vor, Vouch - safe to me Thy grace.
Lord, let me nev - er, nev - er Out - live my love to thee.

O Sacred Head, Now Wounded

1153

Oh, give thanks to the LORD, for He is good! For His mercy endures forever. Psalm 118:1 (NKJV)

Bernard was born into a knight's family in a French castle in 1090. He was educated in the fashion of medieval aristocracy, but he later felt the Lord calling him to the monastic ministry. Being a born leader, he arrived at the monastery of Cîteaux with thirty other young men whom he had persuaded to join him.

Three years later, Bernard, twenty-five, founded his own monastery at Clairvaux, a town near the Swiss border. Here he would remain the rest of his life. He was a brilliant monk, and in time he advised kings and popes from his monastic cell. Historian Harold O. J. Brown wrote, "The ability of one man without political office or power to change history solely by his teaching and example is without parallel until the sixteenth century when Martin Luther would once again transform Europe from his pulpit and professor's chair in a small town in Saxony."

Bernard fought heresy and helped preserve the doctrine of the Trinity. Yet he also supported Christian military orders such as the Knights Templar—soldiers living under monastic discipline who fought to preserve European Christianity and fight Muslims in the Holy Land. He advocated a militant faith that depended on both sword and Spirit.

This man, then, is a paradox to us. We don't know whether to claim him or disdain him. Perhaps it's best to leave that judgment to God and to appreciate him for his songs, such as this pensive hymn on the sufferings of Christ, "O Sacred Head, Now Wounded."

Here are two lesser-known verses of this hymn. Transport yourself to Bernard's cloister, and hear these words echoing through the dimly lit corridors of the monastery. Consider what the Lord did for you during His six hours on Zion's cross.

Now from Thy cheeks has vanished their color once so fair;
From Thy red lips is banished the splendor that was there.
Grim death, with cruel rigor, hath robbed Thee of Thy life;
Thus Thou hast lost Thy vigor, Thy strength in this sad strife.

My burden in Thy Passion, Lord, Thou hast borne for me,
For it was my transgression which brought this woe on Thee.
I cast me down before Thee, wrath were my rightful lot;
Have mercy, I implore Thee; Redeemer, spurn me not!

From Heaven Above to Earth I Come

Martin Luther, translated by Catherine Windworth

Attr. to Martin Luther

1. From heav'n a - bove to earth I come, to bear good news to ev - ery home; glad tid - ings of great joy I bring, Where - of I now will say and sing.

2. To you, this night, is born a Child Of Mar - y, chos - en moth - er mild; This ten - der Child of low - ly birth, Shall be the joy of all your earth.

3. 'Tis Christ our God, who far on high Had heard your sad and bit - ter cry; Him - self will your Sal - va - tion be, Him - self from sin will make you free.

4. These are the to - kens ye shall mark, The swad - dling clothes and man - ger dark; There shall ye find the young Child laid, By Whom the heav'ns and earth were made.

From Heaven Above to Earth I Come

1531

Then God blessed them, and God said to them, "Be fruitful and multiply; fill the earth and subdue it . . ." Genesis 1:28 (NKJV)

Martin Luther never expected to marry, for he had taken a vow of celibacy as an Augustinian monk. Even after discovering the great Reformation truths of *Scripture Alone, Faith Alone,* he still intended to keep his vow. As the Reformation picked up steam and other monks began to marry, he exclaimed, "Good heavens! They won't give me a wife."

It wasn't just monks who were renouncing their celibacy, however; it was nuns, too. When Luther heard that a group of nuns from a nearby cloister wanted to escape their situation (which amounted to virtual captivity) he agreed to help them, though doing so was a serious violation of the law. Enlisting the aid of a local merchant named Leonard Kopp, sixty, Luther arranged for the nuns to be smuggled out in the empty barrels used to deliver herring to the nunnery. It was a fishy plan if ever there was one, but it worked.

Having liberated these women, Luther now felt responsible for placing them in homes. He managed to find husbands for all but one—Katharina Von Bora. Two years passed, and Luther was deeply troubled by his failure to find her a husband. She was now twenty-six years old, brilliant and effervescent, but still unclaimed.

In a visit to his parents, Luther, forty-two, joked that he might have to marry Katharina himself. His dad heartily endorsed the idea, and, to make a long story short, the two were married on June 27, 1525.

By autumn, Katharina informed Martin that she was pregnant, and Luther cheerfully announced, "My Katharina is fulfilling Genesis 1:28"—the verse about being fruitful and multiplying.

"There's about to be born a child of a monk and a nun," he bragged to friends. Accordingly, little Hans was born on June 7, 1526.

Luther was devoted to his son, and five years later he wrote this Christmas carol for him. Luther called it "a Christmas child's song concerning the child Jesus," and it was sung each year during the Christmas Eve festivities at Luther's massive home— a former Augustinian monastery—on the upper end of Wittenberg's main street.

For over five hundred years it has been one of Lutheranism's greatest carols, delighting children today just as it thrilled little Hans in the sixteenth century.

All People That on Earth Do Dwell

William Kethe   *Genevan Psalter*

1. All peo - ple that on earth do dwell,
2. The Lord, ye know, is God in - deed,
3. O, en - ter then His gates with praise,
4. For why? The Lord our God is good,

Sing to the Lord with cheer - ful voice;
With - out our aid He did us make;
Ap - proach with joy His courts un - to;
His mer - cy is for - ev - er sure;

Him serve with mirth His praise forth tell,
We are His flock, He doth us feed,
Praise laud and bless His Name al - ways,
His truth at all times firm - ly stood,

Come ye be - fore Him and re - joice.
And for His sheep He doth us take.
For it is seem - ly so to do.
And shall from age to age en - dure.

All People That on Earth Do Dwell

1561

Serve the LORD with gladness; Come before His presence with singing. Psalm 100:2 (NKJV)

Disagreements about church music are nothing new. When the Reformation swept across Europe in the 1500s, there was a division among Protestants concerning congregational singing. Some of the Reformers, like Martin Luther of Germany, advocated singing hymns and carols. Others, like John Calvin of Geneva, thought that only the Psalms of David should be sung.

Calvin had been born in Noyon, France, in 1509, and educated at the University of Paris. In 1533, he experienced a "sudden conversion" that changed the course of his life. Joining a group of Protestants in Paris, his brilliance and preaching skills elevated him to leadership in the French Protestant movement. That same year, anti-Reformation riots drove him from Paris and he eventually settled in Geneva, Switzerland, which became a center of Reformation life through his ministry.

Calvin was a fierce advocate for the use of metrical versions of the Psalms. He felt that church worship should be simple, consisting of prayer, preaching, and the singing of the Psalms. Like Augustine, he believed that a person cannot "sing things worthy of God unless he has received them from Him," and that there are "no better songs nor more appropriate to the purpose than the Psalms of David which the Holy Spirit made and spoke through him."

In 1551, a hymnbook of Psalms was published in Geneva. In it, Psalm 134 was set to a majestic and beautiful melody composed (or adapted) by a man named Louis Bourgeois.

Ten years later another edition of the Psalter was published, and this time the same majestic, stirring tune was used with the words to Psalm 100 as versified by Rev. William Kethe, who had fled his native Scotland during the persecutions of Queen Mary.

Ever since the publication of the 1561 hymnal, this tune has been called "The Old 100th," because of its association with Psalm 100. Christians today know it as the melody to which the Doxology is typically sung ("Praise God from whom all blessings flow"), but for five hundred years, it has been more closely associated with William Kethe's rendition of Psalm 100.

"All People That on Earth Do Dwell" is known as "Calvin's Reformation Hymn." If you know the melody of the Doxology, take time to sing this old hymn and make a joyful noise unto the Lord.

We Gather Together

Anonymous Dutch Hymn

Dutch Folk Song

1. We gath - er to - geth - er to ask the Lord's bless-ing;
2. Be - side us to guide us, our God with us join-ing,
3. We all do ex - tol Thee, Thou Lead - er tri - um-phant,

He chas - tens and has - tens His will to make known;
Or - dain - ing, main - tain - ing His king - dom di - vine;
And pray that Thou still our De - fend - er wilt be.

The wick - ed op - press-ing now cease from dis - tress-ing,
So from the be - gin - ning the fight we were win-ning:
Let Thy con - gre - ga - tion es - cape tri - bu - la - tion:

Sing prais - es to His name: He for - gets not His own.
Thou, Lord, wast at our side, all glo - ry be Thine!
Thy Name be ev - er praised! O Lord, make us free!

We Gather Together

1597

So the nations shall fear the name of the LORD, *And all the kings of the earth Your glory.* Psalm 102:15 (NKJV)

*T*hose who have visited the Netherlands with its picturesque dikes and windmills may be unaware of the terrific struggle for religious freedom that took place there in the sixteenth and seventeenth centuries. In 1555, the Low Country was given to King Philip II of Spain by his father, Emperor Charles V of Germany. Philip was an arch-Catholic, but the winds of Calvinistic Reformation had reached the Netherlands. Roman Catholic churches were plundered, and the authority of Spain was resisted.

In 1557, King Philip sent the dreaded Duke of Alba (Fernando Alvarez de Toledo) to bring the Netherlands back into the Pope's fold. He established a reign of terror during which ten thousand people were executed and another forty thousand exiled. His ruling counsel was called the "Council of Troubles," but it's better known to history as the "Blood Council." The bodies of thousands of people were hung in the streets and on the doorposts of houses. Alva didn't hesitate to massacre whole cities. An attack on Leiden was stopped only by cutting the dikes and flooding the countryside.

On January 6, 1579, the Catholic southern regions of the Netherlands (modern Belgium) declared their allegiance to Philip; but three weeks later the northern part (modern Holland) refused to submit to the Catholic rule of Spain. In 1581, Holland declared its independence, led by the courageous William of Orange. Holland was devastated by warfare, and in the process William was cut down by an assassin's dagger. But the brave nation would not be denied, and eventually Spain lost its hold on the Dutch Republic.

This hymn, "We Gather Together," which Americans associate with their Thanksgiving holiday, was actually written sometime in 1597 to celebrate Holland's freedom from Spain. Its author, an unknown Dutchman, was full of thanksgiving that his people were finally free from Spanish tyranny and free to worship as they chose. Notice how he expressed this theme in these three beautiful verses:

The wicked oppressing now cease from distressing . . .

. . . so from the beginning the fight we were winning;
Thou, Lord, wast at our side, all glory be Thine!

We all do extol Thee, Thou Leader triumphant,
And pray that Thou still our Defender wilt be.
Let Thy congregation escape tribulation:
Thy Name be ever praised! O Lord, make us free!

9

If Thou But Suffer God to Guide Thee

Georg Neumark

Georg Neumark

1. If thou but suf - fer God to guide thee, and hope in
2. On - ly be still, and wait His lei - sure in cheer - ful
3. Sing, pray, and keep his ways un - swerv - ing, so do thine

Him through all thy ways, He'll give thee strength, what - e'er be - tide thee,
hope, with heart con - tent To take what - e'er Thy Fa - ther's plea - sure
own part faith - ful - ly; And trust His Word, though un - de - serv - ing,

and bear thee through the e - vil days; Who trusts in God's un -
and all - dis - cern - ing love hath sent; Nor doubt our in - most
thou yet shall find it true for thee; God nev - er yet for -

chang - ing love builds on the Rock that naught can move.
wants are known to Him who chose us for His own.
sook at need the soul that trust - ed Him in - deed.

If Thou But Suffer God to Guide Thee

1641

For this is God, Our God forever and ever; He will be our guide Even to death.
Psalm 48:14 (NKJV)

T he newer hymnbooks list this as "If You Will Only Let God Guide You." I still like the older, archaic phrasing, since that's the way I learned it; but never mind—it's a glorious hymn, however it's rendered, especially when you know the tender story behind it.

In 1641, a bright German youth, Georg Neumark, twenty, packed his few belongings and left his home in the Thuringian forests. By hard work and frugality, he had saved enough for his first year at the University of Königsberg. Seeking to travel with others because of roving thieves, Georg joined a group of merchants in Leipzig. But after passing through Magdeburg, they were waylaid and robbed on the Gardelegan Heath. Georg lost everything except his prayer book and a few hidden coins.

His university hopes dashed, the young man retraced his way through villages and towns, looking for work. Months passed, and the onset of winter found Georg poorly fed, scantily clothed, cold, and homeless. Just when he was near despair, a pastor named Nicolaus Becker of Kiel befriended him.

Becker wanted to help Georg secure employment, but how? There was nothing. Just then, a position opened unexpectedly—a tutoring job in the home of a local judge named Henning. Georg was hired on the spot, and that very day he composed "If Thou But Suffer God to Guide Thee."

While tutoring, Georg conserved his money, and the next year he proceeded to Königsberg and enrolled in the university on June 21, 1643. Shortly afterward, he again lost everything, this time in a fire. But by now, he had no doubt in God's ability to both guide and provide.

In 1657, "If Thou But Suffer God to Guide Thee" was published in Neumark's own book of songs, set to a melody he himself had written. The seven stanzas were entitled, "A hymn of consolation. That God will care for and preserve His own in His own time—based on the saying, 'Cast Thy burden upon the Lord, and He shall sustain thee' (Psalm 55:22)."

In later years, Neumark recorded the circumstances of the hymn, saying that his "good fortune, coming suddenly as if it had fallen from heaven, greatly rejoiced me, and on that very day I composed to the honor of my beloved Lord the well-known hymn, 'Wer nur den lieben Gott lässt walten.'"

11

We Sing, Emmanuel, Thy Praise

Paul Gerhardt

Nikolaus Hermann

1. We sing, Em - man - u - el, Thy praise,
2. For Thee, since first the world was made,
3. Now art Thou here, Thou ev - er blest!
4. But I, Thy ser - vant, Lord, to - day

Thou Prince of Life and Fount of grace, Thou Flow'r of
So ma - ny hearts have watched and prayed; The pa - tri -
In low - ly man - ger dost Thou rest. Thou, mak - ing
Con - fess my love and free - ly say, I love Thee

heav'n and Star of morn, Thou Lord of
archs' and proph - ets' throng For Thee have
all things great, art small; So poor art
tru - ly, but I would That I might

lords, Thou vir - gin born. Hal - le - lu - jah!
hoped and wait - ed long. Hal - le - lu - jah!
Thou, yet cloth - est all. Hal - le - lu - jah!
love Thee as I should. Hal - le - lu - jah!

We Sing, Emmanuel, Thy Praise

1654

I will be glad and rejoice in You; I will sing praise to Your name, O Most High.
Psalm 9:2 (NKJV)

P aul Gerhardt might be called the "Charles Wesley of Germany," for he was a prolific hymnist who gave Lutheranism some of its warmest hymns. Paul grew up in Grafenhaynichen, Germany, where his father was mayor. This village near Wittenberg was devastated by the Thirty Years' War, and Paul's childhood was marked by scenes of bloodshed and death. But he had a good mind and heart, and he enrolled at the University of Wittenberg at age twenty-one.

After graduation, Paul found a job in Berlin tutoring children. During this time, encouraged by Johann Crüger, choirmaster at Berlin's St. Nicholas Church, he began writing hymns. When Crüger published a hymnbook in 1648, Paul was delighted to find his hymns in it. Others were added to later editions. In all, Gerhardt wrote 123 hymns. His hymnody reflects the shift from the rugged theological hymns of Luther to the more subjective, devotional songs of German Pietistic revival. Best known are "Give to the Winds Your Fears," "Jesus, Thy Boundless Love to Me," and "O Sacred Head, Now Wounded" (which he translated).

Paul was ordained into the ministry at age forty-four and began preaching in and around Berlin. In 1651, he became chief pastor at Mittenwalde, just outside Berlin, and later he returned to Berlin to labor at St. Nicholas Church alongside his mentor, Johann Crüger.

At that point, however, Paul became embroiled in a conflict with the Elector Friedrich Wilhelm, who wanted Lutheran clergymen to sign an edict limiting their freedom of speech on theological matters. Refusing, Paul was deposed from his pulpit in February of 1666. He was even forbidden to lead private worship in his home. During this time, four of his five children died, and in 1668, his wife also passed away.

Late that year, 1668, Paul assumed the pastorate of the Lutheran church in Lübben an der Spree, where he ministered faithfully until his death on May 27, 1676. He was buried in the crypt beneath the altar of the church where he preached. Today the church is known locally as the "Paul Gerhardt Church," and a monument at the entrance reminds visitors of the church's famous pastor-poet.

This Christmas carol, "We Sing, Emmanuel, Thy Praise," has a hauntingly beautiful melody that seems to express the sorrows through which Gerhardt passed. But the words are full of praise, every verse ending in an exuberant "Hallelujah!"

Just like Paul Gerhardt's life.

Jesu, Joy of Man's Desiring

Martin Janus

Johann Schop
Arr. by J.S. Bach

1. Je - su, joy of man's de - sir - ing,
   Drawn by Thee, our souls as - pir - ing
2. Through the way where hope is guid - ing,
   Where the flock, in Thee con - fid - ing,

Ho - ly wis - dom, love most bright;
Soar to un - cre - a - ted light.
Hark, what peace - ful mu - sic rings;
Drink of joy from death - less springs.

Word of God, our flesh that fash - ioned, With the
Theirs is beau - ty's fair - est plea - sure; Theirs is

fire of life im - pas - sioned, Striv - ing still to
wis - dom's hol - iest trea - sure. Thou dost e - ver

truth un - known, Soar - ing, dy - ing round Thy throne.
lead Thine own In the love of joys un - known.

Jesu, Joy of Man's Desiring

1661

. . . I heard a loud voice of a great multitude in heaven, saying, "Alleluia! Salvation and glory and honor and power belong to the Lord our God!" Revelation 19:1. (NKJV)

omeone said that it doesn't matter who gets the credit so long as the work gets done. Here's Exhibit A: "Jesu, Joy of Man's Desiring," a lovely, lilting classical melody often played at weddings. A recent poll touted it as the overwhelming favorite of all the compositions of the great musician, Johann Sebastian Bach.

But it was actually composed by another Johann—the German musician, Johann Schop. Born about 1590, Schop was a musical prodigy, a gifted youth and accomplished instrumentalist who became one of seventeenth-century Europe's best known composers, conductors, and performers.

In 1614, Schop was appointed probationary musician in the Hofkapelle, the national or royal orchestra of Saxony. His performances on the lute, cornet, and trombone were lauded, but he was exceptionally gifted on the violin. As a result, he was invited to become a permanent member of the Hofkapelle in 1615.

Johann, however, had better offers, and he left Saxony for Copenhagen where he joined the musical staff of King Christian IV. He performed there until 1619 when the plague drove him from Denmark. He returned to Germany, and by 1621, he had become the leading musician in Hamburg, a city that paid him handsomely and was determined to keep him. Johann took charge of the choirs and orchestras, and planned church music for civic occasions. He became Hamburg's musical ambassador to the rest of Germany and to all of Europe, doing much to shape German religious and classical music in the seventeenth century. Many of his melodies found their way into Lutheran hymnals. "Jesu, Joy of Man's Desiring" is a good example, accompanied by words composed in 1661 by Martin Janus, an evangelical pastor in Silesia.

It was the famous Leipzig church musician, Johann Sebastian Bach, who "borrowed" this work and rearranged it into the beautiful piece it is today. Bach began working on this arrangement during the Christmas season of 1716, but it wasn't performed publicly until July 2, 1723, when it appeared as the final choral selection in one of his cantatas. Bach ended up with the credit, but always remember: Behind one Johann stands another. Behind every famous person is a host of faithful, gifted souls, and, in the end, all the glory goes to God.

Or as Bach would say: SDG—Soli Deo Gloria: *To God Alone Be the Glory.*

O That I Had a Thousand Voices

Johann Mentzer

Johann B. König

1. O that I had a thou-sand voic-es And with a thou-sand tongues could tell Of Him in Whom the earth re-joic-es, Who does all things wise-ly and well! My grate-ful heart would then be free To tell what God has done for me.

2. O all you pow'rs that God im-plant-ed, A-rise and si-lence keep no more; Put forth the strength that God has grant-ed, Your no-blest work is to a-dore. O soul and bod-y, join to raise With heart-felt joy our Mak-er's praise!

3. You for-est leaves so green and ten-der, That dance for joy in sum-mer air. You mead-ow grass-es bright and slen-der, You flow'rs so won-drous sweet so fair, You live to show God's praise a-lone. With me now make His glo-ry known.

4. All crea-tures that have breath and mo-tion, That throng the earth, the sea, the sky, Now join with me my heart's de-vo-tion, Help me to raise His prais-es high. My ut-most pow'rs can ne'er a-right De-clare the won-ders of God's might.

O That I Had a Thousand Voices

1704

Behold, bless the LORD, All you servants of the LORD, Who by night stand in the house of the LORD! Lift up your hands in the sanctuary, And bless the LORD.
Psalm 134:1, 2 (NKJV)

salm 134, one of the shortest chapters in the Bible, instructs those who serve the Lord by night to bless Him, to lift up their hands in the sanctuary and bless the Lord. Sometimes our highest praise occurs during the darkest hours.

Johann Mentzer was pastor in the small village of Kemnitz, located in the middle of the forests of Eastern Germany, near the Polish and Czech borders. He began his ministry there in 1696, and became a trusted friend and mentor to the young count, Nicholas Ludwig von Zinzendorf, who was born in 1700 and frequently visited his grandmother in nearby Berthelsdorf (see the story for "Jesus, Thy Blood and Righteousness").

Most of Mentzer's parishioners, however, were poor serfs whose hard work primarily benefited their wealthy masters. Mentzer's heart went out to his people, toiling in poverty and trouble, and he often counseled them to praise the Lord whatever the circumstances.

One evening Johann was returning from a Bible study in a nearby village. The night was dark, but as he approached his church, he grew alarmed at a frightening red glow in the sky. Hurrying onward, he found his own home, the church parsonage, ablaze. It had been set afire during his absence.

As he later inspected the ashes and ruins, he was disturbed and downhearted. Just then a serf tapped him on the shoulder and asked, "So, Pastor, are you still in the mood for praise and thanksgiving?" Johann offered a silent prayer for grace, and at that moment his whole attitude changed. It seemed to him that his praise to God should be louder than the sound of the tongues of flame that had just consumed his own home. The next day, he composed this hymn: "O that I had a thousand voices / and with a thousand tongues could tell / of Him in whom the earth rejoices / who does all things wisely and well."

Years later, Charles Wesley, undoubtedly inspired by this hymn, wrote his more famous, "O for a Thousand Tongues to Sing."

If you're facing difficulty right now, try praise and thanksgiving.

We're Marching to Zion

We're Marching to Zion

1707

Out of Zion, the perfection of beauty, God will shine forth. Psalm 50:2 (NKJV)

O
n the night of November 30, 1940, German planes bombed Southampton, England, and destroyed the Above Bar Congregational Church. The pastor and caretaker were able to rescue the church records, but all else was destroyed—except for a bust of Isaac Watts, the "Father of English Hymnody."

The destruction of those old buildings was a blow to Christian history, for within the walls of the Above Bar Church the hymns of young Isaac Watts were first sung.

Watts was born in Southampton on July 17, 1674, the oldest of nine children. He was a brilliant lad who started learning Latin at age four and Greek and Hebrew soon after. It's said that even before he could speak plainly, he would cry out, "A book! A book! Buy a book!" whenever anyone would give him money.

Isaac advanced so quickly in school that a local physician offered to finance his education at a major university. As members of Above Bar Congregational Church, however, the Watts were committed "Dissenters," Christians who didn't believe in joining the State Church. Dissenters opted instead for establishing independent congregations where they could worship without conforming to government regulations. As such, they were bitterly persecuted, and Isaac's father had even spent time in prison for his beliefs. Nor were dissenters allowed to attend the state universities. So at sixteen, Isaac enrolled instead in an independent academy in London and graduated with honors.

Returning home, Isaac spent two years more living with his parents and attending Above Bar Congregational Church. One day, discontented with the quality of the singing at the church, he wrote a hymn for the church to sing. This was a new and radical innovation, for at that time only the Psalms of David were sung in English churches.

Nonetheless, Above Bar Congregational Church gamely tried the young man's hymn and liked it so much they asked for another. For two and a half years, Isaac churned out hymns for that little congregation. Those two post-college years at home became the "Golden Years" of Watts's hymn writing.

How remarkable that some of the greatest hymns ever sung in the English language—such as "We're Marching to Zion"—should be produced by the "Father of Hymnody" who was only twenty years of age.

The old church building may be gone now, but the hymns first sung there will never die.

When I Survey the Wondrous Cross

Isaac Watts

Gregorian Chant
Arr. by Lowell Mason

1. When I sur - vey the won - drous cross
2. For - bid it, Lord, that I should boast,
3. See, from His head, His hands, His feet,
4. Were the whole realm of na - ture mine,

On which the Prince of glo - ry died,
Save in the death of Christ, my God;
Sor - row and love flow min - gled down;
That were a pres - ent far too small;

My rich - est gain I count but loss,
All the vain things that charm me most,
Did e'er such love and sor - row meet,
Love so a - maz - ing, so di - vine,

And pour con - tempt on all my pride.
I sac - ri - fice them to His blood.
Or thorns com - pose so rich a crown?
De - mands my soul, my life, my all.

When I Survey the Wondrous Cross

1707

But God forbid that I should boast except in the cross of our Lord Jesus Christ, by whom the world has been crucified to me, and I to the world. Galatians 6:14 (NKJV)

fter Isaac Watts finished his college studies and returned home to Southampton, he wrote many of his now-immortalized hymns for Above Bar Congregational Church. In 1696, Isaac, twenty-two, left home for London to become a tutor.

All the while, he was feeling a clear tug toward ministry. On his twenty-fourth birthday, July 17, 1698, Isaac preached his first sermon. The following year, he became assistant pastor of London's Mark Lane Church.

In March of 1700, Isaac received a long letter from his brother, Enoch, urging him to publish the hymns he had written at Southampton. The letter said:

Dear Brother, In your last [letter] you [mentioned] an inclination to oblige the world by showing it your hymns in print, and I heartily wish . . . that you were something more than inclinable thereunto. . . . I am very confident whoever has the happiness of reading your hymns (unless he be either sot or atheist) will have a very favorable opinion of their author. . . . There is . . . a great need of a pen, vigorous and lively as yours, to quicken and revive the dying devotion of the age. . . . Yours now is the old truth, stripped of its ragged ornaments, and appears, if we may say so, younger by ages in a new and fashionable dress.

Isaac, however, hesitated. He had other obligations on his time. On March 8, 1702, he became Mark Lane's pastor. The next year, 1703, the church chose Samuel Price of Wales to assist Isaac, due to the latter's fragile health. Under the preaching of these two, the old, dying church revived. The building grew too small for the crowds, and a new house of worship was built down the street.

Finally in 1707, Watts published his hymns, selling the copyright to a Mr. Lawrence, the publisher, for ten pounds. This volume was an instant success. It was enlarged and republished in 1709.

"When I Survey the Wondrous Cross" appeared in his 1707 book of hymns. Inspired by Galatians 6:14, it was originally titled, "Crucifixion to the World, by the Cross of Christ." Many consider it the finest hymn in English church history, and Charles Wesley reportedly said he would rather have written it than all his own.

Join All the Glorious Names

Isaac Watts, stanzas 2 and 3 Robert J. Morgan   John Darwall

1. Join all the glo - rious names, Of wis - dom, love and
2. The Babe of Beth - le - hem, the Faith - ful Wit - ness,
3. Al - pha, O - me - ga He, One like the Son of

pow'r, That ev - er mor - tals knew, That an - gels
He Is first and last, was dead, now lives to
Man, Ar - rayed in light, He reigned be - fore the

ev - er bore: All are too mean to
set us free. He washed our sins. He
world be - gan. He was, and is, and

speak His worth, Too poor to set my Sav - ior forth.
is the King, the Lord, the Word, to Him we sing.
is to come our Glo - rious Lord, God's on - ly Son.

Join All the Glorious Names

<u>1709</u>

His name will be called Wonderful, Counselor, Mighty God, Everlasting Father, Prince of Peace. Isaiah 9:6 (NKJV)

S hortly after Isaac Watts assumed the pastorate of London's Mark Lane Church, his health broke. Though only in his twenties, he was already famous throughout England for his sermons, books, and hymns. The strain of it all, however, was too much for his constitution; he was very short, thin, and weak. When he offered to resign from his pastorate, Mark Lane Church would have none of it. They hired an able assistant and determined to care for their ailing young pastor.

A wealthy couple, Sir Thomas and Lady Abney, invited him to spend a week at Theobalds (pronounced Tib-balds), their manor house outside London. The week turned into thirty-six years. Theobalds was a perfect environment for the little poet.

An 1875 biography of Watts says of him, "One of the smallest of mortals, he had one of the largest of homes," with "rich rural scenes, the delightful garden, the spreading lawn, and the fragrant and embowered recess all wooing the body back to health and the heart to peace." Watts had his own suite of apartments packed with books, a sort of literary hermitage. During the wee hours, he would study, pray, write his books and sermons, and compose his poems.

His biographer wrote, "For many years he knew little of sleep, except such as could be obtained by medicine. Intense mental application, working upon a weak and nervous constitution, brought about the consequences of insomnia, or sleeplessness; yet his mind seems to have been too calm, too equally balanced, and too completely under the control of highest principles, ever to know such agitations as shake to their centre some poetic natures."

Perhaps it was during the evening hours of many sleepless nights that Isaac studied the wonderful subject of the names of Jesus as revealed in the Bible. There are nearly three hundred names and titles of Jesus in the Bible, and Watts packed some of the richest of them into the twelve original stanzas of "Join All the Glorious Names."

This is my favorite of all Watts's hymns. One of the verses often omitted from today's hymnals says:

Be Thou my Counselor,
My Pattern, and my Guide,
And through this desert land
Still keep me near Thy side;
Nor let my feet e'er run astray
Nor rove nor seek the crooked way.

Joy to the World!

Isaac Watts

George Frederick Handel
Arr. by Lowell Mason

1. Joy to the world! the Lord is come; Let earth re - ceive her
2. Joy to the world! the Sav - ior reigns; Let men their songs em -
3. No more let sin and sor - row grow, Nor thorns in - fest the
4. He rules the world with truth and grace And makes the na - tions

King. Let ev - ery heart pre - pare Him room,
ploy, While fields and floods, Rocks, hills and plains
ground. He comes to make His bless - ings flow
prove The glo - ries of His righ - teous - ness

And heav'n and na - ture sing, And heav'n and na - ture
Re - peat the sound - ing joy, Re - peat the sound - ing
Far as the curse is found, Far as the curse is
And won - ders of His love, And won - ders of His

1. And heav'n and na - ture sing, And

sing, And heav'n, and heav'n and na - ture sing.
joy, Re - peat, re - peat the sound - ing joy.
found, Far as, far as the curse is found.
love, And won - ders, and won - ders of His love.

heav'n and na - ture sing,

Joy to the World!
1719

Shout joyfully to the LORD, all the earth; Break forth in song, rejoice, and sing praises. Psalm 98:4 (NKJV)

Until Isaac Watts came along, most of the singing in British churches was from the Psalms of David. The church—especially the Church of Scotland—had labored over the Psalms with great effort and scholarship, translating them into poems with rhyme and rhythm suitable for singing. As a young man in Southampton, Isaac had become dissatisfied with the quality of singing, and he keenly felt the limitations of being able to only sing these Psalms. So he "invented" the English hymn.

He did not, however, neglect the Psalms. In 1719, he published a unique hymnal—one in which he had translated, interpreted, and paraphrased the Old Testament Psalms through the eyes of New Testament faith. He called it simply, *The Psalms of David Imitated in the Language of the New Testament.* Taking various Psalms, he studied them from the perspective of Jesus and the New Testament, and then formed them into verses for singing.

"I have rather expressed myself as I may suppose David would have done if he lived in the days of Christianity," Watts explained, "and by this means, perhaps, I have sometimes hit upon the true intent of the Spirit of God in those verses farther and clearer than David himself could ever discover."

Watt's archenemy, Thomas Bradbury, was greatly critical of Watts' songs, which he called *whims* instead of *hymns.* He accused Watts of thinking he was King David. Watts replied in a letter, "You tell me that I rival it with David, whether he or I be the sweet psalmist of Israel. I abhor the thought; while yet, at the same time, I am fully persuaded that the Jewish psalm book was never designed to be the only Psalter for the Christian church."

"Joy to the World!" is Isaac Watts' interpretation of Psalm 98, which says: "Shout joyfully to the Lord, all the earth" (verse 4). As he read Psalm 98, Isaac pondered the real reason for shouting joyfully to the Lord—the Messiah has come to redeem us. The result, despite the now-forgotten criticisms of men like Bradbury, has been a timeless carol that has brightened our Christmases for nearly three hundred years.

I'll Praise My Maker While I've Breath

Isaac Watts

Probably by Matthäus Greiter

1. I'll praise my Mak - er while I've breath; And when my voice
2. Hap - py the man whose hopes re - ly On Is - rael's God;
3. The Lord pours eye - sight on the blind; The Lord sup - ports
4. I'll praise Him while He lends me breath; And when my voice

is lost in death, Praise shall em - ploy my no - bler powers.
He made the sky And earth and seas with all their train.
the faint - ing mind; He sends the la - boring con - science peace,
is lost in death, Praise shall em - ploy my no - bler powers.

My days of praise shall ne'er be past, While life, and thought,
His truth for - ev - er stand se - cure, He saves th'op - pressed,
He helps the stran - ger in dis - tress, The wid - ow and
My days of praise shall ne'er be past, While life, and thought,

and be - ing last, Or im - mor - tal - i - ty en - dures.
He feeds the poor, And none shall find His prom - ise vain.
the fa - ther - less, And grants the pris - oner sweet re - lease.
and be - ing last, Or im - mor - tal - i - ty en - dures.

I'll Praise My Maker While I've Breath

1719

While I live I will praise the LORD; *I will sing praises to my God while I have my being.* Psalm 146:2 (NKJV)

everal well-known hymns first appeared in Watts' *Psalms of David,* including "O God Our Help in Ages Past" (from Psalm 90), "Joy to the World!" (Psalm 98), "Jesus Shall Reign Where'er the Sun," (Psalm 72), and "I'll Praise My Maker While I've Breath," Watts' rendition of Psalm 146.

> *I'll praise my Maker while I've breath;*
> *And when my voice is lost in death,*
> *Praise shall employ my nobler powers.*
> *My days of praise shall ne'er be past . . .*

The theme of this hymn reflects Isaac's great interest in the afterlife. One of his most popular books was *The World to Come,* in which he vividly described the Bible's teaching about heaven, hell, and eternity. He wrote, "Death to a good man is but passing through . . . one little dusky room of his Father's house into another that is fair and large, lightsome and glorious, and divinely entertaining."

Then he added this personal note: "Oh, may the rays and splendors of my heavenly apartment shoot far downward and gild the dark entry with such a cheerful beam as to banish every fear when I shall be called to pass through."

It was as he wished. As he lay on his deathbed for three weeks in November of 1748, at age seventy-four, his friends gathered around. Mustering his strength, he exclaimed, "If God should raise me up again, I may finish some more of my papers, or God can make use of me to save a soul, and that will be worth living for. If God has no more service for me to do, through grace I am ready; it is a great mercy to me that I have no manner of fear or dread of death. . . ."

He was buried in London's Bunhill Fields, and this epitaph, prepared by himself, was placed at his tomb:

Isaac Watts, D.D., pastor of a church of Christ in London . . .
after fifty years of feeble labours in the gospel,
interrupted by four years of tiresome sickness, was at last dismissed to his rest . . .
2 Corinthians 5:8: Absent from the body, and present with the Lord.
Colossians 3:4: When Christ, who is my life, shall appear,
then shall I also appear with Him in Glory.

Jesus, Thy Blood and Righteousness

Nickolaus von Zinzendorf   William Gardiner

1. Je - sus, Thy blood and righ - teous - ness My beau - ty are, my glo - rious dress; 'Midst flam - ing worlds, in these ar - rayed, With joy shall I lift up my head.

2. Bold shall I stand in Thy great day, For who aught to my charge shall lay? Ful - ly ab - solved through these I am, From sin and fear, from guilt and shame.

3. Lord, I be - lieve Thy pre - cious blood, Which, at the mer - cy seat of God, For - ev - er doth for sin - ners plead, For me, e'en for my soul, was shed.

4. Lord, I be - lieve were sin - ners more Than sands up - on the o - cean shore, Thou hast for all a ran - som paid, For all a full a - tone - ment made.

Jesus, Thy Blood and Righteousness

1739

But of Him you are in Christ Jesus, who became for us wisdom from God—and righteousness and sanctification and redemption. 1 Corinthians 1:30 (NKJV)

T ravel with me to Germany. After flying into Berlin, we rent a car and drive south to Dresden, then east toward the Polish and Czech borders. There on Highway 178 is the little town of Herrnhut. At first glance, it seems like any other German village; but there in the central square is a large, plainly furnished church, dazzling white on the inside. It's the Moravian Meeting House, rebuilt after having been destroyed by bombs during World War II.

On one side of town is a hillside called "God's Acre," the Moravian Cemetery containing the tomb of the city's founder, Count Nikolaus Ludwig von Zinzendorf. Just beyond "God's Acre," you'll find the ruins of the count's vast manor house.

These are some of the most significant sites in modern Church history.

Count Zinzendorf (1700–1760) was born into wealth, and his family insisted on his pursuing a career as diplomat and statesman. But from childhood, Zinzendorf had a tender heart toward the Lord and felt God's call to the ministry.

The opportunity came unexpectedly. In nearby Moravia, a group of Christians were being persecuted for their faith. They approached Zinzendorf, asking for refuge on his estate. He assisted them in building a community named Herrnhut, a word meaning "Under the Lord's Watch." Zinzendorf became their spiritual leader.

It was in Herrnhut on August 18, 1732, in an extraordinary, emotion-packed service, that two men were commissioned for overseas missionary work. It was a historic moment, for virtually no Protestant group had previously sent out missionaries; but between 1732 to 1742, more than 70 missionaries left Herrnhut, a community of six hundred. This has been called "The Golden Decade," the dawn of Protestant missions.

It was also Zinzendorf's London-based Moravians who later led John and Charles Wesley to genuine faith in Christ and helped launch their history-changing ministry.

The Moravians were a singing people. On the night the two missionaries were commissioned, the church sang one hundred hymns. Zinzendorf wrote many of these songs, the best-known of which is:

Jesus, Thy blood and righteousness
My beauty are, my glorious dress;
'Midst flaming worlds, in these arrayed,
With joy shall I lift up my head.

29

Give to the Winds Thy Fears

Paul Gerhardt, trans. by John Wesley

Samuel Howard

1. Give to the winds Thy fears; Hope
2. Through waves and clouds and storms, He
3. Leave to God's sov - 'reign sway To
4. Let us in life, in death, Thy
5. Far, far a - bove thy thought His

and be un - dis - mayed; God hears Thy sighs and
gent - ly clears Thy way; Wait Thou His time; So
choose and to com - mand; So shall Thou, won - d'ring,
stead - fast truth de - clare, And pub - lish with our
coun - sel shall ap - pear, When ful - ly He the

counts Thy tears, God shall lift up Thy head.
shall this night soon end in joy - ous day.
own that way, How wise, how strong His hand!
lat - est breath Thy love and guard - ian care.
work hath wrought That caused thy need - less fear.

Give to the Winds Thy Fears

1737

I sought the LORD, and He heard me, And delivered me from all my fears. Psalm 34:4 (NKJV)

I t's hard to imagine two brothers making a larger impact on the Christian world than John and Charles Wesley. They were among the nineteen children born to Samuel and Susanna Wesley of little Epworth, England. John was four years older, and because he went off to school at an early age, the two didn't spend extended time together until they found themselves together at Oxford University. There they began praying in small groups, and both began planning for the ministry. Both were ordained in the Church of England. Both went to Georgia as missionaries and returned to England as failures. Both had a transforming experience with Christ the week of May 21, 1738. And both became powerful evangelists, accomplished hymnists, and the founders of the Methodist Movement.

But the two brothers often clashed when it came to personal issues or organizational matters within Methodism. Two examples stand out.

Once, during an illness, John fell in love with his nurse, Grace Murray. He more or less proposed to her, saying, "If I ever marry, I think you will be the person." She more or less accepted. But when Charles heard of it, he flew to Grace's house shouting, "Grace Murray! You have broken my heart," and fainted. When he recovered, he pelted her with objections, saying she would destroy his brother's ministry. She broke the engagement, leaving John to scribble painfully, "We were torn asunder by a whirlwind."

Another painful dispute involved the prospect of Methodism detaching itself from the Anglican Church. Charles spent his sunset years trying to prevent the split, prompting John, eighty-two, to write him, saying, "I do nothing rashly. It is not likely I should. . . . If you will go hand in hand with me, do. But do not hinder me if you will not help . . . With or without help, I creep on."

Despite their differences, however, these two brothers became a dynamic duo for revival, and they changed the world.

They also set the world to singing. Charles wrote most of their hymns, but John often edited Charles's hymns and wrote several of his own.

John also liked to translate German hymns for use by his English Methodists. "Give to the Winds Thy Fears" was originally written by the great German hymnist, Paul Gerhardt. John translated it in 1737, and it became a Methodist favorite, proclaiming the spirit of faith by which they lived.

Where Shall My Wondering Soul Begin?

Charles Wesley

Attr. to Jeremiah Ingalls

Where Shall My Wondering Soul Begin?

1739

And now, LORD, what do I wait for? My hope is in You. Psalm 39:7 (NKJV)

T he great hymnist, Charles Wesley, was converted to Christ on Pentecost Sunday, May 21, 1738. He was staying in the London home of his friend, John Bray. He was ill at the time, and Bray was tending to him both physically and spiritually. Wesley's journal tracks the course of his remarkable conversion:

Thursday, May 11, 1738. Mr. Bray read me many comfortable Scriptures . . . so that I was persuaded I should not leave his house before I believed with my heart unto righteousness.

May 12. This day . . . I spent in discoursing on faith, either with those that had it, or those that sought it.

May 13. I waked without Christ; yet still desirous of finding Him.

May 14. The beginning of the day I was very heavy, weary, and unable to pray . . . I longed to find Christ that I might show Him to all mankind. . . .

May 17. About midnight I was waked by the return of my pleurisy. I felt great pain and straitness at my heart; but found immediate relief by bleeding. I had some discourse with Mr. Bray; thought myself willing to die the next moment, if I might but believe. . . .

May 19. At five this morning the pain and difficulty in breathing returned. The surgeon was sent for; but I fell asleep before he could bleed me a second time. I was easier all day, after taking Dr. Cockburn's medicines. . . . I received the sacrament; but not Christ.

May 20. I waked much disappointed, and continued all day in great dejection. . . . Mr. Bray, too, seemed troubled at my not yet believing. . . .

Sunday, May 21, 1738. I rose and looked into the Scripture. The words that first presented were, "And now, Lord, what is my hope? Truly my hope is even in Thee. . . ." I now found myself at peace with God, and rejoiced in hope of loving Christ. . . . I saw that by faith I stood. . . . I went to bed. . . . confident of Christ's protection.

Within just a day or two, Charles wrote "Where Shall My Wondering Soul Begin?" Some historians believe it is the first of his thousands of hymns, one that expressed the joy of his newfound faith.

O for a Heart to Praise My God

Charles Wesley

A Collection of Hymns and Sacred Poems
Probably arranged by John F. Lampe

1. O for a heart to praise my God, A heart from sin set free, A heart that al - ways feels Thy blood, So free - ly shed for me!
2. A heart re - signed, sub - mis - sive, meek, My great Re - deem - er's throne, Where on - ly Christ is heard to speak, Where Je - sus reigns a - lone.
3. A hum - ble, low - ly, con - trite heart, Be - liev - ing, true and clean; Which nei - ther life nor death can part, From Christ who dwells with - in!
4. A heart in ev - ery thought re - newed, And full of love di - vine; Per - fect and right and pure and good, A cop - y, Lord, of Thine.

O for a Heart to Praise My God

1742

. . . From childhood you have known the Holy Scriptures, which are able to make you wise for salvation through faith which is in Christ Jesus. 2 Timothy 3:15 (NKJV)

Charles Wesley began preaching as soon as he'd been converted. He had already been ordained into the Anglican ministry, but his lack of genuine faith had robbed him of both motivation and message, and his ministry had been a failure. Upon his conversion, he found himself longing to proclaim the New Birth. He began preaching in religious meetings here and there, in a few churches, and in private homes.

At first, Charles followed the custom of the day in writing out his sermons and reading them word for word, but he felt inhibited by this practice. About five months after his conversion, he was invited to preach in a church with a small crowd. Deciding this was the time to experiment, he cast his notes aside. He recorded the results in his journal: "Seeing so few present at St. Antholin's, I thought of preaching extempore: afraid; yet ventured on the promise, 'Lo, I am with you always;' and spake on justification from Romans 3 for three quarters of an hour without hesitation. Glory be to God, who keepeth His promises forever."

Charles was a dynamic, emotional preacher, a bundle of zeal, an opinionated, strong-willed, stubborn evangelist. He was soon preaching to huge crowds; but he was at his best as a personal soul-winner. Here is an entry from his journal for September 27, 1738:

Wed., September 27th. *In our way to Oxford, I talked with my fellow-traveler, Mr. Combes. He expressed his desire of faith: I was moved to sing, "Salvation by Faith," then "Faith in Christ." I told him, if the Spirit had convinced him of unbelief, He could of righteousness also, even before we reached Oxford. I stopped and prayed that he might believe. Immediately he told me he was in such a blessed temper, as he never before experienced. We halted and went to prayers. He testified the great delight he felt, saying, it was heaven if it would but continue. While we were discoursing, the fire within him, he said, diffused itself through every part; he was brim full of joy . . . and eager to praise God. He called upon me to join. . . . We sang and shouted all the way to Oxford.*

Charles sang and shouted all the way through life, as reflected in "O for a Heart to Praise My God," one of his greatest hymns.

Ye Servants of God

Charles Wesley

Probably by William Croft

1. Ye ser-vants of God, your Mas - ter pro - claim,
2. God rul - eth on high, al - might - y to save;
3. "Sal - va - tion to God, who sits on the throne!"
4. Then let us a - dore and give Him His right;

And pub - lish a - broad His won - der - ful Name;
And still He is nigh, His pres - ence we have;
Let all cry a - loud and hon - or the Son:
All glo - ry and pow'r, all wis - dom and might,

The Name all - vic - to - rious of Je - sus ex - tol;
The great con - gre - ga - tion His tri - umph shall sing,
The prais - es of Je - sus the an - gels pro - claim,
All hon - or and bless - ing, with an - gels a - bove,

His king - dom is glo - rious, He rules o - ver all.
As - crib - ing sal - va - tion to Je - sus, our King.
Fall down on their fac - es and wor - ship the Lamb.
And thanks nev - er ceas - ing, and in - fi - nite love.

Ye Servants of God

1744

Praise the LORD! Praise the name of the LORD; Praise Him, O you servants of the LORD! Psalm 135:1 (NKJV)

I n the spring of 1739, Charles Wesley was recruited by his friend, evangelist George Whitefield, to begin preaching in the open air. This was highly unorthodox and would open Wesley up to harsh criticism. But after a period of inward struggling, Charles accepted it as God's will for him, and soon crowds of thousands were gathering in the cities and countryside of Great Britain listening to him and his brother, John, proclaim the gospel.

His journal records:

Tues., May 29th. *Franklyn, a farmer, invited me to preach in his field. I did so, to about five hundred, on, "Repent, for the kingdom of heaven is at hand." I returned to the house rejoicing.*

Wed., May 30th. *I invited near a thousand sinners (with whom the whole house was filled at night) to come weary and heavy-laden to Christ for rest.*

Thur., May 31st. *A Quaker sent me a pressing invitation to preach at Thackstead . . . Many Quakers, and near seven hundred others, attended, while I declared in the highways, "The Scripture hath concluded all under sin."*

Fri., June 1st. *My subject, to above one thousand attentive sinners, was, "He shall save his people from their sins." Many showed their emotion by their tears.*

Sun., June 17th. *My brother preached to above ten thousand people (as was supposed) in Moorfields, and to a still larger congregation on Kennington-Common. I preached twice in the prison.*

Sun., June 24th. *I found near ten thousand helpless sinners waiting for the word, in Moorfields. I invited them in my Master's words, as well as name: "Come unto me, all ye that travail, and are heavy laden and I will give you rest." The Lord was with me . . . At Newington, the Rector, Mr. Motte, desired me to preach. My text was, "All have sinned, and come short of the glory of God; being justified freely," & etc. I walked on to the Commons and cried to multitudes upon multitudes, "Repent ye, and believe the gospel." The Lord was my strength, and my mouth, and my wisdom.*

Charles Wesley's great hymn "Ye Servants of God" is an expression of his powerful evangelistic zeal. *Ye servants of God, your Master proclaim, / And publish abroad His wonderful Name.*

Rejoice, the Lord Is King

Charles Wesley   John Darwall

1. Re - joice, the Lord is King! Your Lord and King a - dore!
2. Je - sus, the Sav - ior reigns, The God of truth and love;
3. His king - dom can - not fail, He rules o'er earth and heaven;
4. Re - joice in glo - rious hope! Je - sus, the judge shall come,

Mor - tals, give thanks, and sing, And tri - umph ev - er - more:
When He had purged our stains, He took His seat a - bove:
The keys of death and hell Are to our Je - sus given:
And take His ser - vants up To their e - ter - nal home:

Lift up your heart; Lift up your voice!
Lift up your heart; Lift up your voice!
Lift up your heart; Lift up your voice!
Lift up your heart; Lift up your voice!

Re - joice, a - gain I say, re - joice!
Re - joice, a - gain I say, re - joice!
Re - joice, a - gain I say, re - joice!
Re - joice, a - gain I say, re - joice!

Rejoice, the Lord Is King

1744

Rejoice greatly, O daughter of Zion! Shout, O daughter of Jerusalem! Behold, your King is coming to you. . . . Zechariah 9:9 (NKJV)

By the 1740s, Charles Wesley was regularly preaching to thousands in the open air, but opposition was developing. He first encountered physical danger when a doctor in Wales, angry over Charles' sermon, stormed up to him and demanded an apology for having been called a "Pharisee."

Charles, who wasn't known for his tact, replied, "I still insist you are a Pharisee. . . . My commission is to show you your sins, and I shall make no apology for so doing. . . . You are a damned sinner."

The doctor struck Charles with his cane, causing a mêlée involving several men and women. This was the beginning of a period of dangerous ministry. Here's an entry in Charles' diary from July 22, 1743:

I had just named my text at St. Ives. . . . when an army of rebels broke in upon us. . . . They began in a most outrageous manner, threatening to murder the people, if they did not go out that moment. They broke the sconces, dashed the windows in pieces, tore away the shutters . . . and all but the stone-walls. I stood silently looking on; but mine eyes were unto the Lord. They swore bitterly I should not preach there again; which I disproved, by immediately telling them Christ died for them all. Several times they lifted up their hands and clubs to strike me; but a stronger arm restrained them. They beat and dragged the women about, particularly one of a great age, and trampled on them without mercy. The longer they stayed, and the more they raged, the more power I found from above. . . .

It was during these days of danger that Charles wrote his triumphant hymn, "Rejoice, the Lord Is King," the third verse of which says:

> *His kingdom cannot fail, He rules o'er earth and heaven;*
> *The keys of death and hell are to our Jesus given:*
> *Lift up your heart; lift up your voice!*
> *Rejoice, again I say, rejoice!*

Interestingly, this entry appeared in Charles's journal a few years later, on Sunday, July 13, 1746: *At St. Ives no one offered to make the least disturbance. Indeed, the whole place is outwardly changed in this respect. I walk the streets with astonishment, scarce believing it St. Ives. It is the same throughout all the county. All opposition falls before us. . . .*

Come, Thou Long-Expected Jesus

Charles Wesley   Rowland H. Prichard

1. Come, Thou long ex - pect - ed Je - sus,
From our fears and sins re - lease us,
2. Born Thy peo - ple to de - liv - er,
Born to reign in us for - ev - er,

Born to set Thy peo - ple free;
Let us find our rest in Thee.
Born a Child and yet a King;
Now Thy gra - cious king - dom bring.

Is - rael's strength and con - so - la - tion, Hope of all the
By Thine own e - ter - nal Spir - it, Rule in all our

earth Thou art; Dear de - sire of ev - ery
hearts a - lone; By Thine all - suf - fi - cient

na - tion, Joy of ev - ery long - ing heart.
mer - it, Raise us to Thy glo - rious throne.

Come, Thou Long-Expected Jesus

1744

You therefore must endure hardship as a good soldier of Jesus Christ. 2 Timothy 2:3 (NKJV)

I t's hard to imagine the difficulties faced by John and Charles Wesley and their fellow evangelists as they traveled by horseback from town to town, facing mobs, enduring harsh conditions and severe weather. Here is a sampling from Charles' journal as he pressed into Wales in March of 1748.

Wed., March 23rd. *I was . . . not to set out till past seven. The continual rain and sharp wind were full in my teeth. I rode all day in great misery, and had a restless, painful night at Tan-y-bwlch.*

Thur., March 24th. *I resolved to push for Garth, finding my strength would never hold out for three more days riding. At five (a.m.), I set out in hard rain, which continued all day. We went through perils of water. I was quite gone when we came at night to a little village. There was no fire in the poor hut. A brother supplied us with some, nailed up our window, and helped us to bed. I had no more rest than the night before.*

Fri., March 23th. *I took horse again at five, the rain attending us still. . . . The weather grew more severe. The violent wind drove the hard rain full in our faces. I rode till I could ride no more; walked the last hour; and by five dropped down at Garth.*

Charles' primary purpose in going to Garth was to preach, but he had another motive as well. It was also to see Miss Sally Gwynee, whom he wanted to marry. Marriage required a regular income, however, and Sally's parents were concerned about Charles' ability to sustain a family with no regular source of finances. Charles agreed to publish two volumes of his *Hymns and Sacred Poems.*

The income from royalties more than satisfied Sally's parents, and the two were married on Saturday, April 8, 1749.

"Come, Thou Long-Expected Jesus" wasn't introduced in this two-volume set of *Hymns and Sacred Songs* containing a total of 455 hymns. It had been published earlier, in a 1745 edition of Christmas hymns entitled, *Hymns for the Nativity of Our Lord.* This little hymnal contained eighteen Christmas carols Charles had written, of which "Come, Thou Long-Expected Jesus" is the best known.

Love Divine, All Loves Excelling

Charles Wesley   John Zundel

1. Love   di - vine, all loves ex - cel - ling,   Joy of heav'n, to   earth come   down!
2. Breathe, O breathe, Thy   lov - ing Spir - it   In - to ev - 'ry   trou - bled   breast!
3. Come,   Al - might - y   to de - liv - er;   Let us   all   Thy   life   re - ceive.
4. Fin - ish, then, Thy   new cre - a - tion;   Pure and spot - less   let   us   be.

Fix   in   us   Thy   hum - ble   dwell - ing;   All   Thy   faith - ful   mer - cies   crown.
Let   us   all   in   Thee   in - her - it;   Let   us   find   Thy   prom - ised   rest.
Sud - den - ly   re - turn, and   nev - er,   Nev - er - more   Thy   tem - ples   leave.
Let   us   see   Thy   great sal - va - tion,   Per - fect - ly   re - stored in   Thee:

Je - sus, Thou art   all com - pas - sion;   Pure, un - bound - ed   love Thou   art.
Take   a - way our   bent   to   sin - ning;   Al - pha and   O - me - ga   be.
Thee   we would be   al - ways bless - ing,   Serve Thee as Thy   hosts   a - bove,
Changed from glo - ry   in - to   glo - ry,   'Til   in heav'n we   take   our   place,

Vis - it   us   with   Thy   sal - va - tion;   En - ter ev - 'ry   trem - bling   heart.
End   of faith, as   its   Be - gin - ning,   Set our hearts at   lib - er - ty.
Pray, and praise Thee   with - out   ceas - ing,   Glo - ry   in Thy   per - fect   love.
Till   we cast   our   crowns be - fore Thee,   Lost in won - der,   love, and   praise.

Love Divine, All Loves Excelling

1747

His divine power has given to us all things that pertain to life and godliness, through the knowledge of Him who called us by glory and virtue. 2 Peter 1:3 (NKJV)

After their marriage, Charles and Sally Wesley set up housekeeping in Bristol, England, heading up the Methodist activities there. Later they moved to London so Charles could work more closely with his brother, John. All the while, however, he was writing hymns. There are few stories behind specific hymns because Charles was just always writing them. He didn't need events to inspire him or quiet stretches of meditative time in which to develop his thoughts. He was just always writing hymns, and afterward he had few if any dramatic stories to tell about the occasions for writing them.

Biographer Arnold Dallimore says about his poetry: "He had inherited this gift from his father and although it had undoubtedly been resident in him since childhood, his conversion unlocked it and set it free. During [his] early ministry he says little in his journal about his composing hymns and, indeed, this is true throughout his life. But he had within him virtually a treasury of poetry. He constantly experienced the emotions of the true poet, his mind instinctively invested words with harmony, and hymn after hymn flowed from his pen."

Henry Moore, one of his friends, later described Charles like this: "When he was nearly eighty he rode a little horse, gray with age. . . . Even in the height of summer he was dressed in winter clothes. As he jogged leisurely along, he jotted down any thought that struck him. He kept a card in his pocket for this purpose, on which he wrote his hymn in shorthand. Not infrequently he had come to our house in City Road, and, having left the pony in the garden in front, he would enter, crying out, 'Pen and ink! Pen and ink!' These being supplied he wrote the hymn he had been composing."

How many hymns did Wesley compose? No one has been able to count them. In all, Charles wrote over nine thousand literary texts of one kind or another, but not all of them should be classified as hymns. Experts put the number somewhere between three thousand and six thousand. Among all of them, "Love Divine, All Loves Excelling" is the favorite of many.

Charles's last hymn was dictated to his beloved Sally as he was on his deathbed, in March, 1788. It was short, simple, and picturesque. Predictably, it, too, became a popular one-verse song among the Methodists:

In age and feebleness extreme, / Who shall a helpless worm redeem?
Jesus, my only hope Thou art, / Strength of my failing flesh and heart,
Oh, could I catch a smile from Thee / And drop into eternity!

Be Still, My Soul

Katherina A. von Schlegel

Jean Sibelius

1. Be still, my soul; the Lord is on thy side. Bear pa-tient-ly the cross of grief or pain; Leave to thy God to or-der and pro-vide. In ev-'ry change He faith-ful will re-main. Be still, my soul; Thy best, Thy heaven-ly Friend Thro' thorn-y ways leads to a joy-ful end.

2. Be still, my soul; Thy God doth un-der-take To guide the fu-ture as He has the past. Thy hope, Thy con-fi-dence let noth-ing shake; All now mys-te-rious shall be bright at last. Be still, my soul; the waves and winds still know His voice Who ruled them while He dwelt be-low.

3. Be still, my soul! The hour is hast'ning on When we shall be for-ev-er with the Lord, When dis-ap-point-ment, grief, and fear are gone, Sor-row for-got, love's pur-est joys re-stored. Be still, my soul; when change and tears are past, All safe and bless-ed we shall meet at last.

Be Still, My Soul

1752

Truly my soul silently waits for God; From Him comes my salvation. Psalm 62:1
(NKJV)

L
ittle is known about Katharina von Schlegel, the German author of this poem. Her words, joined with the haunting strains of "Finlandia" by Sibelius, have made this a classic hymn. It was widely sung during World War II when it comforted an entire nation. Virgil J. Bachman of Our Saviour Lutheran Church in Port Huron, Michigan, is a good example. Writing in his church newsletter, he said:

> "I had probably sung 'Be Still, My Soul' many times before, but it was not until I sang it in a small stucco church in a tiny village in France during World War II that [it] became part of my life.
>
> "The war in Europe was going badly. The news from the front was disheartening. We had suffered reverses. We were edgy, confused, and discouraged. It was at this crucial time that some Chaplain arranged a service in this quaint church somewhere in France. It seemed the roof of that little village church actually opened up as we weary, dirty, GIs blended our voices under the leadership of that Chaplain and the church's old pump organ.
>
> "Halfway through the service it happened. Softly the organ began and we sang, 'Be still my soul, the Lord is on thy side.' How badly it was needed. It was as though the Lord was speaking to me in a very personal way. 'Bear patiently the cross of grief or pain'—the cross of war with its hardships, misery, separation and pain.
>
> "As we began the second stanza, 'Be still my soul, Thy God doth undertake to guide the future as he hath the past,' God seemed to whisper, 'Don't give up, I'm still in command, yes, even here. I'll guide the future as I have the past.'
>
> "The thoughts of dead and missing friends came as through a choked-up throat I sang, 'Be still my soul, though dearest friends depart. . . .' Soothing, personal assurance [came] at that moment and in that spot. With renewed spirit I was able to sing the final stanza, 'Be still my soul, when change and tears are past, all safe and blessed we shall meet at last.'
>
> "Peace! Either here or in eternity.
>
> "As we left that little church, the peace I felt among the horrors of war was nothing but a gift of the Holy Spirit. God did spare me and allow me to return to my loved ones and His service and still preserves me."

I Will Arise and Go to Jesus

Joseph Hart

American Melody

1. Come, ye sin - ners, poor and need - y, Weak and wound-ed, sick and sore;
2. Come, ye thirst - y, come and wel - come, God's free boun - ty glo - ri - fy;
3. Come, ye wea - ry, heav - y - la - den, Lost and ru - ined by the Fall;
4. Let not con-science make you lin - ger, Nor of fit - ness fond - ly dream;

Je - sus read - y stands to save you, Full of pit - y, love and pow'r.
True be - lief and true re - pen - tance, Ev - ery grace that brings you nigh.
If you tar - ry 'til you're bet - ter, You will nev - er come at all.
All the fit - ness He re - quir - eth Is to feel your need of Him.

I will a - rise and go to Je - sus, He will em - brace me in His arms.

In the arms of my dear Sav - ior, O there are ten thou - sand charms.

I Will Arise and Go to Jesus

1759

Because you have kept My command to persevere, I also will keep you from the hour of trial which shall come upon the whole world, to test those who dwell on the earth. Revelation 3:10 (NKJV)

When visiting London, make sure to go to Bunhill Fields, a little cemetery located across City Road from Wesley's House and Chapel. This old graveyard became the final resting place of a host of "Dissenters," spiritual giants who refused to follow the State Church and thus were not allowed burial on "consecrated ground." They were taken to Bunhill Fields. Among the graves, you'll find John Bunyan, author of *Pilgrim's Progress*, Daniel Defoe, author of *Robinson Crusoe*, and the great Puritan, John Owen.

You'll also find some of Britain's greatest hymnwriters. Isaac Watts, Father of English Hymnody, is buried here, as is Susanna Wesley, mother of Charles. William Shrubsole, who wrote the hymn tune, "Miles' Lane," is here. So are hymnists Joseph Swain, David Denham, Samuel Stennett ("On Jordan's Stormy Banks"), and John Rippon ("How Firm a Foundation").

Here also lies Joseph Hart, author of "Come, Ye Sinners, Poor and Needy." Born in London in 1712, he was raised a Christian and given a splendid education. He turned away from the Lord in his twenties and became an enemy of the Cross. Later describing himself as a "monstrous sinner," he wrote, "I ran such dangerous lengths both of carnal and of spiritual wickedness that I outwent professed infidels."

Joseph even wrote an anti-Christian pamphlet entitled, "The Unreasonableness of Religion," in response to a sermon John Wesley had preached from Romans 8:32.

Finally, at age forty-five, after a bout of depression, Joseph fell under deep spiritual conviction. Attending a Moravian service in Fetter Lane, London, on Pentecost Sunday 1757, he was struck by a sermon from Revelation 3:10. Hurrying home, he flung himself on his knees in broken repentance. "My horrors were immediately dispelled," he said, "and such light and comfort flowed into my heart, as no words can paint."

Soon Joseph was writing Christian poems, and when he published them in 1759, they became so popular that he felt compelled to enter the ministry. Acquiring an old wooden meetinghouse on London's Jewin Street, Joseph pastored an independent congregation until his death on May 24, 1768. By then, he was so beloved that 20,000 people attended his funeral at Bunhill Fields.

His greatest hymn is an expression of his testimony:

I will arise and go to Jesus, / He will embrace me in His arms.
In the arms of my dear Savior, / O, there are ten thousand charms.

The Saints Should Never Be Dismayed

William Cowper　　　　　　　　　　　　　　　　Alexander R. Reinagle

1. The saints should nev - er be dis - mayed, Nor sink in hope - less fear; For when they least ex - pect His aid, The Sav - ior will ap - pear.
2. This A - br'am found: he raised the knife; God saw, and said, "For - bear! Yon ram shall yield his mean - er life; Be - hold the vic - tim there."
3. Once Da - vid seemed Saul's cer - tain prey; But hark! the foe's at hand; Saul turns his arms an - oth - er way, To save th'in - vad - ed land.
4. When Jo - nah sunk be - neath the wave, He thought to rise no more; But God pre - pared a fish to save, And bear him to the shore.
5. Blest proofs of pow'r and grace di - vine, That meet us in His Word! May ev - ery deep felt care of mine Be trust - ed with the Lord.
6. Wait for His sea - son - a - ble aid, And though it tar - ry, wait: The pro - mise may be long de - layed, But can - not come too late.

The Saints Should Never Be Dismayed

1779

Oh, love the LORD, all you His saints! For the LORD preserves the faithful. . . .
Psalm 31:23. (NKJV)

The little town of Olney, England, quaintly situated by the River Ouse, is best known for two things. The first is its "Pancake Race," held every year since the mid-fifteenth century. According to legend, the women of Olney, needing to use up their accumulated cooking fats at the beginning of Lent, made pancakes every year on Shrove Tuesday. In 1445, one woman became so engrossed in her pancakes that she forgot the time until the church bells pealed. Dashing from the house in her apron, she raced to the church, skillet in hand. Thus began the custom of Pancake Racing that continues to this day.

Olney's other claim to fame is its association with the famous hymnists John Newton and William Cowper (pronounced Cooper).

All his life, William suffered severe bouts of depression. The son of a minister, he had intended to become a lawyer until disabled by his depression. He found relief in poetry; and when he came to Christ, the poems flowing from his pen were set to music and sung throughout England. Together he and Newton compiled the famous *Olney Hymnal,* still in print today. That's where you'll find hymns like "Amazing Grace," "There Is a Fountain Filled with Blood," and "God Moves in a Mysterious Way."

Here's a lesser-known Olney hymn, one that shows us from biblical examples how we, like Cowper, can fight off the blues:

> *The saints should never be dismayed, nor sink in hopeless fear;*
> *For when they least expect His aid, the Savior will appear.*

> *This Abr'am found: he raised the knife; God saw, and said, "Forbear!*
> *Yon ram shall yield his meaner life; behold the victim there."*

> *Once David seemed Saul's certain prey; but hark! the foe's at hand;*
> *Saul turns his arms another way, to save th'invaded land.*

> *When Jonah sunk beneath the wave, he thought to rise no more;*
> *But God prepared a fish to save, and bear him to the shore.*

> *Blest proofs of power and grace divine, that meet us in His Word!*
> *May every deep felt care of mine be trusted with the Lord.*

> *Wait for His seasonable aid, and though it tarry, wait:*
> *The promise may be long delayed, but cannot come too late.*

Glorious Things of Thee Are Spoken

John Newton

Franz Joseph Haydn

1. Glo - rious things of Thee are spo - ken, Zi - on, cit - y of our God;
2. See, the streams of liv - ing wa - ters, Spring-ing from e - ter - nal Love,
3. Round each hab - i - ta - tion hov - ering, See the cloud and fire ap - pear

He whose word can - not be bro - ken Formed thee for His own a - bode.
Well sup - ply thy sons and daugh - ters, And all fear of want re - move.
For a glo - ry and a cov - ering, Show - ing that the Lord is near!

On the Rock of A - ges found - ed, What can shake thy sure re - pose?
Who can faint while such a riv - er Ev - er flows their thirst as - suage?
Thus de - riv - ing from our ban - ner Light by night and shade by day;

With sal - va - tion's walls sur-round - ed, Thou mayst smile at all thy foes.
Grace which, like the Lord, the Giv - er, Nev - er fails from age to age!
Safe they feed up - on the man - na Which He gives them when they pray.

Glorious Things of Thee Are Spoken

1779

Glorious things are spoken of you, O city of God! Psalm 87:3 (NKJV)

I f you visit England in the future, plan to stop in quaint little Olney, home of John Newton and William Cowper. An excellent museum is dedicated to them, housed in Orchard Side, Cowper's home on Olney's triangular marketplace. Cowper had moved to Olney to be under the ministry of John Newton, who preached in the village church. The two became friends and would often meet in the garden between their houses for long talks. Out of their friendship came one of history's most famous books—the *Olney Hymns*, first published in 1779.

Prior to his conversion, Newton had been a slave trader on the high seas, and a very wicked man. After his conversion, he became a powerful preacher, a leader in the fight against slavery, and a renowned hymnist. His most famous hymn, "Amazing Grace," is an expression of his testimony.

This song, "Glorious Things of Thee Are Spoken," Number 60 in the Olney hymnal, is a powerful hymn about the church, which is metaphorically described here as "Zion." It originally had five verses, built around seven biblical passages, which Newton footnoted in the original hymnal.

If you hear this hymn being played in Germany, you'd better stand to your feet for you'll be hearing the German national anthem. Franz Joseph Haydn's majestic composition, AUSTRIA, was played for the first time on February 12, 1797, to honor the Austrian Emperor Franz Josef on his birthday. It was an immediate hit, and was almost instantly adopted as the Austrian national anthem. Thus it remained until Adolf Hitler rose to power. In 1938 when Austria was annexed into the German Third Reich during the Anschluss, Hitler not only seized Austria, but he seized AUSTRIA, adapting Haydn's musical score as the Nazi national anthem.

After the War, the Austrian people, feeling they could no longer use Haydn's tune as their national song because of its association with the Nazis, chose another melody. The Germans, however, kept Haydn's tune, AUSTRIA, as their own anthem.

As far back as 1802, however, Christians in America and Britain were using Haydn's AUSTRIA as a hymn accompaniment, and this majestic composition is best known today as the melody for John Newton's famous hymn about the church of Jesus Christ, "Glorious Things of Thee Are Spoken."

On Jordan's Stormy Banks

Samuel Stennett

American Folk Melody

1. On Jor-dan's storm - y banks I stand, And cast a wish - ful eye
2. O'er all those wide ex - tend - ed plains Shines one e - ter - nal day;
3. No chill-ing winds nor poi - s'nous breath Can reach that health - ful shore;
4. When I shall reach that hap - py place, And be for - ev - er blest,

To Ca-naan's fair and hap - py land, Where my pos - ses - sions lie.
There God the Son for - ev - er reigns And scat-ters night a - way.
Sick - ness and sor-row, pain and death Are felt and feared no more.
For I shall see my Fa-ther's face, And in His bos - om rest.

I am bound for the Prom - ised Land, I am bound for the Prom - ised Land;

O who will come and go with me? I am bound for the Prom-ised Land.

On Jordan's Stormy Banks

1787

Greater love has no one than this, than to lay down one's life for his friends. John 15:13 (NKJV)

S amuel Stennett, the Seventh Day Baptist who wrote "On Jordan's Stormy Banks," originally titled it "Heaven Anticipated," a sentiment that later comforted a dying twenty-one-year-old spy.

Sam Davis was a student in Nashville when the Civil War broke out. He joined the Confederate army and proved such a fearless soldier that he was selected for an elite group of spies named, "Coleman's Scouts." Sam excelled as an undercover agent. Once he even shared a table at Nashville's St. Cloud Hotel with General William Rosecrans, listening to a discussion of Yankee battle plans.

In November, 1863, Sam was seized in Giles County, Tennessee, and thrown into jail. The maps and papers under his saddle exposed him as a spy. His captors promised to spare his life if he would only reveal the identity of the mysterious "Coleman."

Sam refused, and it fell to Private C. B. Van Pelt to inform him of his sentence. "I read him a copy of his death sentence," Van Pelt later said. "A reprieve was extended which I [also] read to him, if he would inform us where 'Coleman' was. He stood before me, an uncrowned hero, his eyes flashing, and said: 'I will die a thousand deaths rather than betray my [friends].' We were both moved to tears and remained silent for a time."

Unknown to the Yankee soldiers, "Coleman" was really Dr. H. B. Shaw, who at that moment was being held in an adjacent cell and who was later released.

On the eve of his execution, Sam wrote to his dear mother, saying: *Oh, how painful it is to write you! I have got to die tomorrow morning—to be hanged by the Federals. Mother, do not grieve for me. I must bid you good-by forevermore.*

Chaplain James Young spent the day before the hanging praying with Sam. That night in a small worship service, Sam asked if they would sing, "On Jordan's Stormy Banks." Young later said he would never forget the young soldier's animated voice as he sang: "I am bound for the Promised Land; I am bound for the Promised Land."

Today there is a monument honoring Sam Davis on the grounds of the Tennessee State Capitol. Underneath are the words: "Greater love hath no man than this, that a man lay down his life for his friends."

Praise the Lord! Ye Heavens Adore Him

Published by Thomas Coram

John H. Wilcox

1. Praise the Lord! Ye heav'ns a - dore Him; praise Him, an - gels, in the height; Sun and moon, re - joice be - fore Him; praise Him, all ye stars of light. Praise the Lord! for He hath spo - ken; worlds His might - y voice o - beyed: Laws which nev - er shall be bro - ken for their guid-ance He hath made.

2. Praise the Lord! For He is glo - rious; nev - er shall His prom - ise fail; God hath made His saints vic - to - rious; sin and death shall not pre - vail. Praise the God of our sal - va - tion! hosts on high, His pow'r pro - claim; Heav'n and earth and all cre - a - tion, laud and mag - ni - fy His name.

Praise the Lord! Ye Heavens Adore Him

1796

Sing praise to the LORD, you saints of His, And give thanks at the remembrance of His holy name. Psalm 30:4 (NKJV)

*O*ne of Christianity's legacies is its concern for the fatherless. The Bible tells us forty-four times that God regards the plight of the orphans, and that we should do the same. But in seventeenth-century England, little was being done. It was commonplace to see babies left on the doorsteps or abandoned in latrines. London had its fashionable spots, but much of the city was gripped by poverty and disease with thousands living atop one another in mucky slums.

Captain Thomas Coram (1668—1751), a devout Anglican and friend of the Wesleys, determined to do something. Coram (who wasn't really a captain; the title was honorary), was a trader on the high seas who had been sent by a group of merchants to set up the first shipyard in Massachusetts. Returning to London after ten years in the colonies, he was shocked to learn that London had become a city of abandoned babies. "Left to die on dung heaps," he complained to anyone who would listen.

Not being a wealthy man, Coram approached the rich men of London, soliciting donations for a hospital and orphanage for "foundlings" (infants found on the streets). No one would help. "I could no more prevail with them than if I had asked them to pull down their breeches and present their backsides to the King and Queen," he wrote in disgust.

But when he appealed to the wives of London's wealthy men, he found a responsive audience. Finally, the charter was granted, the funds procured, and the foundling hospital opened in 1741. On its first night, hundreds of desperate women gathered at its doors, each with a child in her arms.

Soon London's artists threw their support behind the project, filling the institution with their paintings and music. The great composer George Handel gave benefit performances of his *Messiah* to help raise funds. The London Foundling Hospital became known for its beautiful singing and children's choirs.

In 1796, Coram published a hymnbook entitled *Psalms, Hymns, and Anthems of the Foundling Hospital, London.* Pasted into the cover of this book was an anonymous hymn entitled "Praise the Lord! Ye Heavens Adore Him." To this day, no one knows who wrote it, but it will forever be associated with God's love for children and His concern for the fatherless.

I Love Thy Kingdom, Lord

Timothy Dwight

Aaron Williams

1. I love Thy king - dom Lord, The
2. I love Thy Church, O God! Her
3. For her my tears shall fall, For
4. Be - yond my high - est joy I
5. Sure as Thy truth shall last, To

house of Thine a - bode, The Church our blest Re -
walls be - fore Thee stand Dear as the ap - ple
her my prayers as - cend, To her my cares and
prize her heaven - ly ways, Her sweet com - mu - nion,
Zi - on shall be given The bright - est glo - ries

deem - er saved With His own pre - cious blood.
of Thine eye, And grav - en on Thy hand.
toils be giv'n, Till toils and cares shall end.
sol - emn vows, Her hymns of love and praise.
earth can yield, And bright - er bliss of heaven.

I Love Thy Kingdom, Lord

1800

If I forget you, O Jerusalem, let my right hand forget its skill! If I do not remember you, let my tongue cling to the roof of my mouth— if I do not exalt Jerusalem above my chief joy. Psalm 137:5–6 (NKJV)

Those of us praying for a spiritual revival in America should remember the last two decades of the 1700s. It was a low-water mark for morality, especially on college campuses. The Rationalist movement, sweeping over classroom and dormitory, had turned most professors and students into infidels.

"During the last decade of the eighteenth century," wrote J. Edwin Orr, "the typical Harvard student was atheist. Students at Williams College conducted a mock celebration of Holy Communion. When the Dean at Princeton opened the chapel Bible to read, a pack of playing cards fell out, some radical having cut a rectangle out of each page to fit the pack! Christians were so unpopular they met in secret and kept their minutes in code."

Yale University in Hartford, Connecticut, was no exception. The college church was almost extinct, and Christian students—if there were any—were underground. But God was preparing a man named Timothy Dwight (grandson of Jonathan Edwards) to turn the tide.

As a child, Timothy had been precocious. He learned the alphabet in one lesson and read the Bible at an early age. Once when he didn't show up for dinner, his worried parents found him in the orchard teaching the catechism to a group of Native Americans. He was only four.

Timothy entered Yale at age thirteen, and was so devoted to his studies that he neglected exercise and sleep. He even limited himself to twelve mouthfuls of vegetables at meals, so as not to overeat and dull his mind. He went on to become a pastor and community leader. In 1795, he was elected president of Yale.

Soon he was debating upperclassmen on the subject: "Are the Scriptures of the Old and New Testament the Word of God?" In small numbers, students began considering Christianity, and within a couple of years there were about a dozen believers on campus.

After seven years of preaching, teaching, and praying, Dwight saw a revival break out at Yale in which one-third of the student body was converted. This spiritual resurgence touched other colleges, too: Harvard, Brown, Dartmouth, and many others. This "Second Great Awakening," provided the spiritual leadership America needed for the next generation.

The spirit of revival permeates Dwight's "I Love Thy Kingdom, Lord," which is based on a portion of Psalm 137. It's the oldest American hymn in continual use.

Look, Ye Saints, the Sight Is Glorious

Thomas Kelly

William Owen

1. Look ye saints! The sight is glo - rious; See the Man of Sor - rows now;
2. Crown the Sav - iour, an - gels, crown Him; Rich the tro - phies Je - sus brings;
3. Sin - ners in de - ri - sion scorned Him, Mock - ing thus the Sav - ior's claim;
4. Hark, those bursts of ac - cla - ma - tion! Hark, those loud tri - um - phant chords!

From the fight re - turned vic - to - rious, Ev - ery knee to Him shall bow:
In the seat of power en - throne Him, While the vault of heav - en rings:
Saints and an - gels crowd a - round Him, Spread a - broad the vic - tor's fame.
Je - sus takes the high - est sta - tion; O what joy the sight af - fords:

Crown Him, crown Him, Crown Him, crown Him, Crown Him, crown Him.
Crown Him, crown Him, Crown Him, crown Him, Crown Him, crown Him.
Crown Him, crown Him, Crown Him, crown Him, Crown Him, crown Him.
Crown Him, crown Him, Crown Him, crown Him, Crown Him, crown Him.

Crowns be - come the vic - tor's brow, Crowns be - come the vic - tor's brow.
Crown the Sav - iour King of kings, Crown the Sav - iour King of kings.
Spread a - broad the vic - tor's fame, Spread a - broad the vic - tor's fame.
King of kings, and Lord of lords! King of kings, and Lord of lords!

Come Build a Church

Ken Medema

Come build a church with soul and spir - it, come build a church of flesh and bone.
We need no tow - er ris - ing sky-ward, no house of wood or glass or stone.

Come build a church with hu-man frail-ty. Come build a church of flesh and blood.

Je-sus shall be its sure foun-da-tion, it shall be built by the hand of God.

Text and Music: Ken Medema © 1993. Ken Medema Music Briar Patch Music. All rights reserved. Reprinted (user CCLI #1299l657
Rocky Mountain Conference. UCC one-time use 6 2014

Look, Ye Saints, the Sight Is Glorious

1809

. . . And there were loud voices in heaven, saying, "The kingdoms of this world have become the kingdoms of our Lord and of His Christ, and He shall reign forever and ever!" Revelation 11:15 (NKJV)

Thomas Kelly (1769—1855) was a prolific Irish hymnist who gave us "Praise the Savior, Ye Who Know Him" and many other great hymns—over 750 in all. He's the "Isaac Watts" of Ireland.

As a young man, Thomas honored his father's wishes and enrolled at Dublin University to study law. But while pursing his studies, he came across a book that piqued his interest in Hebrew. This led to his studying the Scriptures with greater diligence and reading books of a spiritual nature. Deeply moved, Thomas abandoned his pursuit of the law, committed his life to Christ, and began studying theology.

In 1792, Thomas was ordained into the Anglican ministry and became friends with the well-known open-air evangelist, Rowland Hill. (It was Rowland Hill who, when asked about the upbeat tempo of some of the Christian music of his day, quipped, "Why should the devil have all the good tunes?")

Such evangelical fervor wasn't welcome in the Anglican Church of that day, and as a result Thomas was suspended from ministry and forbidden to preach. Thus he became a Dissenter—a non-Anglican preacher whose passionate sermons, winning personality, and zealous work with the poor made him a local hero. In one famous incident, a poor Irishman encouraged his wife during an unusually difficult period, saying, "Hold up, Bridget! There's always Mr. Kelly to pull us off of the bog after we've sunk for the last time."

In this way, Kelly pastored in Dublin throughout his life. On his deathbed at age eighty-six, he was heard to pray, "Not my will, but Thine be done." A friend read the 23rd Psalm to him, and Thomas whispered his last words: "The Lord is my all."

Though Kelly's hymn, "Look, Ye Saints, the Sight Is Glorious" was inspired by Revelation 11:15, it's usually associated with the Ascension of Christ. Forty days after His resurrection, Christ took His disciples to the Mount of Olives, where "He was taken up and a cloud received Him out of their sight." According to Acts 1:9–11, the stunned disciples continued staring into the sky until two angels dressed in white broke the spell, asking, "Men of Galilee, why do you stand gazing up into heaven? This same Jesus, who was taken up from you into heaven, will so come in like manner."

The First Noel

Traditional English Carol

Traditional English Melody

1. The first No - el, the an - gel did say, Was to cer - tain poor
2. They look - ed up and saw a star Shin-ing in the
3. And by the light of that same star, Three Wise Men
4. Then en - tered in those Wise Men three, Full rev - erent-

shep - herds, in fields as they lay; In fields where they lay
east, be - yond them far, And to the earth it
came from coun - try far; To seek for a King was
ly up - on their knee, And of - fered there, in

keep-ing their sheep, On a cold win-ter's night that was so deep.
gave great light, And so it con - tin - ued both day and night.
their in - tent, And to fol - low the star, wher - ev - er it went.
His pres - ence, Their gold, and myrrh, and frank - in - cense.

No - el, No - el, No - el, No - el, Born is the King of Is - ra - el.

The First Noel

1823

And there were shepherds living out in the fields nearby, keeping watch over their flocks at night. Luke 2:8 (NIV)

No other carol casts such a spell. The sweet, plaintive strains of "The First Noel," quietly sung on a snow-clad Christmas Eve, bring tears to the eyes and gentle peace to the heart. *Noel, noel, noel, noel. Born is the King of Israel.*

If only we knew who wrote it! It first appeared anonymously in *Some Ancient Christmas Carols*, published by Davis Gilbert in 1823, and the traditional music evidently came from an unknown source in the west of England.

The poetry itself is plain. If we were to recite this rather lengthy piece, we'd get only a garbled sense of the Christmas story. There's no indication in Scripture, for example, that the shepherds saw the Magi's star. And the final verse of the original carol seems anticlimactic. But when combined with its wistful music, the words glow and our hearts are strangely warmed.

The word "Noel" seems to be a French word with Latin roots: *Natalis*, meaning birthday. Modern hymns omit several of the verses. Here is the complete version:

The first Noel the angels did say was to certain poor shepherds in fields as they lay;
In fields where they lay keeping their sheep on a cold winter's night that was so deep.
Noel, Noel, Noel, Noel; Born is the King of Israel.

They looked up and saw a star shining in the East, beyond them far,
And to the earth it gave great light, and so it continued, both day and night.

And by the light of that same star three wise men came from country far,
To seek for a King was their intent, and to follow the star wherever it went.

This star drew nigh to the northwest; o'er Bethlehem it took its rest.
And there it did both stop and stay, right over the place where Jesus lay.

Then they did know assuredly within that house, the King did lie
One entered in then for to see and found the babe in poverty.

Then entered in those wise men three, full reverently, upon bended knee,
And offered there, in His presence, their gold and myrrh and frankincense.

If we in our time do well we shall be free from death and hell
For God hath prepared for us all a resting place in general.
Noel, Noel, Noel, Noel; Born is the King of Israel.

Praise, My Soul, the King of Heaven

Henry F. Lyte

John Goss

Praise, My Soul, the King of Heaven

1834

Praise the LORD, O my soul; all my inmost being, praise His holy name. Psalm 103:1 (NKJV)

ould you like to spend the night in the home of one of England's greatest hymnists? Reserve a room at the elegant Berry Head Hotel in Brixham, on England's southern coast. Years ago, this was the home of Henry Lyte, author of "Abide with Me," "Jesus, I My Cross Have Taken," and "God of Mercy, God of Grace."

For twenty-three years, Henry Lyte pastored the local church in Brixham, on the "English Riviera." How Henry and his wife, Anne, acquired this elegant estate is something of a mystery, but it was most likely provided for them by the King of England in appreciation for Henry's ministry. The estate was at water's edge, and there in the tranquility of that house and grounds Henry wrote most of his sermons, poems, and hymns.

Despite frail health and weak lungs, Henry established a Sunday school of eight hundred children in Brixham. In addition to preaching and tending his flock, he ministered to sailors on the docks and wrote his hymns and poems. In 1834, he published a small book that included this now-famous hymn, based on Psalm 103. (It was later chosen by Princess Elizabeth, now Queen Elizabeth II, for her wedding hymn in Westminster Abbey on November 20, 1947—the one hundredth anniversary of Lyte's death.)

> *Praise, my soul, the King of heaven;*
> *To His feet thy tribute bring.*
> *Ransomed, healed, restored, forgiven,*
> *Evermore His praises sing.*

While in his early fifties Henry realized his lung disorder had deteriorated into tuberculosis. On September 4, 1847, at age fifty-four, he entered his pulpit with difficulty and preached what was to be his last sermon. Henry closed the service by presiding over the Lord's Supper. That afternoon, he walked pensively over the grounds of Berry Head, working on his most enduring hymn, "Abide with Me."

Shortly afterward, Henry departed for warmer climes. Arriving on the French Riviera, he checked into the Hotel de Angleterre in Nice, and there on November 20, 1847, his lungs finally gave out. He was buried in Nice and a white cross now marks his grave.

After Anne's death, Berry Head passed to the Lyte daughter, Mrs. John Hogg, and it remained in the family until 1949, when it was converted into a hotel.

Savior, Like a Shepherd Lead Us

Attr. to Dorothy A. Thrupp

William B. Bradbury

1. Sav - ior, like a Shepherd lead us; Much we need Thy ten-der care.
2. We are Thine; do Thou be - friend us; Be the Guard-ian of our way.
3. Thou hast prom-ised to re - ceive us, Poor and sin - ful tho' we be;
4. Ear - ly let us seek Thy fa - vor; Ear - ly let us do Thy will.

In Thy pleas - ant pas-tures feed us; For our use Thy folds pre - pare.
Keep Thy flock; from sin de - fend us; Seek us when we go a - stray.
Thou hast mer - cy to re - lieve us, Grace to cleanse, and power to free.
Bless - ed Lord and on - ly Sav - ior, With Thy love our bos-oms fill.

Bles - sed Je - sus, bless - ed Je - sus! Thou hast bought us; Thine we are.
Bless - ed Je - sus, bless - ed Je - sus! Hear, O hear us when we pray.
Bless - ed Je - sus, bless - ed Je - sus! We will ear - ly turn to Thee.
Bless - ed Je - sus, bless - ed Je - sus! Thou hast loved us; love us still.

Bless-ed Je - sus, bless - ed Je-sus! Thou hast bought us, Thine we are.
Bless-ed Je - sus, bless-ed Je-sus! Hear, O hear us when we pray.
Bless-ed Je - sus, bless-ed Je-sus! We will ear - ly turn to Thee.
Bless-ed Je - sus bless-ed Je-sus! Thou hast loved us; love us still.

Savior, Like a Shepherd Lead Us

1836

For the Lamb who is in the midst of the throne will shepherd them and lead them to living fountains of waters. And God will wipe away every tear from their eyes. Revelation 7:16, 17 (NKJV)

T his hymn, originally for children, first appeared in an 1836 volume entitled *Hymns for the Young*, compiled by Dorothy A. Thrupp. Many hymnologists have attributed the words to Mrs. Thrupp, but her authorship is uncertain. One early hymnbook attributed it to Henry Francis Lyte; but that, too, is doubtful.

There's no doubt, however, about the composer of the music. It was the famous William Bradbury, one of the most prolific hymnists of the nineteenth century. A native of York, Maine, William moved to Boston at age fourteen to enroll in the Boston Academy of Music. There he joined Lowell Mason's choir at the Bowdoin Street Church.

Lowell Mason was a banker-turned-composer who became the first American to receive a Doctorate in Music from an American university. A dedicated Christian, he had written the tunes for such hymns as "Joy to the World!," "My Faith Looks Up to Thee," "Nearer, My God, to Thee," and "From Greenland's Icy Mountains." Mason was passionate about training children in sacred music.

Recognizing that young William Bradbury had an inborn talent, Mason sought to encourage him at every turn. Soon William was playing the organ under Mason's watchful eye, and earning a whopping $25 a year in the process.

William was so inspired by his mentor that he moved to New York City to do there what Mason had been doing in Boston—encouraging the Christian musical education of children. He organized and led children's singing conventions, encouraged music in the New York school system, and publishing Sunday school songbooks. During his lifetime, fifty-nine separate books appeared under his name.

Bradbury set in motion a great change in American church music. Prior to his work, most hymns were heavy, noble, and stately. William wanted to write lighter melodies that children could sing. His compositions were softer, full of movement, and easier for children to sing.

In so doing, William Bradbury helped usher in the era of gospel music. He may not have realized that adults would sing his hymns as readily as children would, but he paved the way for the likes of Fanny Crosby and Ira Sankey. Today Bradbury is remembered as the musical composer of such favorites as: "He Leadeth Me," "The Solid Rock," "Just As I Am," "Jesus Loves Me," "Sweet Hour of Prayer" and this one—"Savior, Like a Shepherd Lead Us."

Come, Christians, Join to Sing

Christian Henry Bateman

Traditional Spanish Melody
Arr. by Benjamin Carr

1. Come, Chris-tians, join to sing   Al - le - lu - ia!   A - men!
2. Come, lift your hearts on high,   Al - le - lu - ia!   A - men!
3. Praise yet our Christ a - gain,   Al - le - lu - ia!   A - men!

Loud praise to   Christ our King;   Al - le - lu - ia!   A - men!
Let prais - es   fill the sky;   Al - le - lu - ia!   A - men!
Life shall not   end the strain;   Al - le - lu - ia!   A - men!

Let all, with   heart and voice,   Be - fore His   throne re - joice;
He is our   Guide and Friend;   To us He'll   con - des - cend;
On heav - en's   bliss - ful shore   His good - ness   we'll a - dore,

Praise is His   gra - cious choice: Al - le - lu - ia!   A - men!
His love shall nev - er   end: Al - le - lu - ia!   A - men!
Sing - ing for - ev - er - more,   "Al - le - lu - ia!   A - men!"

Come, Christians, Join to Sing

1843

Serve the LORD with gladness; Come before His presence with singing. Psalm 100:2 (NKJV)

Many of our "adult" hymns were originally written for children. "Savior, Like a Shepherd Lead Us," is a good example. So is Isaac Watts' great hymn, "I Sing the Mighty Power of God," which first appeared in his *Divine and Moral Songs for Children.* The rousing "Onward, Christian Soldiers" was written for the youngsters of Horbury, England, to sing on a Monday morning in 1865 as they marched to a nearby village to establish a Sunday school. Even the great anthem, "All Creatures of Our God and King," by Saint Francis of Assisi, was first translated into English and set to music for a 1919 children's festival in Leeds, England.

Here's another instance: "Come, Christians, Join to Sing" first appeared in *Sacred Melodies for Children,* published in Edinburgh in 1843. The original words said, "Come, children, join to sing . . ."

Its author, Christian Henry Bateman, a pastor in Edinburgh, was committed to developing a Sunday school in which children sang the great truths of the Christian faith. Bateman had begun his ministry as a Moravian pastor, but moved to Edinburgh and became a Congregational minister and the pastor of Richmond Place Congregational Church, where he was serving when he wrote "Come, Christians, Join to Sing." He was later ordained in the Church of England and ministered in that communion until his retirement in 1884. He passed away five years later.

"Come, Christians, Join to Sing" originally had five stanzas, but Bateman reduced the hymn to its present form in the 1854 edition of his hymnal, *Sacred Melodies for Sabbath Schools and Families.* This book became one of the best-selling songbooks in Scottish history, selling more than six million copies by 1881 and becoming the standard hymnbook for Scottish Sunday schools for a generation.

The tune, MADRID, was a popular Spanish folk melody arranged for this hymn by Benjamin Carr, who was born in London in 1769, and died in Philadelphia in 1831. In England, Carr was a well-known singer with the London Ancient Concerts. Immigrating to America, he joined his father and brother in a music publishing enterprise, with stores in Philadelphia, New York, and Baltimore. He also served as a church organist and music director in Philadelphia for many years. Benjamin Carr is best known as the first American publisher of "Yankee Doodle"—and for arranging the music to "Come, Christians, Join to Sing."

Come, Ye Thankful People, Come

Henry Alford

George J. Elvey

1. Come, ye thank-ful peo-ple, come; Raise the song of har-vest home.
2. All the world is God's own field, Fruit un-to His praise to yield;
3. For the Lord our God shall come, And shall take His har-vest home;
4. Ev-en so, Lord, quick-ly come To Thy fi-nal har-vest home;

All is safe-ly gath-ered in, Ere the win-ter storms be-gin.
Wheat and tares to-geth-er sown, Un-to joy or sor-row grown;
From His field shall in that day All of-fens-es purge a-way;
Gath-er, Thou, Thy peo-ple in, Free from sor-row, free from sin;

God, our Mak-er, doth pro-vide For our wants to be sup-plied;
First the blade and then the ear, Then the full corn shall ap-pear;
Give His an-gels charge at last In the fire the tares to cast,
There for-ev-er pu-ri-fied, In Thy pres-ence to a-bide.

Come to God's own tem-ple, come; Raise the song of har-vest home.
Lord of har-vest grant that we Whole-some grain and pure may be.
But the fruit-ful ears to store In His gar-ner ev-er-more.
Come, with all Thine an-gels, come; Raise the glo-rious har-vest home.

Come, Ye Thankful People, Come

1844

Let us come before His presence with thanksgiving; Let us shout joyfully to Him with psalms. Psalm 95:2 (NKJV)

C onsider this definition of a gravesite for a Christian: "An Inn of a Pilgrim Traveling to Jerusalem." That's what Henry Alford wrote for his tombstone.

He was born October 7, 1810, in the Bloomsbury area of London, and even from childhood showed remarkable promise. At six, he wrote a biography of the apostle Paul. When he was ten he wrote a pamphlet titled, "Looking unto Jesus: the Believers' Support under Trials and Afflictions."

When sixteen, Henry penned a note in his Bible describing his rededication to Christ: "I do this day in the presence of God and my own soul renew my covenant with God and solemnly determine henceforth to become his and to do his work as far as in me lies."

This committed young man made a mark on Cambridge University as he studied there for the ministry. One of his deans said, "He was morally the bravest man I ever knew. His perfect purity of mind and singleness of purpose seemed to give him a confidence and unobtrusive self-respect which never failed him."

When he was ordained, Henry wrote in his journal: "I went up to town and received the Holy Orders of a Priest; may I be a temple of chastity and holiness, fit and clean. . . . O my beloved Redeemer, my dear Brother and Master, hear my prayer."

Henry was a powerful preacher and a brilliant scholar. He served in the village of Wymeswold for eighteen years before accepting the pastorate of a large London church in 1853. In 1857, he was appointed Dean of Canterbury, an office he held until his rather sudden death on January 12, 1871.

Henry Alford is remembered for his scholarly books, including his classic *Greek New Testament*, the fruit of eighteen years of labor. His two-volume set of psalms and hymns was published in 1844, while he was laboring among his flock in the little farming village of Wymeswold, where he was beloved. He visited every home, loved every soul, taught the Bible simply, and helped the people render thanksgiving.

This hymn, "Come, Ye Thankful People, Come" was written for the English Harvest Festival, the British version of the American Thanksgiving holiday.

Sweet Hour of Prayer

Attr. to William W. Walford

William B. Bradbury

1. Sweet hour of prayer, Sweet hour of prayer, That calls me from a world of care,
2. Sweet hour of prayer, Sweet hour of prayer, Thy wings shall my pe - ti - tion bear
3. Sweet hour of prayer, Sweet hour of prayer, May I Thy con - so - la - tion share,

And bids me at my Fa - ther's throne Make all my wants and wish - es known.
To Him whose truth and faith - ful - ness En - gage the wait - ing soul to bless;
'Til from Mount Pis - gah's loft - y height, I view my home and take my flight.

In sea - sons of dis - tress and grief My soul has of - ten found re - lief,
And since He bids me seek His face, Be - lieve His word, and trust His grace,
This robe of flesh I'll drop, and rise To seize the ev - er - last - ing prize;

And oft es - caped the temp - ter's snare, By Thy re - turn, sweet hour of prayer.
I'll cast on Him my ev - 'ry care, And wait for Thee, sweet hour of prayer.
And shout while pass - ing through the air, Fare - well, fare-well, sweet hour of prayer.

Sweet Hour of Prayer

1845

Hear my cry, O God; Attend to my prayer. Psalm 61:1 (NKJV)

Sweet Hour of Prayer" first appeared in *The New York Observer* on September 13, 1845, accompanied by this explanatory note by a Rev. Thomas Salmon, a British minister recently immigrated to America:

At Coleshill, Warwickshire, England, I became acquainted with W. W. Walford, the blind preacher, a man of obscure birth and connections and no education, but of strong mind and most retentive memory. In the pulpit he never failed to select a lesson well adapted to his subject, giving chapter and verse with unerring precision and scarcely ever misplacing a word in his repetition of the Psalms, every part of the New Testament, the prophecies, and some of the histories, so as to have the reputation of "knowing the whole Bible by heart." He actually sat in the chimney corner, employing his mind in composing a sermon or two for Sabbath delivery. . . . On one occasion, paying him a visit, he repeated two or three pieces he had composed, and having no friend at home to commit them to paper, he had laid them up in the storehouse within. "How will this do?" asked he, as he repeated the following lines . . . ?" I rapidly copied the lines with my pencil as he uttered them, and sent them for insertion in the Observer.

No one, however, has ever found a trace of a blind preacher named W. W. Walford in Coleshill, England. There was a Congregational minister named William Walford who wrote a book about prayer containing striking similarities to this poem, and some believe he was the author. But he was neither blind nor uneducated, and the authorship of this hymn remains a mystery.

There's yet another mystery—a deeper one—connected with this hymn. It's the question Jesus asked Simon Peter in Gethsemane: "What? Could you not watch with Me one hour?" If an hour spent with the Lord is so sweet, why do we race through our day prayerless, then squeeze all our requests into a two-minute segment at bedtime? If prayer is so powerful, why do we neglect it so consistently? An oft-omitted verse to this hymn says:

Sweet hour of prayer! Sweet hour of prayer! The joys I feel, the bliss I share,
Of those whose anxious spirits burn with strong desires for thy return!
With such I hasten to the place where God my Savior shows His face,
And gladly take my station there, and wait for thee, sweet hour of prayer!

O Holy Night

Placide Clappeau

Adolphe Charles Adam

Fall on your knees! O hear the an - gel voic - es! O night di - vine! O night when Christ was born, O night di - vine! O night, O night di - vine!

O Holy Night

1847

. . . The star which they had seen in the East went before them, till it came and stood over where the young Child was. Matthew 2:9 (NKJV)

he words of "O Holy Night" were written in 1847 by a French wine merchant named Placide Clappeau, the mayor of Roquemaure, a town in the south of France. We know little about him except that he wrote poems as a hobby.

We know more about the man who composed the music, a Parisian named Adolphe Charles Adam. The son of a concert pianist, Adams was trained almost from infancy in music and piano. In his mid-twenties, he wrote his first opera and thereafter wrote two operas a year until his death at age fifty-two. Near the end of his life, he lost his savings in a failed business venture involving the French national opera, but the Paris Conservatory rescued him by appointing him professor of music.

It was John Dwight, son of Yale's president, Timothy Dwight ("I Love Thy Kingdom, Lord"), who discovered this French Carol, "Christian Midnight," and translated it into the English hymn, "O Holy Night."

After graduating from Harvard and Cambridge, John was ordained as minister of the Unitarian church in Northampton, but his pastoring experience wasn't happy. In 1841, George and Sophia Ripley founded a commune named Brook Farm "to prepare a society of liberal, intelligent, and cultivated persons, whose relations with each other would permit a more simple and wholesome life." John was hired as director of the Brook Farm School and began writing a regular column on music for the commune's publication.

Greatly influenced by the liberal views of Ralph Waldo Emerson, he became fascinated by the German culture, especially the symphonic music of Ludwig van Beethoven, and it was largely his influence that introduced Americans to Beethoven's genius.

When Brook Farm collapsed in 1847, John Dwight moved into a cooperative house in Boston and established a career in music journalism. He penned articles on music for major publications, and in 1852 he launched his own publication, *Dwight's Journal of Music*. He became America's first influential classical music critic. He was opinionated, sometime difficult, a great promoter of European classical music, and an early advocate of Transcendentalism.

How odd that a wine merchant, a penniless Parisian, and liberal clergyman should give Christianity one of its holiest hymns about the birth of Jesus Christ, Savior of the world.

All Things Bright and Beautiful

Cecil F. Alexander   17th Century English Melody

Unison All things bright and beau - ti - ful, All crea - tures great and small,

All things wise and won - der - ful, The Lord God made them all.

Fine

1. Each lit - tle flow'r that o - pens, Each lit - tle bird that sings,
2. The pur - ple - head - ed moun - tains, The riv - er run - ning by,
3. The cold wind in the win - ter, The pleas - ant sum - mer sun,
4. He gave us eyes to see them, And lips that we might tell

He made their glow - ing col - ors, He made their ti - ny wings.
The sun - set and the morn - ing, That bright - ens up the sky.
The ripe fruits in the gar - den, He made them ev - 'ry one.
How great is God Al - might - y, Who has made all things well.

D.C.

All Things Bright and Beautiful

1848

Then God saw everything that He had made, and indeed it was very good. Genesis 1:31 (NKJV)

One day, Mrs. Cecil Frances Alexander was working with one of her pupils in Sunday school—a little boy who happened to be her godson. He was struggling to understand the Apostles' Creed and certain portions of the catechism. Mrs. Alexander began to mull the possibility of converting the Apostles' Creed into songs for children, using simple little hymns to explain the phrases and truths of the Christian faith to little ones.

The Apostles' Creed begins: *I believe in God, the Father Almighty, Maker of heaven and earth, and in Jesus Christ, His only Son, our Lord.* For the phrase, "Maker of heaven and earth . . ." she wrote this lovely little song, "All Things Bright and Beautiful." She based the hymn on Genesis 1:31: "Then God saw everything that He had made, and indeed it was very good."

The Apostles' Creed goes on to say about Jesus Christ: ". . . who was conceived of the Holy Spirit, born of the Virgin Mary . . ." That spurred the writing of "Once in Royal David's City."

The next phrase, ". . . suffered under Pontius Pilate, was crucified, died, and was buried," became the basis for Mrs. Alexander's hymn, "There Is a Green Hill Far Away."

According to one account, the imagery Mrs. Alexander used for that hymn came about as she was driving into the city of Derry, Ireland, to do some shopping. Alongside the road near the old city walls was a little grass-covered hill. Somehow, this knoll helped her visualize Calvary, and from that came the inspiration for the hymn.

The Creed goes on to speak of the Second Coming of Christ, prompting Mrs. Alexander to write a lesser-known but still beautiful hymn entitled, "He Is Coming! He Is Coming!" which contrasts the Lord's First Coming as a babe with His return in power and glory.

These hymns were published in 1848 in Mrs. Alexander's book, *Hymns for Little Children.* It became one of the most successful hymn-publishing projects in history, going through over one hundred editions.

Cecil Frances Alexander published many other books and hymnals, including: *Verses from the Holy Scriptures* (1846), *Narrative Hymns for Village Schools* (1853), *Poems on Subjects in the Old Testament* (1854), *Hymns Descriptive and Devotional* (1858), and *The Legend of the Golden Prayer* (1859). But nothing has stood the test of time like the powerful combination of the Apostles' Creed with her own gift for song.

My God, How Wonderful Thou Art

Frederick W. Faber   Carl G. Gläser; arr. by Lowell Mason

1. My God, how won - der - ful Thou art, Thy
2. How dread are Thine e - ter - nal years, O
3. How won - der - ful, how beau - ti - ful The
4. O how I fear Thee, liv - ing God, With
5. Yet I may love Thee too, O Lord, Al -

maj - es - ty how bright! How beau - ti - ful Thy
ev - er - last - ing Lord, By pros - trate spir - its
sight of Thee must be. Thine end - less wis - dom,
deep - est ten - d'rest fears; And wor - ship Thee with
might - y as Thou art; For Thou hast stooped to

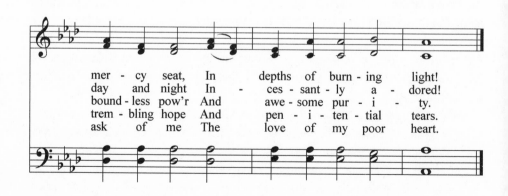

mer - cy seat, In depths of burn - ing light!
day and night In - ces - sant - ly a - dored!
bound - less pow'r And awe - some pur - i - ty.
trem - bling hope And pen - i - ten - tial tears.
ask of me The love of my poor heart.

My God, How Wonderful Thou Art

1849

Oh, that men would give thanks to the LORD for His goodness, And for His wonderful works to the children of men! Psalm 107:15 (NKJV)

Frederick William Faber is a Roman Catholic whom Christians of every stripe and stamp love to read. A. W. Tozer, for example, was forever quoting his poetry and worshiping with his hymns. Faber was deeply devotional. His passion was to provide English Catholics with a body of hymns such as John Newton and William Cowper had given English Protestants in the *Olney Hymns*.

In the end, Faber provided all of Christianity with some of its richest songs, including "Faith of Our Fathers," "There's a Wideness to God's Mercy," and this song, "My God, How Wonderful Thou Art."

He was born on June 28, 1814, midway up the English coast in the village of Calverley, Yorkshire. His father was a Church of England pastor. During his college years at Balliol College at Oxford, Faber was torn between his Calvinistic roots and the reverent liturgy of Roman Catholicism. Following his studies, he was ordained an Anglican priest.

But these were the days of John Henry Newman, a British clergyman who had converted to Roman Catholicism. Under Newman's influence, the Church of England lost 250 of their best pastors to Roman Catholicism. This was known as the Oxford Movement. Faber couldn't shake Newman's influence, and, in 1846, he converted to Catholicism, was rebaptized, and took the name Wilfrid. He began ministering in and around the village of Cheadle in Staffordshire, and managed to convert the whole town, except, "the parson, the pew-opener, and two drunken men."

From 1849 until his death in 1863, he headed the Brompton Oratory in London. He was given a makeshift chapel in a former tavern, and there he established schools for the poor, conducted nightly services, and wrote his great hymns. He also authored a series of devotional books with titles like *All for Jesus* (1853), *The Foot of the Cross* (1858), and *The Precious Blood* (1860).

A lesser-known Faber hymn highlights the distinctive Christian doctrine of the deity of Jesus Christ—that Jesus was, is, and always will be God, proclaiming:

> *Jesus is God! O! could I now but compass earth and sea,*
> *To teach and tell the single truth, how happy should I be!*
> *O! had I but an angel's voice, I would proclaim so loud,*
> *Jesus, the good, the beautiful, is everlasting God.*

Faith of Our Fathers

Frederick W. Faber

Henri F. Hemy

1. Faith of our fa - thers, liv - ing still In spite of dun-geon,
2. Our fa-thers, chained in pris - ons dark, Were still in heart and
3. Faith of our fa - thers, we will love Both friend and foe in

fire and sword! O how our hearts beat high with joy
con - science free. How sweet would be their chil - dren's fate
all our strife; And preach Thee, too, as love knows how,

When-e'er we hear that glo - rious word! Faith of our fa - thers!
If they, like them could die for thee! Faith of our fa - thers!
By kind - ly words and vir - tuous life. Faith of our fa - thers!

Ho - ly faith! We will be true to Thee till death!
Ho - ly faith! We will be true to Thee till death!
Ho - ly faith! We will be true to Thee till death!

Faith of Our Fathers

1849

Now faith is the substance of things hoped for, the evidence of things not seen. For by it the elders obtained a good testimony. Hebrews 11:1, 2 (NKJV)

Frederick William Faber was raised in an Anglican parsonage in Calverley, Yorkshire, England; but both his parents died when he was young. When he moved to Oxford University as a young man, he came under the influence of the great Roman Catholic, John Henry Newman, author of "Lead, Kindly Light." Following graduation, Faber entered the Anglican ministry, but his soul was troubled. He was drawn to the historic, reverent liturgy of the Catholic faith. On Sunday night, November 16, 1845, he announced to his congregation that he intended to leave the Church of England and be ordained as a Roman Catholic.

For the remainder of his short life—Faber died at fifty-nine—he endeavored to provide a body of hymns for English Catholics to sing. Perhaps his most enduring is "Faith of Our Fathers."

What most Protestants don't know is that Faber wrote this song to remind the Catholic Church of its martyrs during the days of the Protestant King Henry VIII and Queen Elizabeth I. "Good Queen Bess," for example, used fines, gallows, gibbets, racks, and whips against those who said Mass, honored the pope, or harbored a priest. Often in the middle of the night, thugs would burst into Catholic homes and drag them away to be scourged, fined, or seared with glowing irons. The dungeons were choked with victims.

Nicholas Owen was such a victim. Probably a builder by trade, Owen designed countless hiding places for endangered Catholics. He hid them in secret rooms, between the walls, and under the floors. He hid them in stone fences and in underground passages. He designed nooks and crannies that looked like anything but hiding places.

When Nicholas was at last betrayed, he was dragged to the Tower of London and his arms were fixed to iron rings. There he hung for hours, his body dangling. Weights added to his feet increased the suffering. The tortures continued until March 2, 1606, when "his bowels broke in a terrible way" and he passed to his reward.

It was for these Catholic heroes, martyred at the hands of so-called "Protestant" monarchs, that "Faith of Our Fathers" was originally written. Now, of course, this great hymn reminds us all of the noble sacrifices made by those in every branch of the Christian family who have passed on their faith to us ". . . in spite of dungeon, fire and sword."

O Come, O Come, Emmanuel

Latin Hymn, 9th cent.
Translated by John M. Neale

Thomas Helmore

1. O come, O come, Em - man - u - el, And ran - som cap - tive
2. O come, thou Wis - dom from on high, Who or - der est all things
3. O come, De - sire of na - tions, bind All peo - ples in one
4. O come, thou Day - spring, come and cheer Our spir - its by Thine

Is - ra - el, That mourns in lone - ly ex - ile here
might - i - ly; To us the path of knowl - edge show
heart and mind. From dust Thou brought us forth to life;
ad - vent here; Dis - perse the gloom - y clouds of night,

Un - til the Son of God ap - pear.
And teach us in her ways to go. Re - joice! Re - joice! Em-
De - liv - er us from earth - ly strife.
And death's dark shad - ows put to flight.

man - u - el, Shall come to thee, O Is - ra - el!

O Come, O Come, Emmanuel

1851

Behold, the virgin shall be with child, and bear a Son, and they shall call His name Immanuel. Matthew 1:23 (NKJV)

T he origins of this plaintive carol date to medieval times. In the 800s, a series of Latin hymns were sung each day during Christmas Vespers from December 17 to 23. Each of these hymns began with the word "O," and were called the "Great" or "O" Antiphons (the word *antiphon* meaning psalm or anthem). These hymns were apparently restructured into verse form in the 1100s, and finally published in Latin in 1710. In the mid-1800s, they were discovered by an English minister named John Mason Neale, who wove together segments of them to produce the first draft of "O Come, O Come, Emmanuel," which was published in 1851. Neale's original version said, "Draw nigh, draw nigh, Emmanuel."

Neale is a man worth knowing. He was born in London on January 24, 1818, the son of an evangelical Anglican clergyman. He attended Cambridge University and proved to be a brilliant student and prize-winning poet. While there, Neale was influenced by the Oxford Movement and became attracted to Roman Catholicism. In 1841, he was ordained into the Anglican ministry; but his poor health and Catholic leanings prevented him from gaining a parish ministry.

He was appointed instead as the director of Sackville College, a home for old men. (Sackville College, started by Robert Sackville, Earl of Dorset, in the early 1600s as a home for the elderly, is still going strong today in East Grinstead, Sussex.) This was the perfect job for Neale, for he was a compassionate man with a great heart for the needy, but he was also a scholar needing time for research and writing.

As a high church traditionalist, Neale disliked the hymns of Isaac Watts and longed to return Christianity to the liturgical dignity of church history. He was an outspoken advocate of returning church buildings to their former glory. He campaigned, for example, against certain types of stoves that spoiled the tastefulness and charm of English churches. He also worked hard to translate ancient Greek and Latin hymns into English.

In today's hymnals, we find Neale and Watts side-by-side, the old differences having been forgotten. We owe a debt of gratitude to John Mason Neale every time we sing one of his Christmas carols: "Good King Wenceslas," "O Come, O Come, Emmanuel," "Good Christian Men, Rejoice," and his Palm Sunday hymn, "All Glory, Laud, and Honor."

Children of the Heavenly Father

Carolina W. Sandell-Berg

Swedish Melody

1. Chil - dren of the heaven - ly Fa - ther, Safe - ly
2. God His own doth tend and nour - ish, In His
3. Nei - ther life nor death shall ev - er, From the
4. Though He giv - eth or He tak - eth, God His

in His bos - om gath - er; Nest - ling bird nor star in
ho - ly courts they flour - ish; From all e - vil things He
Lord His chil - dren sev - er; Un - to them His grace He
chil - dren ne'er for - sak - eth; His the lov - ing pur - pose

heav - en Such a ref - uge e'er was giv - en.
spares them, In His might - y arms He bears them.
show - eth, And their sor - rows all He know - eth.
sole - ly To pre - serve them pure and ho - ly.

Children of the Heavenly Father

1855

Behold what manner of love the Father has bestowed on us, that we should be called children of God! 1 John 3:1 (NKJV)

T his Scandinavian hymn was penned by Carolina (Lina) Sandell-Berg, the "Fanny Crosby of Sweden." She was born in a parsonage in Fröderyd, Sweden, on October 3, 1832, into a home full of music and literature. Lina (pronounced Lie-nah) was a "daddy's girl" in childhood, for her frail health often kept her indoors, in his study, when other children were outside playing.

When she was twelve, she fell ill and was paralyzed. Eventually Lina regained her health, and out of the experience came her first book of poems, published when she was a teenager. But another tragedy awaited her.

When she was twenty-six, she and her dad were traveling by boat outside the harbor of Göteborg when he fell overboard and drowned. Out of this experience came a flood of poems and hymns, including her classic, "Day by Day, and with Each Passing Moment."

Some hymn histories claim that "Children of the Heavenly Father" was one of the hymns written in response to her father's death; but it was first published in 1855, three years before this tragedy. This has prompted other historians to claim it was one of the poems she wrote as a teenager. All we know is that "Children of the Heavenly Father" first appeared in Lina's book, *Andeliga Dagg-Droppar* in 1855, when she was twenty-three.

The simple, lilting tune to "Children of Our Heavenly Father" is a Swedish folk melody called *"Tryggare Kan Ingen Vara,"* which translated, is: "No One Can Be Safer." Its origins are unknown, but "Sweden's Spiritual Troubadour," Oskar Ahnfelt, a Lutheran Pietist who helped introduce evangelical hymns to the Swedish Church, set many of Lina's poems to music. At the time, the state-sponsored church didn't allow simple pietistic hymns like "Children of the Heavenly Father." But Ahnfelt sang them anyway, traveling around with his ten-string guitar. When opposition arose, he was ordered to sing before King Karl XV. To the chagrin of church officials, the king loved Ahnfelt's simple melodies and tender hymns, saying, "You may sing them as much as you desire in both of my kingdoms."

He did, and many of his texts were written by Lina Sandell-Berg, who wrote about six hundred fifty hymns and poems during her lifetime. "Ahnfelt has sung my songs into the hearts of the people," she later said.

O How I Love Jesus

Frederick Whitfield

American Melody

1. There is a name I love to hear, I love to sing its worth;
2. It tells me of a Sav-ior's love, Who died to set me free;
3. It tells me what my Fa-ther hath, In store for ev - 'ry day;
4. It tells of One whose lov-ing heart, Can feel my deep - est woe;

It sounds like mu - sic in my ear, The sweet - est Name on earth.
It tells me of His pre-cious blood, The sin - ner's per-fect plea.
And tho' I tread a dark-some path, Yields sun - shine all the way.
Who in each sor - row bears a part, That none can bear be - low.

O how I love Je - sus, O how I love Je - sus,

O how I love Je - sus; Be - cause He first loved me.

O How I Love Jesus

1855

We love Him because He first loved us. 1 John 4:19 (NKJV)

Frederick Whitfield was born on a cold January day in 1829, in tiny Threapwood, England, population about 250. He attended college in Dublin, Ireland, and devoted his life to pastoral ministry in the Church of England. His greatest legacy is this hymn about the name of Jesus, written when he was a student. Generations of Christians have loved "There Is a Name I Love to Hear" with its peppy refrain: *"O how I love Jesus, / O how I love Jesus, / O how I love Jesus, / because He first loved me."*

You might be interested to know that while Whitfield wrote the *verses* to this hymn, he didn't compose its famous chorus.

Both the simple words and the nimble tune of "O How I Love Jesus" are American inventions of unknown origin. They floated around like orphans, attaching themselves to various hymns in the nineteenth century. One hymnologist found forty-two occurrences of this chorus in early songbooks. Even such stately hymns as "Amazing Grace" and "Alas! And Did My Savior Bleed" were occasionally sung to this lighthearted melody, with "O How I Love Jesus" used as the refrain.

But when "O How I Love Jesus" was finally wedded to Whitfield's "There Is a Name I Love to Hear," it was a marriage made in heaven. We've been singing it ever since. Some of Whitfield's original verses have fallen by the wayside, which is too bad; every verse tells us what the Name of Jesus can do in our lives:

> *It tells me what my Father hath / in store for every day,*
> *And though I tread a darksome path, / yields sunshine all the way.*
>
> *It tells of One whose loving heart / can feel my deepest woe;*
> *Who in each sorrow bears a part / that none can bear below.*
>
> *It bids my trembling heart rejoice; / it dries each rising tear.*
> *It tells me, in a "still small voice," / to trust and never fear.*
>
> *This Name shall shed its fragrance still / along this thorny road,*
> *Shall sweetly smooth the rugged hill / that leads me up to God.*
>
> *And there with all the blood-bought throng, / from sin and sorrow free,*
> *I'll sing the new eternal song / of Jesus' love for me.*

Little Brown Church in the Vale

William S. Pitts

William S. Pitts

1. There's a church in the val-ley by the wild-wood, No love - li - er
2. There close by the side of that loved one, To the trees where the
3. How sweet on a clear Sab-bath morn - ing, To list to the
4. From the church in the val-ley by the wild-wood, When day fades a -

spot in the dale; No place is so dear to my child - hood
wild flow - ers bloom; Where the fare - well hymn will be chant - ed,
clear ring - ing bell; Its tones so sweet - ly are call - ing,
way in - to night. I would fain from this spot of my child - hood,

No spot is so dear To my child - hood

Fine

As the lit - tle brown church In the vale.
I shall rest by her side in the tomb. Oh, come, come, come, come
Oh, come to the church In the vale.
Wing my way to the man - sions of light.

As the lit - tle brown church in the vale.

D.S. al Fine

Come to the church in the wild - wood, Oh, come to the church in the vale;

Little Brown Church in the Vale

1857

Remember the Sabbath day, to keep it holy. Exodus 20:8 (NKJV)

T he Little Brown Church in the Vale sits in a beautiful park alongside Highway 218 in the town of Bradford, near Nashua, in northern Iowa. But it wasn't there when the song was written.

A New York native named William Pitts, about twenty-seven, was traveling by stagecoach from his home in Wisconsin to Fredericksburg, Iowa, to see his girlfriend. It was a bright afternoon in 1857. When the stagecoach made a pit stop in Bradford, Pitts took a stroll among the trees to stretch his legs. The gently sloping hills formed a slight valley, and the Cedar River flowed peacefully by. That grove of trees, it seemed to Pitts, would be the perfect setting for a church.

Unable to erase the scene from his mind, Pitts returned home and composed the words and music to "Little Brown Church in the Vale." Nothing came of his song, however, and he filed it away.

Five years later, Pitts, now married to his sweetheart, relocated to Iowa to be near his elderly in-laws and to teach music at Bradford Academy. Imagine his surprise when he saw a church building sitting in the very spot he had previously envisioned it. Christians in the community, growing tired of meeting in abandoned stores, had determined to build a church. The Civil War was raging and times were hard; but by 1862, the building was up. It had to be painted using the cheapest color—which was brown.

When Pitts saw the little brown church in the vale, he rushed home and found "Little Brown Church in the Vale," packed among his papers. He sang his hymn at the building's dedication in 1864. Soon afterward, he sold his manuscript to a publisher in Chicago for $25. He used the money to enroll in Rush Medical College, and William spent the rest of his life as the town physician in Fredericksburg, Iowa, about fourteen miles from Bradford.

Today the Little Brown Church boasts a membership of about 100, but it's best known for the hundreds of weddings and thousands of tourists who flock there each year to see the church in the valley by the wildwood, the little brown church in the vale.

We Three Kings of Orient Are

John H. Hopkins, Jr.   John H. Hopkins, Jr.

1. We three kings of O - ri - ent are, Bear-ing gifts we trav - erse a - far;
2. Born a King on Beth - le - hem's plain, Gold I bring to crown Him a - gain;
3. Frank-in - cense to of - fer have I, In-cense owns a De - i - ty nigh;
4. Myrrh is mine, its bit - ter per - fume, Breathes a life of gath - er-ing gloom;
5. Glo - rious now be - hold Him a - rise, King and God and Sac - ri - fice;

Field and foun - tain, moor and moun - tain, Fol - low-ing yon - der star.
King for - ev - er, ceas - ing nev - er, O - ver us all to reign.
Prayer and prais - ing, all men rais - ing, Wor - ship Him, God on high.
Sor - rowing, sigh - ing, bleed - ing, dy - ing, Sealed in the stone cold tomb.
Al - le - lu - ia, al - le - lu - ia! Earth to heav'n re - plies.

O star of won - der, star of night, Star with roy - al beau - ty bright;

West - ward lead - ing, still pro - ceed - ing, Guide us to Thy per - fect light.

We Three Kings
of Orient Are
1857

Now after Jesus was born in Bethlehem of Judea in the days of Herod the king, behold, wise men from the East came to Jerusalem . . . Matthew 2:1 (NKJV)

S trange but true: A visit from St. Nicholas paved the way for "We Three Kings." It happened like this. After the War of 1812, Anglicans in America decided to establish their own seminary for training Episcopalian ministers. The proposal was first made in 1814; and in 1817, the Episcopalian General Convention voted to locate the school in New York City. But where in New York?

Clement Clarke Moore, son of New York's Episcopalian Bishop, was an up-and-coming land developer. He had recently become well-known because of a poem he had written, which began:

> *'Twas the night before Christmas, when all through the house*
> *not a creature was stirring, not even a mouse . . . .*

The popularity of his poem (reportedly written following a sleigh ride home from Greenwich Village) made his name a household word. The fame and increased income made him a more generous and sought-after layman.

Moore owned a large estate in the undeveloped northern regions of Manhattan. He referred to it as "a quiet, rural retreat on the picturesque banks of the Hudson." Hearing that the Episcopalians needed land for their seminary, he offered a portion of his estate, and thus was born General Theological Seminary. Moore, also a linguist and Hebrew scholar, became one of General's first professors, teaching biblical languages.

Some years later, a reporter named John H. Hopkins, Jr., enrolled in this seminary. Born in Pittsburgh, Hopkins had matriculated at the University of Vermont before moving to New York to pursue legal studies. But he fell in love with the Lord's work, enrolled in General, and graduated from the seminary in 1850. In 1855, he was hired as the school's first instructor of church music.

Hopkins wrote "We Three Kings" as part of a Christmas pageant produced by General Theological Seminary in 1857. In 1863 it was published in his *Carols, Hymns, and Songs*. This hymnal went through three editions by 1882, establishing Hopkins as a leader in Episcopalian hymnody. He wrote other hymns, but most have fallen into obscurity. "We Three Kings" was his crowning achievement, made possible, in a way, through the generosity of another poet whose most famous work ends:

> *But I heard him exclaim, 'ere he drove out of sight,*
> *Merry Christmas to all, and to all a good night!*

Praise Ye the Triune God

Elizabeth R. Charles

Friedrich F. Flemming

1. Praise ye the Fa - ther! For His lov - ing kind - ness,
2. Praise ye the Sa - vior! Great is His com - pas - sion,
3. Praise ye the Spir - it! Com - fort - er of Is - rael,

ten - der - ly cares He For His err - ing
gra - cious - ly cares He for His cho - sen
sent of the Fa - ther and the Son to

chil - dren; Praise Him, ye an - gels, praise Him in the
peo - ple; young men and maid - ens, ye old men and
bless us; praise to the Fa - ther, Son and Ho - ly

heav - ens, praise ye Je - ho - - - vah!
chil - dren, praise ye the Sav - - - ior!
Spir - it, praise ye the tri - une God!

Praise Ye the Triune God

1858

Go therefore and make disciples of all the nations, baptizing them in the name of the Father and of the Son and of the Holy Spirit. Matthew 28:19 (NKJV)

Elizabeth Rundle Charles was blessed with an idyllic childhood in a picturesque village on the southwestern tip of England. Her father, John Rundle, was a banker and a Member of Parliament. Her mother, Joana, provided a well-ordered home where the hymns of Watts and Wesley were often sung. Elizabeth was an only child, but a brood of cousins lived nearby; together they were educated by governesses, and Elizabeth was well-trained in the liberal arts and foreign languages.

As a teenager, she began realizing that a Christian environment wasn't enough. She needed Christ Himself. One sunny afternoon after talking with a Swiss friend, César Malan, Elizabeth gave her heart to the Lord Jesus. She was eighteen. "For the first time I seemed to forget and lose myself altogether," she wrote. "I began to see that the work of our Redemption is not ours but God's, that Christ has borne away our sins. . . . The Spirit bore witness with my spirit that I was His child. I loved Him because He first loved me! For hours I was conscious of nothing but the absorbing joy. *'My Father! I am Thy child!'* " (italics hers).

Out of this experience she wrote one of her best-known hymns, "Come and Rejoice with Me," which she called "Eureka," meaning "I have found Him!"

Five years later, Elizabeth married Andrew Charles and they settled down in Hampstead, where Charles was part-owner in a factory. There she ministered among the poor around the factory, engaged in benevolent work, and wrote books and poems. This great hymn, "Praise Ye the Triune God" was published when she was about thirty. Every stanza is a verse of praise to one of the members of the Godhead—Father, Son, and Holy Spirit. It is unusual in that the lyrics do not rhyme.

Elizabeth's father later faced bankruptcy and her husband died, leaving her a widow at forty. She assumed financial care of her parents, and God provided through royalties from her fifty or so books. So great was her skill as a poet, novelist, devotional writer, linguist, musician, and painter that she became one of the best-known women in England during the nineteenth century—to which she would simply say: "Praise Ye the Triune God."*

---

*I am indebted to Virginia Davis of www.hiddenpearls.com for her willingness to share with me her original research on the extraordinary life of Elizabeth Rundle Charles.

Angels We Have Heard on High

French Carol

French Melody

1. An - gels we have heard on high Sweet - ly sing - ing o'er the plains,
2. Shep - herds, why this ju - bi - lee? Why your joy - ous strains pro - long?
3. Come to Beth - le - hem and see Him whose birth the an - gels sing;

And the moun - tains in re - ply Ech - o - ing their joy - ous strains.
What the glad - some tid - ings be, Which in - spire your heav'n - ly song?
Come a - dore on bend - ed knee, Christ the Lord, the new - born King.

Glo - - - - - - - - - ri - a

in ex - cel - sis De - o! Glo - - - - -

ri - a in ex - cel - sis De - o!

Angels We Have Heard on High

1855

And suddenly there was with the angel a multitude of the heavenly host praising God and saying: Glory to God in the highest, And on earth peace, goodwill toward men! Luke 2:13, 14 (NKJV)

*L*es Anges dans nos Campagnes" was a French carol dating from the 1700s, which appeared in several different versions. It was published in English in 1862, the words saying:

> *Angels we have heard on high | Sweetly singing o'er the plains,*
> *And the mountains in reply | Echoing their joyous strains.*
> Gloria, in excelsis Deo!

An older version had the title, "Harken All! What Holy Singing!" The words, translated into English, said:

> *Hearken, all! What holy singing | Now is sounding from the sky!*
> *'Tis a hymn with grandeur ringing, | Sung by voices clear and high.*
> Gloria, in excelsis Deo!

Still another primitive version speaks from the shepherds' vantage point, saying:

> *Shepherds in the field abiding, | Tell us when the seraph bright*
> *Greeted you with wondrous tiding, | What you saw and heard that night.*
> Gloria, in excelsis Deo!

Hymns are usually authored by human beings like us, but in this case obscure verses by unknown French poets were coupled with a refrain that was literally composed by angels in heaven: *Gloria, in excelsis Deo.* That's the Latin wording for the angelic anthem, "Glory to God in the highest!" It comes from Luke 2:14 in the Vulgate, the Latin version of the Bible. The Latin word *Gloria* means *Glory*, and *in excelsis* is the phrase for *in the highest*. Our English words *excel* and *excellent* come from the same root, meaning *to rise* or *to ascend* or *to be high*. The Latin word *Deo* means *God*.

This was the song proclaimed by the angels over Shepherds' Field the night Christ was born. The musical score stretches out and emphasizes the words in a way that is uniquely fun to sing and deeply stirring, as we lift our voices to proclaim: Jesus has come! Hope has arrived on earth! A Savior is born! Glory to God on High! *Gloria, in excelsis Deo!*

Thou Didst Leave Thy Throne

Emily E. S. Elliott

Timothy R. Matthews

1. Thou didst leave Thy throne and Thy king - ly crown When Thou cam - est to earth for me, But in Beth - le - hem's home was there found no room For Thy ho - ly na - tiv - i - ty. O come to my heart, Lord Je - sus: There is room in my heart for Thee!

2. Heav - en's arch - es rang when the an - gels sang, Pro - claim - ing Thy roy - al de - cree, But of low - ly birth didst Thou come to earth And in great hu - mil - i - ty. O come to my heart, Lord Je - sus. There is room in my heart for Thee!

3. The fox - es found rest, and the birds their nest In the shade of the for - est tree; But Thy couch was the sod, O Thou Son of God, In the des - erts of Gal - i - lee. O come to my heart, Lord Je - sus. There is room in my heart for Thee!

4. Thou cam - est, O Lord, with the liv - ing word That should set Thy peo - ple free; But with mock - ing scorn and with crown of thorn They bore Thee to Cal - va - ry. O come to my heart, Lord Je - sus. There is room in my heart for Thee!

5. When the heavens shall ring and the an - gels sing At Thy com - ing to vic - tor - y, Let Thy voice call me home, say - ing, "Yet there is room, There is room at My side for thee." And my heart shall re - joice, Lord Je - sus, When Thou com - est and call - est me.

Thou Didst Leave Thy Throne

1864

And she brought forth her firstborn Son, and wrapped Him in swaddling cloths, and laid Him in a manger, because there was no room for them in the inn. Luke 2:7 (NKJV)

 mily Elliott was born south of London in the little holiday town of Brighton on the English Channel in 1836. Her father, Edward Elliott, was pastor of St. Mark's Church there. His invalid aunt—Charlotte Elliott, well-known hymnist and the author of the invitational hymn, "Just as I Am"—lived nearby.

While working with children in the church choir and the local parish school, Emily, in her late twenties, wanted to use the Christmas season to teach them about the entire life and mission of the Savior. As she studied Luke 2:7, she wrote this hymn. The first and second verses speak of our Lord's birth, but the third verse describes His life as an itinerate preacher. The next stanza describes His death on Calvary, and the last verse proclaims His Second Coming.

Emily had her hymn privately printed, and it was first performed in her father's church during the Christmas season of 1864. Six years later, she included it in a magazine she edited called "Church Missionary Juvenile Instructor."

Several years later, Emily inserted this carol into her book of poems and hymns entitled *Chimes for Daily Service.* "Thou Didst Leave Thy Throne" first appeared in the United States in *The Sunday School Hymnal,* published in Boston in 1871.

Emily devoted her life to Sunday school work, to ministering to the down-and-out in Brighton's rescue missions, and to sharing the message of Christ through poems, hymns, and the printed page. Another of her carols was widely used for many years during the Christmas season, though it isn't well-known today. The words are ideally suited for the children Emily so loved. This carol, too, encompasses our Lord's entire life and mission:

There came a little Child to earth long ago;
And the angels of God proclaimed His birth, high and low.

Out on the night, so calm and still, their song was heard;
For they knew that the Child on Bethlehem's hill was Christ the Lord.

In mortal weakness, want and pain, He came to die,
That the children of earth might in glory reign with Him on high.

And evermore in robes so fair and undefiled,
Those ransomed children His praise declare, who was a Child.

I Heard the Bells on Christmas Day

Henry Wadsworth Longfellow

Jean Baptiste Calkin

1. I heard the bells on Christ - mas day Their
2. And thought how, as the day had come, The
3. And in de - spair I bowed my head: "There
4. Then pealed the bells more loud and deep: "God
5. Till ring - ing, sing - ing on its way, The

old fa - mil - iar car - ols play, And wild and sweet the
bel - fries of all Chris - ten - dom Had rolled a - long th'un -
is no peace on earth," I said, "For hate is strong, and
is not dead, nor doth He sleep; The wrong shall fail, the
world re - volved from night to day, A voice, a chime, a

words re - peat, Of peace on earth, good - will to men.
bro - ken song Of peace on earth, good - will to men.
mocks the song Of peace on earth, good - will to men."
right pre - vail, With peace on earth, good - will to men."
chant sub - lime, Of peace on earth, good - will to men!

I Heard the Bells on Christmas Day

1864

Behold, He who keeps Israel shall neither slumber nor sleep. Psalm 121:4 (NKJV)

T he famous Longfellow brothers were born and raised in Portland, Maine, in the 1800s. Henry Wadsworth was born in 1807, and younger brother Samuel arrived in 1819. Henry became a Harvard professor of literature and one of America's greatest writers, and Samuel became a Unitarian minister and a hymnist.

While Henry was publishing his books, however, dark clouds were gathering over his life and over all America. In 1861, his wife tragically died when her dress caught fire in their home in Cambridge, Massachusetts. That same year, the Civil War broke out, tearing the nation apart. Two years later, during the fiercest days of the conflict, Henry's son, Charley, seventeen, ran away from home and hopped aboard a train to join President Lincoln's army.

Charley proved a brave and popular soldier. He saw action at the Battle of Chancellorsville in 1863, but in early June he contracted typhoid fever and malaria and was sent home to recover. He missed the Battle of Gettysburg, but by August, Charley was well enough to return to the field. On November 27, during the battle of New Hope Church in Virginia, he was shot through the left shoulder. The bullet nicked his spine and came close to paralyzing him. He was carried into the church and later taken to Washington to recuperate.

Receiving the news on December 1, 1863, Henry left immediately for Washington. He found his son well enough to travel and they headed back to Cambridge, arriving home on December 8. For weeks Henry sat by his son's bedside, slowly nursing his boy back to health.

On Christmas Day, December 25, 1863, Henry gave vent to his feelings in this plaintive carol that can only be understood against the backdrop of war. Two stanzas now omitted from most hymnals speak of the cannons thundering in the South and of hatred tearing apart "the hearth-stones of a continent." The poet feels like dropping his head in despair, but then he hears the Christmas bells. Their triumphant pealing reminds him that "God is not dead, nor doth He sleep."

The Sunday school children of the Unitarian Church of the Disciples in Boston first sang this song during that year's Christmas celebration. How wonderful that such a song should emerge from the bloody clouds of the War Between the States.

For All the Saints

William W. How

Ralph Vaughan Williams

1. For all the saints Who from their la - bors rest,
2. Thou wast their Rock, their fort - ress and their might;
3. O blest com - mu - nion, fel - low - ship di - vine!
4. And when the strife is fierce, the war - fare long,
5. From earth's wide bounds and o - cean's far - thest coast,

Who Thee by faith be - fore the world con - fessed, Thy
Thou, Lord, their Cap - tain in the well - fought fight;
We fee - bly strug - gle; they in glo - ry shine. Yet
Steals on the ear the dis - tant tri - umph song, And
Through gates of pearl streams in the count - less host,

name, O Je - sus, be for - ev - er blest.
Thou in the dark - ness drear, their one true light.
all are one in Thee, for all are Thine.
hearts are brave a - gain and arms are strong.
Sing - ing to Fa - ther, Son and Ho - ly Ghost.

Al - - le - lu - ia! Al - le - lu - ia!

For All the Saints

1864

But the saints of the Most High shall receive the kingdom, and possess the kingdom forever, even forever and ever. Daniel 7:18 (NKJV)

William Walsham How was born into a wealthy British home just before Christmas in 1823. His father was a lawyer and his grandfather a preacher. William attended Oxford to study law, but after graduation he entered the Anglican ministry. He proved very capable and was offered the Bishopric of Manchester; but he turned it down without even telling his family of the offer. He also refused the Bishopric of Durham, England, with its large salary and prestige. He wanted to serve in humbler places.

In 1851, he became a country parson in the rural parish of Whittington near the Welsh border. He labored there for twenty-eight years, during which time he wrote most of his nearly sixty hymns. In 1879, he moved to London and began working tirelessly among the poor as an assisting (suffragen) Bishop.

He was called the "Omnibus Bishop" for he refused to ride in the private coach afforded bishops. He preferred public transportation. He was also called "the Poor Man's Bishop" because of his concern for the poverty-stricken of Victorian London.

William tended toward liberalism in his theology and was influenced by the intellectual trends of his day, including the theory of evolution. His son once said, "My father considered evolution to be the wonderful way in which 'the Lord formed man out of the dust of the ground.'"

Nevertheless, William was a passionate soul-winner and an evangelical hymnist. He once said a minister "should be a man pure, holy, and spotless in his life; a man of much prayer; in character meek, lowly . . . devoting his days and nights to lightening the burdens of humanity." And he said about his poems: "A good hymn should be like a good prayer—simple, real, earnest, and reverent."

In 1897, How was asked to write the national hymn for the British Empire's observance of Queen Victoria's Jubilee, but he had little time to enjoy the honor. He died on August 10 that year while vacationing in Ireland.

One of William's greatest hymns is "For All the Saints," originally titled "Saints Day Hymn—Cloud of Witnesses—Hebrews 12:1." It was written for All Saints' Day (November 1) and is often used as a processional in church services on that day due to its majestic tune. It was first published in 1864 in Earl Nelson's *Hymns for Saint's Days and Other Hymns*.

We Give Thee But Thine Own

William W. How

Lowell Mason and George J. Webb

1. We give Thee but Thine own, What-e'er the gift may be. All that we have is Thine a-lone, A trust, O Lord, from Thee.

2. May we Thy boun-ties thus As stew-ards true re-ceive. And glad-ly, as Thou bless-est us, To Thee our first-fruits give.

3. To com-fort and to bless, To find a balm for woe, To tend the lone and fa-ther-less, Is an-gels' work be-low.

4. And we be-lieve Thy word, Though dim our faith may be. What-ev-er task we do, O Lord, We do it un-to Thee.

We Give Thee But Thine Own

1864

. . . We thank You And praise Your glorious name. . . . For all things come from You, And of Your own we have given You. 1 Chronicles 29:13, 14 (NKJV)

A recent newspaper report said that if American Christians would simply give the biblical tithe to the Lord, an additional $143 billion dollars would flow annually into His worldwide work. Despite being the most affluent generation in history, only a fraction of believers tithe from their income to the ministry of the gospel.

Perhaps it's because they don't understand 1 Chronicles 29:14. When King David was planning the temple in Jerusalem, he gave liberally of his wealth and asked his people to do the same. When the money came in, David was ecstatic: "But who am I, and who are my people," he exclaimed, "that we should be able to offer so willingly as this? For all things come from You, and of Your own we have given You."

William How, a nineteenth-century English bishop, put David's words into verse form in this great stewardship hymn:

> *We give Thee but Thine own, whate'er the gift may be;*
> *All that we have is Thine alone, a trust, O Lord, from Thee.*

How had a burning desire to minister to the masses of London. This was the era of the Industrial Revolution, when multitudes had left the tranquility of the English countryside to work in the burgeoning factories and dockyards of London's East Side. It was the stuff of a Dickens' novel. Endless slums. Child labor. Long hours. Poverty. Alcoholism. Squalor. William How was called the "Poor Man's Bishop" as he visited, counseled, preached, evangelized, and provided for the needs of the desperate. His concern is seen in a frequently omitted stanza of this hymn:

> *To comfort and to bless, to find a balm for woe,*
> *To tend the lone and fatherless is angels' work below.*

If only we would realize that when we give to God we're only giving from what He has already given us. Someone said, "It isn't whether we're going to give ten percent of *our* income to God. It's whether we're going to keep ninety percent of *His* money for ourselves."

Coming to Christ, we give Him all we are and have, and we become His stewards. "So let each one give as he purposes in his heart," says 1 Corinthians 8:9, "not grudgingly or of necessity; for God loves a cheerful giver."

What Child Is This?

William C. Dix

English Melody

1. What child is this, who laid to rest, on Mar-y's lap is sleep-ing?
2. Why lies He in such mean es - tate, where ox and ass are feed-ing?
3. So bring Him in - cense, gold, and myrrh; come peas-ant, king to own Him.

Whom an - gels greet with an-thems sweet, while shep - herds watch are keep - ing?
Good Chris-tian, fear; for sin-ners here the si - lent Word is plead - ing.
The King of kings, sal - va-tion brings, let lov - ing hearts en - throne Him.

This, this is Christ the King, whom shep-herds guard and an - gels sing;
Nails, spear, shall pierce Him thro', the cross be borne, for me, for you.
Raise, raise the song on high, The vir - gin sings her lul - la - by.

Haste, haste to bring Him laud, the Babe, the Son of Mar - y.
Hail, hail the Word made flesh, the Babe, the Son of Mar - y.
Joy, joy for Christ is born, the Babe, the Son of Mar - y.

What Child Is This?

1865

. . . When the angels had gone away from them into heaven, that the shepherds said to one another, "Let us now go to Bethlehem . . ." Luke 2:15 (NKJV)

eelings of sadness come over me whenever I hear this deeply moving carol. It is, after all, set in the key of E minor, the "saddest of all keys." Yet triumphant joy dispels the sadness as we exclaim: "This, this is Christ the King, whom shepherds guard and angels sing."

The melancholic melody is a famous old British tune called "Greensleeves," originally a ballad about a man pining for his lost love, the fair Lady Greensleeves. Tradition says it was composed by King Henry VIII for Anne Boleyn. That's unlikely, but we do know that Henry's daughter, Queen Elizabeth I, danced to the tune.

Shakespeare referred to it twice in his play, *The Merry Wives of Windsor.* In Act V, for example, Falstaff said, "Let the sky rain potatoes; let it thunder to the tune of 'Green Sleeves.'"

It was licensed to two different printers in 1580, and soon thereafter was being used with religious texts. Its first association with Christmas came in 1642, in a book titled *New Christmas Carols,* in which it was used with the poem "The Old Year Now Away Has Fled." The last verse says: *Come, give's more liquor when I doe call, / I'll drink to each one in this hall . . . And God send us a happy new yeare!*

For nearly 150 years, however, "Greensleeves" has been most identified with "What Child Is This?" The words of this carol are taken from a longer poem written by an insurance agent named William Chatterton Dix, born in Bristol, England, in 1837. His father was a surgeon who wanted his son to follow his footsteps. But having no interest in medicine, William left Bristol Grammar School, moved to Glasgow, and sold insurance.

His greatest love was his prose and poetry for Christ. He wrote two devotional books, a book for children, and scores of hymns, two of which remain popular Christmas carols: "What Child Is This?" and "As with Gladness Men of Old."

All of Dix's hymns should be more widely sung today, for they are masterpieces of poetry, filled with rich scriptural truth. Here's the way he begins his exultant hymn, "Alleluia!"

> *Alleluia! Sing to Jesus! His the scepter, His the throne.*
> *Alleluia! His the triumph, His the victory alone.*

Ring the Bells of Heaven

William O. Cushing

George F. Root

1. Ring the bells of heav-en! There is joy to-day, For a soul re-
2. Ring the bells of heav-en! There is joy to-day, For the wan-d'rer
3. Ring the bells of heav-en! Spread the feast to-day! An-gels swell the

turn-ing from the wild! See! the Fa-ther meets Him out up-on the way,
now is rec-on-ciled; Yes, a soul is res-cued from His sin-ful way,
glad tri-um-phant strain! Tell the joy-ful ti-dings, bear it far a-way!

Wel-com-ing His wea-ry, wan-d'ring child.
And is born a-new a ran-somed child. Glo-ry! Glo-ry! How the
For a pre-cious soul is born a-gain.

an-gels sing! Glo-ry! Glo-ry! How the loud harps ring! 'Tis the ran-somed

ar-my, like a might-y sea, Peal-ing forth the an-them of the free.

Ring the Bells of Heaven
1866

. . . I say to you, there is joy in the presence of the angels of God over one sinner who repents. Luke 15:10 (NKJV)

Civil War musician George Root wrote a song entitled, "Glory! Glory! (The Little Octoroon)." The word "octoroon" was a term defining a person of one-eighth African ancestry. In Root's song, a little octoroon named Rosa was sitting with her mother on a Southern plantation at the close of day when they heard the sounds of Northern troops in the distance. The mother, a slave, knew that this might be Rosa's one and only chance for freedom. With heart-tugging courage, she told little Rosa to "Fly, my precious darling to the Union camp; / I will keep the hounds and hunters here. / Go right through the forest though 'tis dark and damp, / God will keep you, dear one, never fear." The chorus said:

> *Glory! glory! How the Freedmen sang!*
> *Glory! glory! How the old woods rang!*
> *'Twas the loyal army sweeping to the sea,*
> *Flinging out the banner of the Free!*

Some time later, Christian hymnist William Cushing, hearing it, determined to claim the tune for gospel music. In his autobiography, *Story of a Musical Life*, he wrote:

"The melody ran in my head all day long, chiming and flowing in its sweet musical cadence. I wished greatly that I might secure the tune for use in Sunday school and for other Christian purposes. When I heard the bells of heaven ringing of some sinner that had returned . . . the word(s) 'Ring the Bells of Heaven' at once flowed down into the waiting melody."

As Cushing wrote it, the chorus said:

> *Glory! Glory! How the angels sing:*
> *Glory! Glory! How the loud harps ring!*
> *'Tis the ransomed army, like a mighty sea,*
> *Pealing forth the anthem of the free.*

George Root, who also wrote gospel songs, was pleased with the changes and published "Ring the Bells of Heaven" in 1866 in one of his own music books, *Chapel Gems for Sunday School.*

This was the second of Root's Civil War songs to be "Christianized." The first was "Tramp! Tramp! Tramp!" which became the noted children's song, "Jesus Loves the Little Children."*

---

*This story is told in the author's first volume of hymn stories, *Then Sings My Soul* (Nashville: Thomas Nelson, 2002).

The Church's One Foundation

Samuel J. Stone   Samuel S. Wesley

1. The Church-'s one foun - da-tion Is   Je - sus Christ her   Lord,
2. She   is   from ev - 'ry   na-tion, Yet one o'er   all   the   earth,
3. 'Mid toil and trib - u - la-tion, And tu - mult of her   war,
4. Yet   she   on earth hath un - ion With God the Three in   One,

She   is His new cre - a - tion By   wa - ter and the   word;
Her   char - ter of sal - va-tion, One Lord, one faith, one birth;
She   waits the con - sum - ma-tion Of peace for - ev - er - more;
And   mys - tic sweet com - mu-nion With those whose rest is   won;

From heav'n He came and sought her To   be His ho - ly   bride;
One   ho - ly name she bless - es, Par - takes one ho - ly   food,
Till   with the vi - sion glo - rious Her long - ing eyes are blest,
With   all her sons and daugh-ters, who by the Mas-ter's   hand

With   His own blood He bought her, And for her   life He died.
And   to   one hope she press - es, With ev - 'ry grace en - dued.
And   the great Church vic - to - rious Shall be the Church at rest.
Led   through the death - ly   wa - ters, Re - pose in Ed - en land.

The Church's One Foundation

1866

For no other foundation can anyone lay than that which is laid, which is Jesus Christ. 1 Corinthians 3:11 (NKJV)

This great hymn emerged from a ragged and wearing controversy that threatened to tear asunder the Church of England. In the mid-1800s, the liberal views of German theologians drifted like a poisonous fog over Anglicans worldwide. In South Africa, Bishop John William Colenso, influenced by the German "higher critics," questioned whether Moses had really written the first five books of the Bible. He also took liberal views toward Paul's Book of Romans, denying the doctrine of eternal punishment. Colenso had been a tireless missionary bishop, serving the Zulu people in northeastern South Africa with laudable passion, but his emerging liberalism sent shock waves among evangelical Anglican leaders.

In 1853, Bishop Robert Gray of Capetown, defending the historic faith, removed Colenso from his post. Colenso fought the order and was reinstated by a London court of law. The resulting conflict shook the Anglican Church to its foundations.

One man on the side of evangelical truth was Samuel Stone, the curate at Windsor in the shadow of Windsor Castle. In 1866, he wrote twelve hymns based on the twelve articles of the Apostles' Creed. "The Church's One Foundation" was based on the ninth article of the creed, which says: "I believe in the holy catholic (universal) church: the communion of saints."

The next year, Anglican bishops from around the world assembled for a theological enclave that became known as the first Lambeth Conference. The tone of the proceedings was set by Stone's hymn, "The Church's One Foundation," which had been set to music by Samuel Wesley, the grandson of Charles Wesley. It became the processional for that conference, and has been one of the church's best-loved hymns ever since. Not all the verses, however, are sung today. Here is a stanza you may never have sung, but which helps us understand the passion of Samuel Stone as he wrote in defense of the integrity of Christ's holy church:

Though with a scornful wonder men see her sore oppressed,
By schisms rent asunder, by heresies distressed:
Yet saints their watch are keeping, their cry goes up, "How long?"
And soon the night of weeping shall be the morn of song!

I Love to Tell the Story

A. Katherine Hankey

William G. Fischer

1. I love to tell the sto - ry Of un - seen things a - bove,
2. I love to tell the sto - ry, More won - der - ful it seems
3. I love to tell the sto - ry, 'Tis pleas - ant to re - peat
4. I love to tell the sto - ry, For those who know it best

Of Je - sus and His glo - ry, Of Je - sus and His love.
Than all the gold - en fan - cies Of all our gold - en dreams.
What seems, each time I tell it, More won - der - ful - ly sweet.
Seem hun - ger - ing and thirst - ing To hear it like the rest.

I love to tell the sto - ry Be - cause I know 'tis true,
I love to tell the sto - ry, It did so much for me;
I love to tell the sto - ry, For some have nev - er heard
And when in scenes of glo - ry I sing the new, new song,

It sat - is - fies my long - ings As noth - ing else can do.
And that is just the rea - son I tell it now to thee.
The mes - sage of sal - va - tion From God's own ho - ly Word.
'Twill be the old, old sto - ry That I have loved so long.

I Love to Tell the Story

1866

Then they will see the Son of Man coming in the clouds with great power and glory.
Mark 13:26 (NKJV)

William Wilberforce, the Christian statesman and abolitionist, led a fierce campaign in nineteenth-century England to eradicate slavery from the British Empire. The geographical center of the campaign was a wealthy neighborhood in the south of London known as Clapham, where a group of Anglican evangelicals lived. The "Clapham Sect" also advocated prison reform, education for children, and the expansion of missionary efforts overseas. Though lampooned for their efforts, they changed the world.

Arabella Katherine Hankey was born into this environment in 1834. Her father was a banker in Clapham and a leader in the Clapham Group. Early in life, Kate became involved in religious work. As a young girl, she taught Sunday school; and when she was eighteen she organized a Bible study for factory girls in London. (This Bible study was never large, but the girls became close and fifty years later, five of them met together at Kate's funeral.) When her brother fell ill in Africa, Kate traveled there to bring him home. That trip sparked a passion for foreign missions, and in later life Kate devoted all proceeds from her writing to missionary work.

During the winter of 1865–1866, Kate, thirty, became seriously ill. The doctors warned her to abandon her Christian activities and remain in bed for a full year. To occupy her time, Kate wrote a poem of one hundred stanzas entitled "The Old, Old Story." She began the first section, "The Story Wanted," on January 29, 1866. Later that year, she wrote a second section entitled, "The Story Told."

The following year, at the international convention of the Young Men's Christian Association, Major General Russell ended his powerful sermon by quoting from Kate's poem. It left the audience breathless. Songwriter William Doane, in the crowd that day, put a portion of Kate's poem to music, giving birth to the hymn, "Tell Me the Old, Old Story."

Another composer, William G. Fischer, set a second portion of Kate's poem to a musical score he named HANKEY, and thus we have this hymn, "I Love to Tell the Story." It was first published in an American hymnbook in 1869, and was later popularized around the world in the great evangelistic campaigns of D. L. Moody and Ira Sankey.

The Cleansing Wave

Phoebe W. Palmer

Phoebe P. Knapp

1. O now I see the crim - son wave, The foun-tain deep and wide;
2. I see the new cre - a - tion rise, I hear the speak-ing blood;
3. I rise to walk in heav'n's own light, A - bove the world and sin;
4. A - maz-ing grace! 'tis heav'n be - low, To feel the blood ap - plied;

Je - sus, my Lord, might - y to save, Points to His wound - ed side.
It speaks! pol - lut - ed na - ture dies, Sinks 'neath the crim - son flood.
With heart made pure and gar-ments white, And Christ en-throned with - in.
And Je - sus, on - ly Je - sus know, My Je - sus cru - ci - fied.

The cleans-ing stream I see, I see! I plunge, and Oh, it cleans-eth me;

Oh praise the Lord, it cleans-eth me, It cleans-eth me, yes, cleans-eth me.

The Cleansing Wave

1867

. . . He was crucified in weakness, yet He lives by the power of God. . . . we also are weak in Him, but we shall live with Him by the power of God toward you. 2 Corinthians 13:4 (NKJV)

Today the cleansing stream I see! I see! I plunge, and oh, it cleanses me!" says this exuberant hymn about the soul-cleansing blood of Jesus. It was written by an unusual mother/daughter team, Phoebe Palmer and Phoebe Knapp.

The mother, Phoebe Palmer, was born in New York City in 1807. At age twenty, she married Walter C. Palmer, a physician, and several years later during a revival at New York's Allen Street Methodist Church, Phoebe and Walter knelt in prayer and pledged their lives to promoting holiness.

Soon Phoebe was leading a women's prayer meeting in her home. Before long, men were slipping in to enjoy Phoebe's teaching, including bishops, theologians, and ministers. Phoebe and Walter began traveling throughout the area, preaching and promoting revival. Though Phoebe spoke to great crowds, she insisted she wasn't "preaching" but "giving exhortations." The articles and books flowing from her pen magnified her impact, and she is now considered the "Mother of the Holiness Movement in the United States." It was this woman who wrote the words to "The Cleansing Wave."

Her daughter, Phoebe Knapp, composed the lively tune. Phoebe Palmer Knapp grew up in an atmosphere of revival. At age 16, she married a man who would later become an executive of the Metropolitan Life Insurance Company. They lived lives of high society, often entertaining the most famous people of their day. Their vast wealth allowed Phoebe to focus on her first love—Christian music. The Knapp Mansion had one of the nation's finest music rooms, and Phoebe even had a large pipe organ installed in her home.

One of her closest friends was the blind hymnist, Fanny Crosby. One day when Fanny was visiting, Phoebe went to the piano and played a melody she had written and asked Fanny what the tune seemed to say. The little hymnist replied, "Blessed Assurance, Jesus Is Mine." Fanny composed the words at once, and a great hymn was born.

Incidentally, Phoebe Knapp may have been one of the first hymnists to hear her own song on a phonograph. In February 1909, Thomas Edison's National Phonograph Company of Orange, New Jersey, released a wax cylinder recording of "Blessed Assurance," sung by the Edison Mixed Quartette. It's likely that Phoebe heard the original recording prior to her death.

Whispering Hope

Alice Hawthorne

Alice Hawthorne

Soft as the voice of an an - gel, Breathing a les-son un - heard,

Hope with a gen - tle per - sua - sion Whis-pers her com-fort-ing word:

Wait till the dark - ness is o - ver, Wait till life's tem-pest is done,

Hope for the sun-shine to - mor - row, Aft - er the show-er is gone.

Whis - per-ing hope, O how wel - come thy voice,

Whis-per-ing hope, whis-per-ing hope, Wel-come thy voice, O how wel-come thy voice,

Mak - ing my heart in its sor - row re - joice.

Mak-ing my heart, Mak-ing my heart in its sor-row, its sor-row re - joice.

Whispering Hope
1868

This hope we have as an anchor of the soul, both sure and steadfast . . . Hebrews
6:19 (NKJV)

T he background of this hymn offers a few surprises, the first being the
author's identity. Though published under the name "Alice Hawthorne,"
it was actually written by a man named Septimus Winner. Second, he's
also the author of such classic folk tunes as "Oh Where, Oh Where Has My
Little Dog Gone?" Third, he was once charged with treason against the government of
the United States of America.

Septimus Winner was born into a musical family in 1827 in Philadelphia. He was
the seventh child in the family, hence the name Septimus. His father was a violin
maker and a crafter of instruments, and Septimus showed early signs of musical
prowess. After attending Philadelphia's Central High School, Septimus joined one of
his brothers in forming a music publishing business. By age twenty, he was also
running his own music shop. Though largely self-taught, he became a popular music
instructor in Philadelphia, giving lessons in violin, guitar, and banjo and performing
with several of the city's bands and orchestras.

Septimus is best remembered, however, for his popular songs which he usually
published under the name of Alice Hawthorne. They are known in American folk
music history as "Hawthorne's Ballads." His most popular were "Listen to the Mock-
ing Bird" (which he reportedly sold to another Philadelphia publisher for five dollars)
and "Oh Where, Oh Where Has My Little Dog Gone?" written to a German tune.

Perhaps the most interesting moment of his life occurred in 1862, after Abraham
Lincoln had fired General George B. McClellan for delays in following up and attack-
ing the Confederate Army. There was great support for the popular McClellan, and
his firing incensed Septimus. He instantly published a song entitled, "Give Us Back
Our Old Commander: Little Mac, the People's Pride." It sold 80,000 copies in the
first two days, leading to Winner's arrest for treason. He was released when he agreed
to destroy all the remaining copies of the song.

Septimus Winner produced over two hundred instructional books for more than
twenty-three instruments, and he wrote thousands of musical arrangements. He was
inducted into the Songwriters Hall of Fame in 1970.

"Whispering Hope," published in 1868, was his last successful composition, and
is based on Hebrews 6:19: "This hope we have as an anchor of the soul, both sure
and steadfast, and which enters the Presence behind the veil."

Yield Not to Temptation

Horatio R. Palmer

Horatio R. Palmer

1. Yield not to temp - ta - tion, For yield - ing is sin;
2. Shun e - vil com - pan - ions, Bad lan - guage dis - dain;
3. To him that o'er - com - eth God giv - eth a crown;

Each vic - t'ry will help you Some oth - er to win;
God's name hold in rev - 'rence, Nor take it in vain;
Thro' faith we shall con - quer, Though of - ten cast down;

Fight man - ful - ly on - ward, Dark pas - sions sub - due;
Be thought - ful and ear - nest, Kind - heart - ed and true;
He who is our Sav - ior, Our strength will re - new;

Look ev - er to Je - sus, He will car - ry you through.
Look ev - er to Je - sus, He will car - ry you through.
Look ev - er to Je - sus, He will car - ry you through.

Yield Not to Temptation

1868

. . . He said to them, "Pray that you may not enter into temptation." Luke 22:40 (NKJV)

Horatio Palmer was one of New York's favorite musicians. Born in the middle of the state in 1834, Horatio grew up in a musical family. He joined the church choir conducted by his father when he was only seven. As a young man, he traveled to Rushford, New York, south of Buffalo, to attend Rushford Academy, a newly established institution of higher learning. He stayed after his graduation to become music professor for ten years, serving also as the choir director for the local Baptist church.

After further training in Europe, Horatio moved to Chicago, where he wrote theory books, edited a musical journal, served on the staff of a church, and worked hard to develop choral unions and music festivals. He was also an enthusiastic promoter of the hymns of Clara Scott, author of "Open My Eyes That I Might See."

Moving back to New York in 1873, Palmer became dean of the summer school of music at Chautauqua, New York. He also organized a massive church choral union in New York City that eventually grew to twenty thousand singers. On one occasion, he filled Madison Square Garden as he led a four-thousand-voice choir in a concert of sacred music.

About "Yield Not to Temptation," Palmer said: "I am reverently thankful God gave me the song, and has used it as a power for good. The song is an inspiration. I was at work on the dry subject of 'Theory' when the complete idea flashed upon my mind. I laid aside the theoretical work and hurriedly penned both words and music as fast as I could write them."

All his life, Palmer worked with young people and this was one of several hymns he wrote on the subject of temptation. Another, lesser-known hymn, is entitled "Have Courage to Say No."

You're starting, my boy, on life's journey,
Along the grand highway of life;
You'll meet with a thousand temptations—
Each city with evil is rife.
This world is a stage of excitement,
There's danger wherever you go;
But if you are tempted to weakness,
Have courage, my boy, to say No!

Beneath the Cross of Jesus

Elizabeth C. Clephane

Frederick C. Maker

1. Be - neath the cross of Je - sus I fain would take my stand:
2. Up - on the cross of Je - sus Mine eyes at times can see
3. I take, O cross, thy shad - ow For my a - bid - ing place;

The shad - ow of a might - y Rock With - in a wea - ry land,
The ver - y dy - ing form of One Who suf - fered there for me;
I ask no oth - er sun - shine than The sun - shine of His face,

A home with - in the wil - der - ness, A rest up - on the way,
And from my strick - en heart with tears, Two won - ders I con - fess:
Con - tent to let the world go by, To know no gain nor loss,

From the burn - ing of the noon-tide heat And the bur - den of the day.
The won - ders of re - deem - ing love And my un - wor - thi - ness.
My sin - ful self, my on - ly shame, My glo - ry all the cross.

Beneath the Cross of Jesus

1868

For the message of the cross is ... to us who are being saved ... the power of God.
1 Corinthians 1:18 (NKJV)

T he author of this hymn, Elizabeth Clephane, was born in Edinburgh, where her father was Sheriff of Fife. One of her siblings later wrote: "My sister was a very quiet little child, shrinking from notice and was always absorbed in books. The loss of both her parents at an early age taught her sorrow. As she grew up she was recognized as the cleverest one of our family. She was first in her class and a favorite at school. Her love for poetry was a passion. Among the sick and suffering she won the name, 'My Sunbeam.'" (Elizabeth's own comment on her nickname is written into a line of this hymn: "I take, O Cross, thy shadow for my abiding place; / I ask no other sunshine than the sunshine of His face.")

At some point, Elizabeth's family moved to Melrose, southeast of Edinburgh, where she spent her remaining years. Though frail, she was a diligent Bible student, a sympathetic listener, and a worker among the poor. She and her sisters raised money for the unfortunate, on one occasion selling their horse and carriage for a needy family.

Elizabeth's poems were published in the Scottish magazine, *The Family Treasury*. This one, appearing after her death, was discovered by Ira Sankey and introduced in the great Moody/Sankey meetings in Britain. In his autobiography, Sankey stated: "The author of this hymn, Elizabeth Celphane, also wrote the widely known hymn, 'The Ninety and Nine,' and these two were her only hymns. The first time this hymn was sung is still fresh in my memory. The morning after I had composed the music, Rev. W. H. Aitkin was to speak at our mission in London. . . . Before the sermon, I sang 'Beneath the Cross of Jesus' as a solo; and as in the case of 'The Ninety and Nine,' much blessing came from its use for the first time. With eyes filled with tears and deeply moved, the preacher said to the audience: 'Dear friends, I had intended to speak to you this morning upon work for the Master, but this new hymn has made such an impression on my heart, and evidently upon your own, that I will defer my proposed address and speak to you on "The Cross of Jesus." ' "

Sankey's tune has since been replaced in popular usage by St. Christopher, music composed for this hymn by Frederick C. Maker.

Pass Me Not, O Gentle Savior

Fanny J. Crosby

William H. Doane

1. Pass me not, O gen - tle Sav - ior; Hear my hum - ble cry!
2. Let me at Thy throne of mer - cy Find a sweet re - lief;
3. Trust-ing on - ly in Thy mer - it, Would I seek Thy face.
4. Thou, the Spring of all my com - fort, More than life to me!

While on oth - ers Thou art call - ing, Do not pass me by.
Kneel - ing there in deep con - tri - tion, Help my un - be - lief.
Heal my wound - ed, bro - ken spir - it, Save me by Thy grace.
Whom have I on earth be - side Thee? Whom in heaven but Thee?

Sav - ior, Sav - ior, hear my hum - ble cry!

While on oth - ers Thou art call - ing, Do not pass me by.

Pass Me Not,
O Gentle Savior

1868

And it shall come to pass That whoever calls on the name of the LORD shall be saved. Acts 2:21 (NKJV)

Born in Connecticut in 1832, William Doane grew up in a devout family and was converted to Christ in high school. At eighteen, he was hired by J. A. Fay & Co. of Norwich, Connecticut, one of America's largest woodworking machinery factories. Within ten years he had become the managing partner of the Cincinnati factory, and by his thirtieth birthday, he was the company's president.

That's when he suffered a heart attack and almost died. As he recovered, Doane felt his illness hadn't been caused by long hours or hard work. He determined that God was chastening him for not devoting more time to gospel music. He began writing music and publishing volumes of Sunday school songs. But he was frustrated because he didn't have quality poems. He needed a gifted and godly lyricist.

In 1867, while in New York on business, Doane visited his friend, Dr. W. C. Van Meter, director of Five Points Rescue Mission. Van Meter asked Doane to write a song for the mission's upcoming anniversary. The businessman said he'd be glad to write the music, but who would write the words?

Returning to his hotel room, Doane knelt and laid the need before the Lord. At once, there was a knock at the door. It was a messenger from the blind poet, Fanny Crosby, bearing this note: "Mr. Doane, I have never met you, but I feel impelled to send you this hymn. May God bless it."

The words of the poem began: "More like Jesus would I be, / Let my Savior dwell with me." Doane composed the music that night and it was used with great success as the anniversary hymn for the Five Points Mission.

Thus began a wonderful partnership that produced such "hits" as "I Am Thine, O Lord," "Near the Cross," "Rescue the Perishing," "Safe in the Arms of Jesus," "Savior, More Than Life to Me," "'Tis the Blessed Hour of Prayer," "Will Jesus Find Us Watching," "To God Be the Glory," and this hymn, "Pass Me Not."

In all, Doane wrote about two thousand tunes and published some forty collections of songs. For a quarter century, he also served as superintendent of the Sunday school of Cincinnati's Mount Auburn Baptist Church. After his death on Christmas Eve, 1915, Doane's vast estate went to his two daughters, who used much of it to fund Christian missionary and educational causes in the twentieth century.

Near the Cross

Fanny J. Crosby

William H. Doane

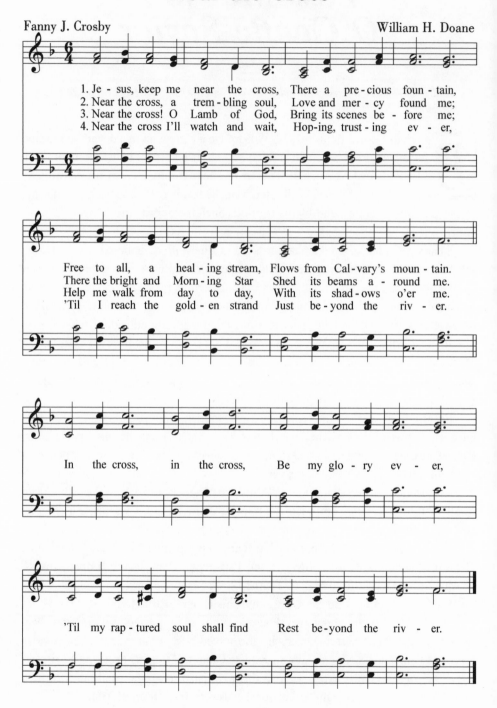

1. Je - sus, keep me near the cross, There a pre - cious foun - tain,
2. Near the cross, a trem - bling soul, Love and mer - cy found me;
3. Near the cross! O Lamb of God, Bring its scenes be - fore me;
4. Near the cross I'll watch and wait, Hop-ing, trust - ing ev - er,

Free to all, a heal - ing stream, Flows from Cal-vary's moun - tain.
There the bright and Morn - ing Star Shed its beams a - round me.
Help me walk from day to day, With its shad - ows o'er me.
'Til I reach the gold - en strand Just be - yond the riv - er.

In the cross, in the cross, Be my glo - ry ev - er,

'Til my rap - tured soul shall find Rest be-yond the riv - er.

Near the Cross

1869

And He, bearing His cross, went out to a place called the Place of a Skull, which is called in Hebrew, Golgotha. John 19:17 (NKJV)

Fanny Crosby was born in Putnam County, New York, in 1820, and was blinded in infancy through the malpractice of a doctor. In 1835, she enrolled in a school for the blind in New York City, staying there twelve years, first as a student then as a teacher. Her remarkable poetry brought widespread acclaim to the school, and she frequently recited her work for visiting dignitaries.

In 1850, Fanny, thirty, attended a revival meeting at New York's Thirtieth Street Methodist Church. During these services, she felt something was missing in her life. On two occasions during the meetings, she prayed with counselors, but without gaining assurance of a personal relationship with God. On November 20, 1850, as the altar call was given, Fanny went forward and found Christ as her Savior. The congregation was singing Isaac Watts' great hymn about the cross:

> *At the cross, at the cross where I first saw the light,*
> *And the burden of my heart rolled away,*
> *It was there by faith I received my sight,*
> *And now I am happy all the day.*

Shortly thereafter, Fanny turned her poetic skills to hymn writing, and many of her songs focused on the theme of the cross, such as "At the Cross, There's Room," "Blessed Cross," "Room at the Cross," "Save Me at the Cross," and this one, "Jesus Keep Me Near the Cross." It was composed after Cincinnati businessman William Doane gave her a melody he had written. Fanny, listening to it, felt it said, "Jesus, keep me near the cross," and she promptly wrote the words.

Fanny Crosby wrote approximately 8,000 hymns. We aren't surprised, then, to discover that many of her later hymns were little more than rewritten versions of earlier ones. In 1893, she and Phoebe Knapp published a gospel song similar to "Near the Cross." The 1893 hymn, entitled, "Nearer the Cross," said:

> *"Nearer the cross!" my heart can say I am coming nearer,*
> *Nearer the cross from day to day, I am coming nearer;*
> *Nearer the cross where Jesus died,*
> *Nearer the fountain's crimson tide,*
> *Nearer my Savior's wounded side,*
> *I am coming nearer, I am coming nearer.*

Christ for the World We Sing

Samuel Wolcott

Felice de Giardini

1. Christ for the world we sing! The world to
2. Christ for the world we sing! The world to
3. Christ for the world we sing! The world to
4. Christ for the world we sing! The world to

Christ we bring, With lov - ing zeal; The poor, and
Christ we bring, With fer - vent prayer; The way - ward
Christ we bring, With one ac - cord; With us the
Christ we bring, With joy - ful song; The new - born

them that mourn, The faint and ov - er - borne,
and the lost, By rest - less pas - sions tossed,
work to share, With us re - proach to dare,
souls whose days, Re - claimed from er - ror's ways,

Sin - sick and sor - row worn, Whom Christ doth heal.
Re - deemed at count - less cost, From dark de - spair.
With us the cross to bear, For Christ our Lord.
In - spired with hope and praise, To Christ be - long.

Christ for the World We Sing

1869

... "I will declare Your name to My brethren; In the midst of the assembly I will sing praise to You." Hebrews 2:12 (NKJV)

L ooking back on his teen years, George Williams described himself as a "careless, thoughtless, godless, swearing young fellow." But then he met Christ as Savior. "I cannot describe to you the joy and peace which flowed into my soul when first I saw that the Lord Jesus had died for my sins, and that they were all forgiven," he later wrote.

In June 1844, George, twenty, found a job as sales clerk at a drapery store in London. But his heart was torn by the masses of young men he saw living on the streets, in bars and brothels, occupied with gambling and fighting. On June 6, 1844, he began a program to win young men to Christ and to help them grow strong in body, mind, and soul. It was called the Young Men's Christian Association—the YMCA.

Williams' idea spread to America, and in 1869, Dr. Samuel Wolcott, pastor of Plymouth Congregational Church in Cleveland, Ohio, and a former missionary to Syria, hosted the local branch of the YMCA in his church. At the rally, he listened carefully to the speakers and noticed the banner over the pulpit that said, "Christ for the World and the World for Christ."

Wolcott had first attempted to write hymns at age fifty-six. Though he had "never put two rhymes together" and felt he could no more compose a hymn as perform a miracle, he felt strangely led to write a hymn of five stanzas. Imagine his surprise when his first hymn, "Father! I Own Thy Voice" was published.

He was trying to find a subject for his second hymn when the local chapter of the YMCA asked to use his church for their rally. That day in 1868, as Wolcott sat listening to the speakers and reading the banner over their heads, he received his inspiration. Walking home alone through the streets of Cleveland after the meeting, Dr. Wolcutt composed all four stanzas of "Christ for the World We Sing."

Samuel Wolcott went on to write over two hundred hymns, but this one—his second attempt—is the only one still in popular usage. It came about because of a London sales clerk who cared about the souls of lost young men, and of a local pastor in Cleveland who shared the burden of winning "Christ for the World and the World for Christ."

Take the Name of Jesus with You

Lydia Baxter

William H. Doane

1. Take the name of Je-sus with you, Child of sor-row and of woe.
2. Take the name of Je-sus ev - er As a shield from ev - ery snare;
3. At the name of Je-sus bow-ing, Fall-ing pros-trate at His feet;

It will joy and com-fort give you; Take it then wher-e'er you go.
If temp - ta - tions 'round you gath - er, Breathe that ho - ly name in prayer.
King of kings, we'll glad - ly crown Him When our jour-ney is com - plete.

Pre - cious name, O how sweet! Hope of earth and joy of heaven.

Pre - cious name, O how sweet! Hope of earth and joy of heaven.

Take the Name of Jesus with You

1870

Repent, and let every one of you be baptized in the name of Jesus Christ for the remission of sins . . . Acts 2:38 (NKJV)

I have a very special armor," Lydia Baxter once told friends who asked her how she could be so radiant despite her health problems. "I have the name of Jesus. When the tempter tries to make me blue or despondent, I mention the name of Jesus, and he can't get through to me anymore."

Lydia, born in Petersburg, New York, on September 8, 1809, was converted alongside her sister under the preaching of a Baptist evangelist named Eben Tucker. She married Colonel John C. Baxter and moved to New York City, where she worked tirelessly for Christ until a severe illness left her bedridden. Her attitude, however, was so sunny that the Baxter home became a gathering place for Christian workers.

Lydia also wrote gospel songs. One of her favorites, "The Gate Ajar," spoke of Christ's leaving the gate open for us. The chorus said: "O depth of mercy! Can it be / That gate was left ajar for me?"

In his memoirs, song leader Ira Sankey wrote of how popular this song became during D. L. Moody's Great Britain Campaign of 1873–74. "It was sung at the watchnight service in 1873," Sankey said, "in the Free Assembly Hall of Edinburgh. A young woman—Maggie Lindsay, of Aberdeen, Scotland—was much impressed by the hymn, and those seated by her side heard her exclaim, 'O, heavenly Father, is it true that the gate is standing ajar for me? If it is so, I will go in.' That night she became a disciple of the Lord Jesus. . . . Scarcely a month later, on January 28, Maggie took a train for her home, but she never reached there alive. . . . A collision took place, (and) a number of passengers were killed. Maggie, all crushed and broken, was found in the wreck. In one of her hands was a copy of her favorite hymn, 'There Is a Gate That Stands Ajar.'"

"The Gate Ajar" is seldom sung now, but Lydia's other popular hymn has stood the test of time. "Take the Name of Jesus with You" sprang from Lydia's own study of the precious name of Jesus in the Bible. It was written four years before her death and published in 1871 by William Doane and Robert Lowry.

O Zion, Haste

Mary A. Thomson

James Walch

1. O Zi - on, haste, Thy mis - sion high ful - fill - ing, To tell to
2. Be - hold how man - y thou-sands still are ly - ing, Bound in the
3. Pro - claim to ev - ery peo - ple, tongue, and na - tion that God in
4. Give of Thy sons to bear the mes - sage glo - rious, Give of thy

all the world that God is light; That He who made all na - tions
dark - some pris - on house of sin. With none to tell them of the
whom they live and move is love; Tell how He stooped to save His
wealth to speed them on their way; Pour out Thy soul for them in

is not will - ing One soul should per - ish, lost in shades of night.
Sav - ior's dy - ing, Or of the life He died for them to win.
lost cre - a - tion, And died on earth that we might live a - bove.
prayer vic - to - rious, O Zi - on, haste to bring the bright - er day.

Pub - lish glad tid - ings, Tid - ings of peace,

Tid - ings of Je - sus, Re - demp - tion and re - lease.

O Zion, Haste

1871

"Behold, I lay in Zion a stumbling stone and rock of offense, And whoever believes on Him will not be put to shame." Romans 9:33 (NKJV)

U ntold numbers of missionaries have been sent off to the regions beyond by congregations singing this rousing Episcopalian missionary hymn that exhorts the church ("Zion") to hurry and fulfill its mission of telling "all the world that God is light." But few realize it was written by a worried mother sitting at the bedside of her dangerously ill son.

Mary Ann Fulkner, the author of "O Zion, Haste," was born in London in 1834, and her family immigrated to America when she was young. After marrying John Thomson, the first librarian of the Free Library in Philadelphia, she and her husband joined the Church of the Annunciation (Episcopalian) in Philadelphia, where they served many years.

Mary Ann, who enjoyed writing poetry, penned more than forty hymns, though only "O Zion, Haste" has lasted in the hymnals. This is what she had to say about writing her most famous hymn:

> *I wrote the greater part of the hymn, "O Sion, Haste," in the year 1868. I had written many hymns before, and one night, while I was sitting up with one of my children who was ill with typhoid fever, I thought I should like to write a missionary hymn to the tune of the hymn, 'Hark, Hark my Soul! Angelic Songs are Swelling,' as I was fond of that tune, but I could not then get the refrain I liked. I left the hymn unfinished and about three years later I finished it by writing the refrain which now forms a part of it."*

Most hymnals omit some of Thomson's original verses, one of which says:

> *'Tis Thine to save from peril of perdition*
> *The souls for whom the Lord His life laid down;*
> *Beware lest, slothful to fulfill thy mission,*
> *Thou lose one jewel that should deck His crown.*

127

The Rock That Is Higher Than I

Erastus Johnson

William G. Fischer

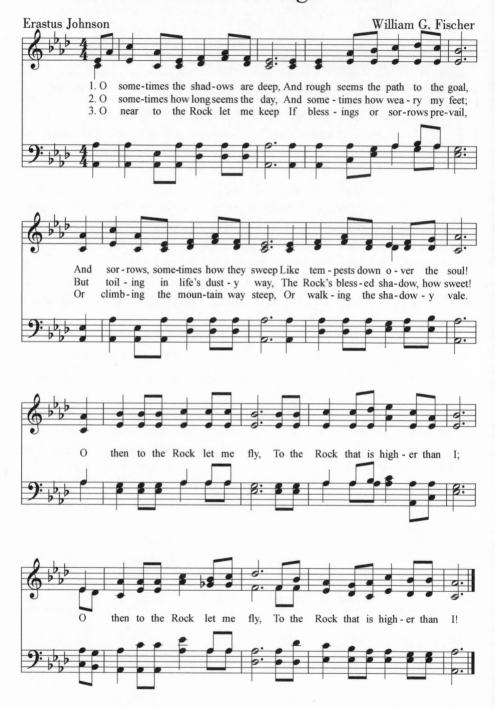

1. O some-times the shad-ows are deep, And rough seems the path to the goal,
2. O some-times how long seems the day, And some-times how wea-ry my feet;
3. O near to the Rock let me keep If bless-ings or sor-rows pre-vail,

And sor-rows, some-times how they sweep Like tem-pests down o-ver the soul!
But toil-ing in life's dust-y way, The Rock's bless-ed sha-dow, how sweet!
Or climb-ing the moun-tain way steep, Or walk-ing the sha-dow-y vale.

O then to the Rock let me fly, To the Rock that is high-er than I;

O then to the Rock let me fly, To the Rock that is high-er than I!

The Rock That Is Higher Than I

1871

... For they drank of that spiritual Rock that followed them, and that Rock was Christ. 1 Corinthians 10:4 (NKJV)

rom the end of the earth I will cry to You, when my heart is overwhelmed," wrote King David in Psalm 61, "lead me to the rock that is higher than I." What a prayer to memorize and hold in reserve in our hearts. It's appropriate for all of life's situations, even financial disaster.

It was in such a crisis that Erastus Johnson wrote a hymn based on that verse: "The Rock That Is Higher Than I," with its resounding chorus: *On then to the Rock let me fly, / To the Rock that is higher than I.*

Erastus was born in a logging camp on the banks of the Penobscot River north of Bangor, Maine, in the spring of 1826. He wanted to enter the ministry, but his poor health and eyesight prevented his attending seminary. At age seventeen, he became a schoolteacher. In his mid-twenties, he followed his brothers to California in search of gold. After living in San Francisco several years, he returned East and settled down in Pittsburgh, farming and working in oil. In 1861, he attended a YMCA convention in nearby Carlisle, Pennsylvania, and it was there he wrote this hymn. His autobiography says:

> There was a convention of the Y.M.C.A. at Carlisle, Pa., which I attended as a delegate, and John Wanamaker was president of the convention. About the second day there came a telegram from Philadelphia that the banking house of Jay Cook & Co. had failed, in which Mr. Wanamaker had $70,000 which to him at that time in life was a great amount to lose. Soon followed reports of other firms throughout the country, indicating a general panic. As a matter of course, it threw a pall of gloom over the convention, for nearly all its members were men of business. As an expression of the common feeling I wrote "The Rock That Is Higher Than I." Mr. Wm. Fisher of Philadelphia, the composer of many tunes for gospel hymns, was at the convention, and in conjunction with Brother William, led the singing. I gave the words to him and he set them to music, sang them, and they with the music immediately became popular in the convention, especially with Mr. Wanamaker, who several times called for it. And soon it found its way into many publications.

All for Jesus

Mary D. James

Source Unknown

1. All for Je - sus, all for Je - sus! All my be - ing's ran - somed powers:
2. Let my hands per - form His bid - ding, Let my feet run in His ways;
3. Since my eyes were fixed on Je - sus, I've lost sight of all be - side,
4. O what won - der! how a - maz - ing! Je - sus, glo - rious King of kings,

All my thoughts and words and do - ings, All my days and all my hours:
Let my eyes see Je - sus on - ly, Let my lips speak forth His praise:
So en - chained my spir - it's vi - sion, Look - ing at the Cru - ci - fied:
Deigns to call me His be - lov - ed, Lets me rest be - neath His wings:

All for Je - sus! all for Je - sus! All my days and all my hours;
All for Je - sus! all for Je - sus! Let my lips speak forth His praise;
All for Je - sus! all for Je - sus! Look - ing at the Cru - ci - fied;
All for Je - sus! all for Je - sus! Rest - ing now be - neath His wings;

All for Je - sus! all for Je - sus! All my days and all my hours.
All for Je - sus! all for Je - sus! Let my lips speak forth His praise.
All for Je - sus! all for Je - sus! Look - ing at the Cru - ci - fied.
All for Je - sus! all for Je - sus! Rest - ing now be - neath His wings.

All for Jesus
1871

Jesus said to him, "You shall love the LORD your God with all your heart, with all your soul, and with all your mind." Matthew 22:37 (NKJV)

How sweetly does her life exhibit the beauty of holiness," someone said of Mary James, author of this hymn. "I think I never saw an individual more fully possessed by that love that thinketh no evil, than our beloved Sister James, yet as she professes the enjoyment of a state of holiness, she has her trials."

Mary was born in 1810, and began teaching Sunday school in her Methodist Episcopal Church when she was only thirteen. She had about a dozen girls in her class, and soon she was visiting them in their homes, often bearing gifts her mother had made. It was the beginning of a lifetime for Jesus.

As an adult, Mary's greatest love was traveling to Methodist camp meetings, especially in Ocean Park, New Jersey. There she led prayer meetings, engaged in personal counseling, taught Bible classes, organized workers, shared her testimony, and sometimes preached. She became a close associate of Methodist Holiness leader, Phoebe Palmer, author of "The Cleansing Wave."

Letter-writing was another arena for Mary's gifts, and she frequently penned letters of encouragement to young pastors just starting their ministries. She authored many articles and was a frequent contributor to popular Christian magazines of the day. Her habit was to rise early in the day and scribble down the essence of her freshest thoughts, laying them aside for additional work later.

Her writings included one book, a biography entitled *The Soul Winner: A Sketch of Edmund J. Yard*, published in 1883, the year of her death. (Her son, Rev. Joseph H. James published Mary's biography three years later.)

Occasionally Mary's scribblings would result in a hymn. In all, she wrote about fifty gospel songs, but only "All for Jesus" remains popular. It was written for her New Year's letter of 1871. Reviewing the previous year, Mary thanked God for the progress of her ministry. "I have written more, talked more, prayed more, and thought more of Jesus than in any previous year," she wrote, "and had more peace of mind, resulting from a stronger and more simple faith in Him." She attached this poem of consecration, "All for Jesus," as a commitment for the coming year.

Mary had a dozen more years of ministry before being laid to rest in a cemetery in Trenton, New Jersey. Inscribed on her gravestone are the simple words: "All for Jesus."

Jesus, Savior, Pilot Me

Edward Hopper   John E. Gould

1. Je - sus, Sav - ior, pi - lot me, O - ver
2. As a moth - er stills her child, Thou canst
3. When at last I near the shore, And the

life's tem - pes - tuous sea; Un - known waves be - fore me
hush the o - cean wild; Bois - t'rous waves o - bey Thy
fear - ful break - ers roar 'Twixt me and the peace - ful

roll, Hid - ing rocks and treach - 'rous shoal; Chart and
will When Thou say'st to them, "Be still!" Won - drous
rest, Then while lean - ing on Thy breast, May I

com - pass came from Thee- Je - sus, Sav - ior, pi - lot me!
Sov - 'reign of the sea, Je - sus, Sav - ior, pi - lot me!
hear Thee say to me, "Fear not, I will pi - lot thee!"

Jesus, Savior, Pilot Me
1871

"Why are you fearful, O you of little faith?" Then He arose and rebuked the winds and the sea, and there was a great calm. Matthew 8:26 (NKJV)

V isitors to Manhattan should take time to visit the First Chinese Presbyterian Church at the corner of Henry Street and Market on the Lower East Side, not far from the Manhattan and Brooklyn Bridges. This grand old building is a Gothic historical landmark, the second oldest church building in New York City. Dutch Reformed Christians built it in 1819. When that group disbanded their church in 1864, the building was acquired by another congregation who chose an unusual name for their church: The Church of Sea and Land.

This was the busy harbor section of New York, with thousands of sailors filling the streets every day. The pastor of the Church of Sea and Land was Edward Hooper, a lifelong New Yorker and a graduate of both the University of the City of New York and Union Theological Seminary in the heart of Manhattan. After pastorates in Greenville, New York, and later in Long Island, Hopper returned to Manhattan to engage in pastoral and evangelistic work among the sailors. Hopper often composed hymns for his sailors, including one titled, "Wrecked and Struggling in Mid-Ocean."

On May 3, 1871, this poem-prayer, "Jesus, Savior, Pilot Me," appeared without attribution in *The Sailor's Magazine.*

In Philadelphia, an ailing composer named John Edgar Gould, saw a copy of this poem and, deeply moved, composed music for it the night before he sailed to Africa in an effort to regain his health. Gould died in Algiers four years later. But "Jesus, Savior, Pilot Me" developed a healthy following in churches across America, especially among those ministering to seafaring men. The sailors and parishioners at the Church of Sea and Land numbered this among their favorite hymns, dubbing it "The Sailor's Hymn," though they had no idea that their own pastor was its author. That fact remained hidden for years, until Hopper finally disclosed it at a special anniversary celebration of New York's Seamen's Friend Society.

On April 23, 1888, suffering from heart disease, Hooper sat in the easy chair of his study, preparing to write another hymn. At the top of the page he put its title— "Heaven"—then he slumped over dead. Among the papers found in his study was the original manuscript of "Jesus Savior, Pilot Me."

Almost Persuaded

Philip B. Bliss

Philip B. Bliss

1. "Al - most per - suad - ed" now to be - lieve;
2. "Al - most per - suad - ed," come, come to - day;
3. "Al - most per - suad - ed," har - vest is past!

"Al - most per - suad - ed" Christ to re - ceive:
"Al - most per - suad - ed," turn not a - way:
"Al - most per - suad - ed," doom comes at last!

Seems now some soul to say, "Go, Spir - it, go Thy way;
Je - sus in - vites you here, An - gels are lin - gering near,
"Al - most" can - not a - vail, "Al - most" is but to fail!

Some more con - ven - ient day On Thee I'll call."
Prayers rise from hearts so dear, O wan - derer, come.
Sad, sad, that bit - ter wail, "Al - most," but lost!

Almost Persuaded

1871

Then Agrippa said to Paul, "You almost persuade me to become a Christian." Acts 26:28 (NKJV)

No one in the history of gospel music is more revered than Philip P. Bliss, a gifted young musician who died tragically at age thirty-five in a train disaster. Interestingly, just a year before his death, this hymn—which he wrote—had a profound influence in his decision to give himself to full-time gospel ministry.

Philip, his wife Lucy, and their two small children lived in Chicago where Philip worked for a publishing company, writing sacred and secular songs. He was considered a rising star on the American music scene. As time allowed, he also volunteered as a soloist and song leader in evangelist meetings.

One day he was assisting a preacher named Rev. Brundage. During the sermon, the evangelist quoted Acts 26:28 and declared: "He who is almost persuaded is almost saved, and to be almost saved is to be entirely lost!" Struck by those words, Philip penned this hymn, "Almost Persuaded."

Shortly afterward, Philip received a letter from evangelist D. L. Moody, urging him to "sing the gospel" by becoming a fulltime evangelistic song leader. As they prayed over the decision, Philip and Lucy were understandably cautious, for it would mean the end of a stable, regular income. It would cost Bliss's career in secular music and entail a nomadic lifestyle of itinerate evangelism. "I am willing," Lucy wrote, "that Mr. Bliss should do anything that we can be sure is the Lord's will, and I can trust the Lord to provide for us, but I don't want him to take such a step simply on Mr. Moody's will."

Shortly afterward, evangelist Daniel Whittle requested Philip's help with evangelistic rallies in Waukegan, Illinois. The meetings started slowly, but on March 26, 1871, as Philip sang his new hymn, "Almost Persuaded," an unusual power swept over the crowd. Lucy wrote, "In different parts of the house, sinners arose as he sang, presenting themselves for prayer, and souls that night rejoiced in Christ. Our hearts were very full, and a great responsibility was upon us."

The next day, Philip made a formal commitment to the Lord to leave all secular concerns and engage himself in fulltime ministry. In the year left to him, Philip Bliss exerted a lasting influence on gospel music, singing multitudes into the Kingdom and writing many of the hymns we love today.

Nobody Knows the Trouble I've Seen

African-American spiritual

African-American spiritual

No-bo-dy knows the trou-ble I've seen; No-bo-dy knows but Je-sus.

No-bo-dy knows the trou-ble I've seen; Glo-ry hal-le-lu-jah.

1. Some - times I'm up; some - times I'm down; Oh yes, Lord.
2. Al - though You see me goin' a - long, Oh yes, Lord,
3. What makes old Sa - tan hate me so? Oh yes, Lord;

Some - times I'm al - most to the ground; Oh yes, Lord.
I have my trou - bles here be - low; Oh yes, Lord.
He got me once and let me go; Oh yes, Lord

Nobody Knows the Trouble I've Seen

1872

"Let not your heart be troubled; you believe in God, believe also in Me." John 14:1
(NKJV)

F isk University in Nashville, Tennessee, opened its doors in 1866, at the close of the Civil War. It was one of the schools established for liberated slaves by the American Missionary Association. As students and professors arrived on campus, they found themselves living in abandoned Union Army hospital barracks built on the site of old slave pens.

Among the arriving professors was a New York Yankee, a white man named White. As music instructor, George White taught his students classical cantatas and patriotic songs, but he was particularly intrigued by the old plantation melodies and slave songs he overheard in the dorms and among the students between classes. White had trouble coaxing his students to sing him those songs; it seemed a particularly private type of hand-me-down music. There were no written scores or words—just plaintive strains passed voice to voice between the generations.

Within a few years, the old buildings at Fisk started rotting. The university found itself in crisis, without even money to buy food for its four hundred students. Regretfully, the Missionary Association decided to close the school. When White approached the trustees suggesting a series of fund-raising concerts, the board refused (they called his scheme "a wild goose chase"). White decided to try it anyway. "I'm depending on God, not you," he told the board.

Selecting nine students (most of them former slaves), White and his wife sold their jewelry and personal belongings to finance the first tour. On October 6, 1871, the singers boarded a train in Nashville for the Midwest. It was a hard trip, and at times the young people had to relinquish their seats to white folks. Other times they were evicted from trains or hotels. Sometimes the little group, braving threats, insults, obscenities, and indignities, sang in nearly empty halls and churches.

At the National Council of Congregational Churches meeting in Oberlin, Ohio, some of the delegates protested giving time to the "colored students from Fisk University." The problem was the pressing nature of denominational business. Their slate was full, and the delegates didn't want interruptions in their business sessions. But George White wouldn't be denied, and finally the Fisk students sang one song during a recess as the delegates were milling around in little groups and leaving the building.

What happened next changed the course of American music.

Continued in the next story . . .

Swing Low, Sweet Chariot

African-American spiritual

African-American spiritual

Swing low, sweet char-i-ot, Com-in' for to car-ry me home;

Swing low, sweet char-i-ot, Com-in' for to car-ry me home.

1. I looked o-ver Jor-dan and what did I see, Com-in' for to car-ry me home?
2. If you get there be-fore I do, Com-in' for to car-ry me home,

A band of an - gels com-in' af-ter me; Com-in' for to car-ry me home.
Just tell my friends I'm com-in'home too; Com-in' for to car-ry me home.

Swing Low, Sweet Chariot

1872

The chariots of God are twenty thousand, Even thousands of thousands; The Lord is among them . . . Psalm 68:17 (NKJV)

I t had been a gray, overcast day in Oberlin, Ohio. Delegates to the National Council of Congregational Churches were weary from the dismal weather and long business sessions. When the meeting recessed, singers from Fisk University filed quietly into the choir loft. Suddenly the clouds parted and sunshine streamed through the windows. Delegates stopped talking, and every face turned toward the music. "Steal away, steal away, steal away to Jesus," came the song in beautiful, brooding harmony. After a moment of stunned silence, the convention burst into wild applause and cries for more.

Among the delegates was Henry Ward Beecher, a noted pastor from Brooklyn who immediately begged the group to cancel its tour and come directly to his church in New York. Unable to do that, director George White offered the group for a December concert.

Knowing the importance of this engagement, White agonized about naming his group; and in Columbus, Ohio, after spending much of the night in prayer, he found the answer. They would be the Jubilee Singers, the biblical year of Jubilee in Leviticus 25 being a time of liberation for slaves.

On December 27, 1871, the Jubilee Singers sang at Plymouth Church in Brooklyn. Rev. Beecher, deeply moved, stood and said, "Ladies and gentlemen, I'm going to do what I want every person in this house to do." He turned his pockets inside out, giving all the money to the Jubilee Singers. That night the offering was $1,300! Newspapers picked up the story, and soon the Jubilee Singers had engagements around the world.

In their concerts, the section that most stirred their audiences was their "spirituals"—those soulful plantation songs born of slavery and full of yearning.

In 1872, gospel music publisher Biglow & Main hired a musician to meet the Jubilee Singers and record these timeless, authorless songs on paper. Later that year, a little volume was published under the title: *Jubilee Songs: Complete. As Sung by the Jubilee Singers of Fisk University.* It was a milestone for both gospel and popular music; it introduced the "Negro Spiritual" to America and to the world. Among the favorites were "Nobody Knows the Trouble I've Seen" and "Swing Low, Sweet Chariot."

Thanks to the Jubilee Singers, Fisk University is still training young people today—and still sending out its Jubilee Singers to churches and concert halls across America and around the world.

Whiter Than Snow

James Nicholson

William G. Fischer

1. Lord Je - sus, I long to be per - fect - ly whole; I
2. Lord Je - sus, look down from Thy throne in the skies And
3. Lord Je - sus, be - fore You I pa - tient - ly wait; Come

want Thee for - ev - er to live in my soul. Break down ev - ery
help me to make a com - plete sac - ri - fice. I give up my -
now and with - in me a new heart cre - ate. To those who have

i - dol, cast out ev - ery foe. Now wash me and I shall be
self and what - ev - er I know, Now wash me and I shall be
sought Thee, Thou nev - er saidst, "No." Now wash me and I shall be

whit - er than snow. Whit - er than snow, Yes, whit - er than

snow, Now wash me and I shall be Whit - er than snow.

Whiter Than Snow

1872

Wash me, and I shall be whiter than snow. Psalm 51:7 (NKJV)

J ames Nicholson, author of "Whiter than Snow," was a dedicated Christian who lived in Washington, D.C., where he worked for the post office. Born in Ireland in the 1820s, James had immigrated to America in the 1850s, originally settling in Philadelphia where he became active in the Wharton Street Methodist Episcopal Church as a Sunday school and evangelistic worker. In 1871, he moved to Washington to assume his new duties with the post office, and the next year he published this hymn.

"Whiter Than Snow" is based on Psalm 51:7, the prayer of repentance offered by King David after his sin with Bathsheba: "Wash me, and I shall be whiter than snow." It originally had six stanzas, all of them beginning, "Dear Jesus . . ." An unknown editor later altered the words to "Lord Jesus." "Whiter Than Snow" was first published in 1872 by the Methodist Episcopal Book Room in Philadelphia, in a sixteen-page pamphlet entitled, *Joyful Songs No. 4.*

Philadelphia musician William Gustavus Fischer composed the music to this hymn. He learned to read music while attending singing classes at a German-speaking church in Philadelphia. When he started his life's occupation as a bookbinder, he still spent his evenings pursuing music. He was eventually hired to teach music at a Philadelphia college, and late in life he entered the piano business.

Fischer was best known as a popular song leader for revival meetings. In 1875, he led the 1,000-voice choir at the D. L. Moody/Ira Sankey Campaign in the great tabernacle at Thirteenth and Market Streets in Philadelphia. He composed over two hundred hymn tunes, including this one. He also composed the melody for "I Love to Tell the Story."

The splendor of snowfall is only one of the pictures used in Scripture to illustrate God's forgiveness of sin. Micah 7:19 says God casts our sins into the ocean. Psalm 103 says He removes them as far from us as East from West. According to Isaiah 38:17, God casts them behind His back. Colossians 2:14 says they are wiped out like erased handwriting. If you're suffering pangs of guilt and regret, needing a fresh experience of God's forgiveness, try singing this old hymn with new sincerity:

Break down every idol, cast out every foe,
Now wash me, and I shall be whiter than snow.

There's a Song in the Air

Josiah G. Holland

Karl P. Harrington

1. There's a song in the air! There's a star in the sky!
2. There's a tu-mult of joy O'er the won-der-ful birth,
3. In the light of that star Lie the a-ges im-pearled;
4. We re-joice in the light, And we ech-o the song

There's a moth-er's deep prayer, And a ba-by's low cry!
For a Vir-gin's sweet Boy, Is the Lord of the earth.
And that song from a-far Has swept o-ver the world.
That comes down thro' the night From the heav-en-ly throng.

And the star rains its fire while the beau-ti-ful sing,
Lo, the star rains its fire while the beau-ti-ful sing,
Ev-ery hearth is a-flame, and the beau-ti-ful sing
Ay! we shout to the love-ly E-van-gel they bring,

For the man-ger of Beth-le-hem, cra-dles a King!
For the man-ger of Beth-le-hem, cra-dles a King!
In the homes of the na-tions that Je-sus is King!
As we greet in His cra-dle our Sav-ior and King!

There's a Song in the Air

1872

Praise the LORD! Sing to the LORD a new song, And His praise in the assembly of saints. Psalm 149:1 (NKJV)

F or a long time, Josiah Gilbert Holland was known to his friends as a failure at just about everything he tried. Dropping out of high school, he tried his hand at photography, then calligraphy. When those professions didn't pan out, Josiah, twenty-one, enrolled in Berkshire Medical College. After graduation, he practiced medicine in Springfield, Massachusetts for a while before quitting to start a newspaper. The paper folded after six months. At length, he joined the editorial staff of another newspaper, *The Springfield Republican,* and there he finally found his niche in writing.

In 1865, the world was stunned by the tragic assassination of Abraham Lincoln. The next year, it was Josiah Holland who published the first major biography of Lincoln. In it, he presented Lincoln as a "true-hearted Christian" and provided a number of stories to reinforce the point. When Lincoln's free-thinking law partner, William Herndon, read the book, he refuted it. Lincoln was an "infidel," declared Herndon, and he died as an "unbeliever." To this day, historians argue about Lincoln's religious faith, or lack of it. But the notoriety put Josiah Holland on the literary map of his day.

In 1870, he became a founder and the senior editor of *Scribner's Magazine.* He continued publishing books and was quite prolific. In 1872, he published *The Marble Prophecy and Other Poems.* In it were the four stanzas of "There's a Song in the Air." It was an unusual poem, in that the first four lines of each stanza contained six syllables each, but the fifth and sixth lines were twice as long. Two years later, it was set to music in a collection of Sunday school songs, but didn't achieve widespread popularity.

Several years after Josiah's death in 1881, a Latin professor named Karl Pomeroy Harrington read "There's a Song in the Air." Harrington was an amateur musician who had begun writing melodies as a youngster on the small organ in his childhood home. Harrington later inherited that old Estey organ and moved it to his vacation cottage in North Woodstock, New Hampshire. While spending the summer there in 1904, he sat down at the old instrument, pumping the bellows with the foot pedals, and hammered out the lovely melodic tune to which "There's a Song in the Air" is now widely sung.

Christ Arose!

Robert Lowry   Robert Lowry

1. Low in the grave He lay, Je - sus, my Sav - ior! Wait-ing the
2. Vain - ly they watched His bed, Je - sus, my Sav - ior! Vain - ly they
3. Death can-not keep his prey, Je - sus, my Sav - ior! He tore the

com - ing day, Je - sus, my Lord! Up from the grave He a - rose,
seal the dead, Je - sus, my Lord!
bars a - way, Je - sus, my Lord! He a - rose,

With a might - y tri - umph o'er His foes; He a - rose a vic - tor from the
He a - rose;

dark do - main, And He lives for - ev - er with His saints to reign; He a -

rose! He a - rose! Hal - le - lu - jah! Christ a - rose!
He a - rose! He a - rose!

Christ Arose!

1874

He is not here, but is risen! Luke 24:6 (NKJV)

W hat can exhausted pastors do to relax on Sunday nights after a hard day's work? Baptist preacher Robert Lowry went home to his wife and three sons—and wrote hymns. "Dr. Lowry will continue to preach the gospel in his hymns long after his sermons have been forgotten," Ira Sankey once wrote. "Many of his hymns were written after the Sunday evening service, when his body was weary but his mind refused to rest."

Robert Lowry was born in Pennsylvania in 1826. At his conversion at age seventeen, he joined a Baptist church. Shortly afterward, he enrolled at the University of Lewisburg (now Bucknell University in Lewisburg, Pennsylvania). After graduating, he pastored churches in New York, New Jersey, and Pennsylvania. He also taught at Bucknell and at one time served as its chancellor. Lowry gained a reputation for keen biblical scholarship and powerful, picturesque preaching.

When gospel song editor William Bradbury died in 1868, Lowry was chosen to replace him as a publisher of Sunday school music. He's best known, however, for his own gospel songs, including:

"Nothing But the Blood" (words and music)
"Shall We Gather at the River?" (words and music)
"Where Is My Wandering Boy Tonight?" (words and music)
"All the Way My Savior Leads Me" (music)
"I Need Thee Every Hour" (music)
"Marching to Zion" (music)

"Music, with me has been a side issue," he once said. "I would rather preach a gospel sermon to an appreciative audience than write a hymn. I have always looked upon myself as a preacher and felt a sort of depreciation when I began to be known more as a composer."

This hymn, "Christ Arose!" was written one evening during the Easter season of 1874 while Lowry was engaged in his devotions. He became deeply impressed with Luke 24:6–8, especially the words of the angel at the tomb of Christ: "Why do you seek the living among the dead? He is not here, but is risen!"

The words and music began forming together in his mind. Going to the little pump organ in his home, Lowry soon completed what was to become one of our greatest resurrection hymns.

To God Be the Glory

Fanny J. Crosby

William H. Doane

1. To God be the glory, great things He hath done. So loved He the world that He gave us His Son, Who yield - ed His life, an a - tone-ment for sin, And o - pened the life-gate, that all may go in.

Praise the Lord, praise the Lord, Let the earth hear His voice! Praise the Lord, praise the Lord, Let the peo - ple re - joice! O come to the Fa - ther thru Je - sus the Son, And give Him the glo - ry, great things He hath done.

To God Be the Glory

<u>1875</u>

Be exalted, O God, above the heavens, And Your glory above all the earth. Psalm 108:5 (NKJV)

O ccasionally a hymn drops into the furrows of history to be buried and forgotten awhile, only to later spring to life for future generations. That's what happened with Fanny Crosby's "To God Be the Glory." It first appeared in *Brightest and Best*, a little volume of hymns published in 1875 by William Doane and Robert Lowry. This small hymnal proved to be a treasure trove, introducing such classics as "Christ Arose," "All the Way My Savior Leads Me," "Savior, More Than Life to Me," "I Am Thine, O Lord," "Rescue the Perishing," "Jesus, Keep Me Near the Cross," and this one—"Praise for Redemption" (as it was originally called).

As it turned out, "Praise for Redemption" wasn't much of a hit. It wasn't widely sung nor included in many hymnals; it just lay hidden for eighty years.

In 1954, Billy Graham was planning an evangelistic crusade at London's Harringay Arena. As Cliff Barrows, music director for the Graham team, was compiling hymns for the *Greater London Crusade Song Book*, Rev. Frank Colquhoun, a prolific British preacher at Norwich Cathedral and a great lover of hymns, approached him. Colquhoun gave Barrows a copy of "Praise for Redemption," with its exuberant chorus: "Praise the Lord! Praise the Lord! Let the earth hear His voice!" Though unfamiliar with the hymn, Barrows decided to use it anyway.

Meanwhile problems were mounting for Graham. The British Press was critical of the young evangelist and an Anglican bishop predicted he would return to America with "his tail between his legs." Funds were short, forcing the Graham team to take pay cuts. A Member of Parliament threatened a challenge in the House of Commons, accusing Graham of interfering in British politics under the guise of religion. Friends in high places were advising Graham to cancel or postpone the meetings. Graham, shaken, dropped to his knees repeatedly, beseeching help from heaven.

As it turned out, Harringay Arena was packed for three months, and the crusade sparked a sense of revival across Great Britain. "To God Be the Glory" seemed a fitting theme. Fanny Crosby's old hymn was sung almost every night in Harringay, launching it into worldwide popularity as one of Christianity's favorite hymns.

I Am Thine, O Lord

Fanny J. Crosby

William H. Doane

1. I am Thine O Lord; I have heard Thy voice, And it told Thy
2. Con - se - crate me now to Thy ser - vice Lord, By the power of
3. O the pure de - light of a sin - gle hour That be - fore Thy
4. There are depths of love that I can - not know 'Til I cross the

love to me. But I long to rise in the arms of faith,
grace di - vine; Let my soul look up with a stead - fast hope,
throne I spend, When I kneel in prayer, and with Thee my God,
nar - row sea; There are heights of joy that I may not reach

And be clos - er drawn to Thee.
And my will be lost in Thine. Draw me near - er, near - er bless-ed Lord,
I com - mune as friend with friend!
'Til I rest in peace with Thee.

To the cross where Thou hast died. Draw me near - er, near - er,

near - er bless - ed Lord, To Thy pre - cious bleed - ing side.

I Am Thine, O Lord

1875

Let us draw near with a true heart in full assurance of faith. Hebrews 10:22 (NKJV)

She's called the "Queen of American Hymn Writers," and the "Mother of Congregational Singing in America." During her ninety-five years, Fanny Crosby wrote over eight thousand hymns. In addition, she was one of the three most prominent evangelical leaders in America during the last part of the 1800s, the others being D. L. Moody and Ira Sankey. She was one of America's most popular preachers and lecturers; in many cases lines of people would circle the block where she was scheduled to speak, hoping to get a seat.

When she traveled, it was usually by train; and she was fiercely independent, insisting on traveling alone, despite her blindness, until she was up in her eighties. Fanny lived in the rundown tenements of lower Manhattan so she'd be nearer her beloved Rescue Missions where she worked with the homeless and addicted.

But to me, the most remarkable thing about Fanny Crosby was her phenomenal memory. After her eyes were blinded in infancy, her grandmother Eunice took a special interest in teaching her Bible verses. Later a woman named Mrs. Hawley, the Crosbys' landlady, took over the job, committed to helping Fanny memorize the entire Bible! Every week, the child was given a certain number of chapters to learn, and Mrs. Hawley drilled them into her during their review sessions together. Fanny learned by heart all of Genesis, Exodus, Leviticus, Numbers, and Deuteronomy, plus the four Gospels, most of the Psalms, all of Proverbs, and many portions of the rest of the Bible.

From the fountainhead of these Scriptures flowed her hymns.

Ira Sankey, in his autobiography, gives us the story behind this particular hymn: "Fanny Crosby was visiting Mr. W. H. Doane, in his home in Cincinnati, Ohio. They were talking together about the nearness of God, as the sun was setting and evening shadows were gathering around them. The subject so impressed the well-known hymn-writer, that before retiring she had written the words to this hymn, which has become one of the most useful she has ever written. The music by Mr. Doane so well fitted the words that the hymn has become a special favorite wherever the gospel hymns are known."

It was first published in 1875 in the little hidden treasure of hymns called *Brightest and Best*. Underneath the hymn was this Scripture quotation: "Let us draw near with a true heart" (Heb. 10:22).

Peace, Perfect Peace

Edward H. Bickersteth

Orlando Gibbons

1. Peace, per-fect peace, in this dark world of sin?
2. Peace, per-fect peace, by throng - ing du - ties pressed?
3. Peace, per-fect peace, with sor - rows surg - ing round?
4. Peace, per-fect peace, with loved ones far a - way?
5. Peace, per-fect peace, our fu - ture all un - known?

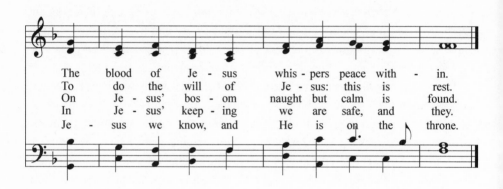

The blood of Je - sus whis - pers peace with - in.
To do the will of Je - sus: this is rest.
On Je - sus' bos - om naught but calm is found.
In Je - sus' keep - ing we are safe, and they.
Je - sus we know, and He is on the throne.

Peace, Perfect Peace

<u>1875</u>

You will keep him in perfect peace, Whose mind is stayed on You, because he trusts in You. Isaiah 26:3 (NKJV)

dward Bickersteth, author of this hymn, was born in London, into a clergyman's family, in 1825. After attending Cambridge, he entered the Anglican ministry. He wrote a number of hymns, but "Peace, Perfect Peace" is his most popular. His son explained how it came to be written:

It was written in Harrogate, in a house facing the Stray, in August 1875. On a Sunday morning, the Vicar of Harrogate, Canon Gibbon, preached from the text, "Thou wilt keep him in perfect peace, whose mind is stayed on Thee" and alluded to the fact that in the Hebrew the words are "Peace, peace," twice repeated, and happily translated in our version by the phrase, "Perfect peace." This sermon set my father's mind working on the subject. He always found it easier to express in verse what was on his mind, so that when on that afternoon he visited an aged and dying relative, Archdeacon Hill of Liverpool, and found him somewhat troubled in mind, it was natural to him to express in verse the spiritual comfort which he desired to convey. Taking up a sheet of paper, he there and then wrote down the hymn exactly as it stands, and read it to this dying Christian.

I was with my father at the time, being home from school for the summer holiday: I well recollect his coming in to tea, a meal we always had with him on Sunday afternoon, and saying, "Children, I have written you a hymn," and reading us "Peace, Perfect Peace." I may add that it was his custom to expect each one of us on Sunday at tea to repeat a hymn, and he did the same, unless, as frequently happened, he wrote us a special hymn himself. . . .

It is not always noticed that the first line of each verse of "Peace, Perfect Peace" is in the form of a question, referring to some one or other of the disturbing experiences of life, and the second line of each verse endeavors to give the answer. The hymn has been translated into many languages, and for many years I doubt if my father went many days without receiving from different people assurances of the comfort and help which the hymn had been to them.

Hallelujah, What a Savior!

Philip P. Bliss

Philip P. Bliss

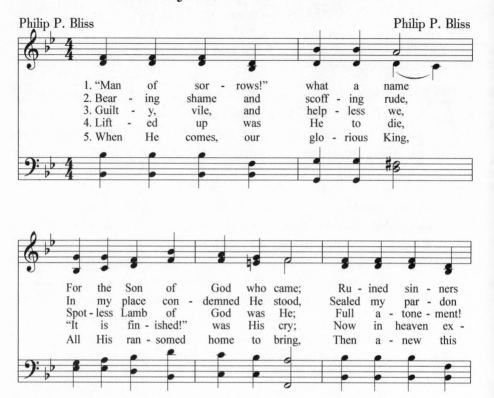

1. "Man of sor - rows!" what a name
2. Bear - ing shame and scoff - ing rude,
3. Guilt - y, vile, and help - less we,
4. Lift - ed up was He to die,
5. When He comes, our glo - rious King,

For the Son of God who came; Ru - ined sin - ners
In my place con - demned He stood, Sealed my par - don
Spot - less Lamb of God was He; Full a - tone - ment!
"It is fin - ished!" was His cry; Now in heaven ex -
All His ran - somed home to bring, Then a - new this

to re - claim! Hal - le - lu - jah! What a Sav - ior!
with His blood; Hal - le - lu - jah! What a Sav - ior!
Can it be? Hal - le - lu - jah! What a Sav - ior!
alt - ed high, Hal - le - lu - jah! What a Sav - ior!
song we'll sing, Hal - le - lu - jah! What a Sav - ior!

Hallelujah, What a Savior!

1875

And my spirit has rejoiced in God my Savior. Luke 1:47 (NKJV)

hilip Bliss and Lucy Young, deeply in love, were married on June 1, 1859. Philip was twenty years old at the time, with a strong physique and a remarkable talent for music. The young couple was devoted to Christ and they often thrilled fellow church members with beautiful duets.

Believing God had given her husband a special talent, Lucy schemed for ways to afford him proper musical training. With her encouragement, he began traveling on an old horse from town to town, carrying a twenty-dollar melodeon and holding singing schools.

When Lucy's grandmother gave them thirty dollars, Philip attended a six-week course at the Normal Academy of Music in New York. Upon completion, he became a full-time music teacher and was soon recognized as a local music authority.

Philip and Lucy moved to Chicago so he could pursue a ministry of music there. Between 1865 and 1873, he held music conventions, singing schools, and church meetings. In 1869, he attracted the attention of evangelist D. L. Moody, who continually urged him to enter the full-time ministry of music.

Moody would later write: "In my estimate, he was the most highly honored of God of any man of his time as a writer and singer of gospel songs, and with all his gifts he was the most humble man I ever knew. I loved him as a brother."

With Lucy's encouragement, Philip joined Moody's associate, Major Daniel W. Whittle, as song leader in a series of evangelistic campaigns; and "Whittle and Bliss" became almost as famous as "Moody and Sankey." Successful crusades were held in Illinois, Wisconsin, Pennsylvania, Kentucky, Minnesota, Mississippi, Alabama, and Georgia.

Philip wrote such favorites as "Wonderful Words of Life," "Almost Persuaded," "Dare to Be a Daniel," "Hold the Fort," "Jesus Loves Even Me," "Let the Lower Lights Be Burning," "The Light of the World Is Jesus," "I Will Sing of My Redeemer," and the music to "It Is Well with My Soul." By 1876, Philip, only thirty-six, was known as one of the greatest hymnists of his generation.

Late that year, Philip conducted a service for inmates at the Michigan State Prison and sang one of his last hymns, "Hallelujah, What a Savior!" Many of the prisoners wept openly and confessed Christ as Savior.

No one dreamed that the young songwriter and his wife had but a month remaining to live.

The Light of the World Is Jesus

Philip P. Bliss

Philip P. Bliss

1. The whole world was lost in the dark-ness of sin; The Light of the
2. No dark-ness have we who in Je - sus a - bide; The Light of the
3. Ye dwell - ers in dark-ness with sin-blind - ed eyes, The Light of the
4. No need of the sun-light in Heav - en, we're told, The Light of the

world is Je - sus; Like sun - shine at noon-day His glo - ry shone in,
world is Je - sus; We walk in the Light when we fol - low our Guide;
world is Je - sus; Go, wash at His bid - ding, and light will a - rise,
world is Je - sus; The Lamb is the light in the Cit - y of Gold;

The Light of the world is Je - sus. Come to the Light, 'tis

shin - ing for thee! Sweet-ly the Light has dawned up-on me; Once I was

blind, but now I can see; The Light of the world is Je - sus!

The Light of the World Is Jesus

<u>1875</u>

You are the light of the world. A city that is set on a hill cannot be hidden. Matthew 5:14 (NKJV)

O n the last Thursday of 1876, Philip Bliss prayed with his boys, Paul, two, and George, four, and explained that he and Lucy were leaving by train for Chicago to sing at D. L. Moody's Tabernacle at year's end. "I would far rather stay than go if it were God's will," he told them, "but I must be about the Master's work." The boys were left in the care of relatives.

Another passenger on the Chicago-bound train, Mr. J. E. Burchell, later told the story: "There were eleven cars on the train that left Buffalo at two o'clock Friday afternoon . . . in a blinding snowstorm. We neared the bridge (over the Ashtabula River in Ohio) at about 7:45. . . . We ran on the structure at a rate of about ten miles an hour, and the whole train was on the bridge when it gave way. The bridge is about 200 feet long, and only the first engine had passed over when the crash came. . . . The first thing I heard was a cracking in the front part of the car, and then the same cracking in the rear. Then . . . a sickening oscillation and a sudden sinking, and I was thrown stunned from my seat. . . . The iron work bent and twisted like snakes, and everything took horrid shapes. I heard a lady scream in anguish . . . then I heard the cry of fire . . . The crackling of the flames, the whistling wind, the screaming of the hurt, made a pandemonium of that little valley, and the water of the freezing creek was red with blood or black with the flying cinders. . . . The fire stole swiftly along the wreck, and in a few moments the cars were all in flames. The sight was sickening. The whole wreck was then on fire, and from out the frozen valley came great bursts of flame. . . ."

According to Mr. Burchell, Philip initially survived the wreck but crawled back through a window to save his wife. Both perished together.

Among Philip's last hymns was "The Light of the World Is Jesus" with its fitting final lines:

> *No need of the sunlight in Heaven we're told,*
> *The Light of the world is Jesus!*
> *The Lamb is the Light in the city of gold,*
> *The Light of the world is Jesus!**

---

*The Bliss family home in Rome, Pennsylvania, is now the P. P. Bliss Gospel Songwriters Museum.

Beulah Land

Edgar P. Stites   John R. Sweney

1. I've reached the land of joy di - vine, And all its beau - ty now is mine,
2. The Sav - iour comes and walks with me, And sweet com - mu - nion here have we;
3. A sweet per - fume up - on the breeze, Is borne from ev - er ver - nal trees,
4. The zeph - yrs seem to float to me, Sweet sounds of heav - en's mel - o - dy,

Here shines un - dimmed one bliss - ful day, For all my night has passed a - way.
He gent - ly leads me with His hand, For this is heav - en's bor - der-land.
And flow'rs that nev - er fad - ing grow Where streams of life for - ev - er flow.
As an - gels, with the white-robed throng, Join in the sweet re - demp - tion song.

O Beu - lah Land, sweet Beu - lah Land, As on thy high - est mount I stand,

I look a - way a - cross the sea, Where man - sions are pre - pared for me,

And view the shin - ing glo - ry shore, My heav'n, my home for - ev - er more!

Beulah Land
1876

You shall be called Hephzibah, and your land Beulah; for the LORD delights in you . . . Isaiah 62:4 (NKJV)

T he author of this hymn, Edgar Stites, was a descendant of John Howland, who came to America on the *Mayflower*. He was born in Cape May, New Jersey, in March of 1836, and was born again in Philadelphia during the Revival of 1857. He served Union Forces during the Civil War by feeding the troops that passed through Philadelphia.

After the war Edgar became a riverboat pilot on the Delaware River and a Methodist preacher. He also served a stint as home missionary to South Dakota. For more than sixty years, he was a member of the First Methodist Episcopal Church of Cape May, New Jersey. In 1870 he joined a number of other ministers and laymen in founding the Ocean Grove Camp Meeting Association. Today Ocean Grove is a full-fledged town as well as Christian community and conference center.

It was in Ocean Grove that "Beulah Land" was first sung.

The word "Beulah" is an Old Testament term that occurs only in Isaiah 62:4: "You shall no longer be termed Forsaken, nor shall your land be Desolate; but you shall be called Hephzibah, and your land Beulah; for the Lord delights in you, and your land shall be married." "Beulah" comes from a Hebrew word meaning "to marry." The idea is a land that is loved, that is as delightful to the Lord as a beautiful bride. As such, it has come to represent heaven.

"It was in 1876 that I wrote 'Beulah Land,'" Edgar Stites said. "I could write only two verses and the chorus, when I was overcome and fell on my face. That was one Sunday. On the following Sunday I wrote the third and fourth verses, and again I was so influenced by emotion that I could only pray and weep. The first time it was sung was at the regular Monday morning meeting of Methodists in Philadelphia. Bishop McCabe sang it to the assembled ministers. Since then it is known wherever religious people congregate. I have never received a cent for my songs. Perhaps that is why they have had such a wide popularity. I could not do work for the Master and receive pay for it."

Trusting Jesus

Edgar P. Stites

Ira D. Sankey

1. Sim - ply trust - ing ev - ery day, Trust-ing through a storm - y way;
2. Bright - ly doth His Spir - it shine In - to this poor heart of mine.
3. Sing - ing if my way is clear, Pray-ing if the path be drear;
4. Trust - ing Him while life shall last, Trust-ing Him till earth be past;

E - ven when my faith is small, Trust - ing Je - sus, that is all.
While He leads I can - not fall, Trust - ing Je - sus, that is all.
If in dan - ger, for Him call, Trust - ing Je - sus, that is all.
'Til I hear His fi - nal call, Trust - ing Je - sus, that is all.

Trust - ing as the mo - ments fly, Trust - ing as the days go by;

Trust - ing Him what - e'er be - fall, Trust - ing Je - sus, that is all.

Trusting Jesus
1876

The word of the LORD is proven; He is a shield to all who trust in Him. 2 Samuel 22:31 (NKJV)

R iverboat pilot turned Methodist preacher, Edgar Stites, the author of "Beulah Land," also wrote another well-known hymn, "Trusting Jesus." It was published in a newspaper, and a clipping of the poem was handed to D. L. Moody in Chicago. Moody, reading the poem, passed it to his song leader, Ira Sankey, asking Sankey to write a tune. Sankey agreed on condition that Moody vouch for the doctrine taught in the verses, which he did.

Who was this Ira Sankey who wrote the popular tune to "Trusting Jesus"? Sometimes called the "Father of Gospel Music," Sankey was born in 1840 in Pennsylvania and came to Christ as a teenager in a revival meeting. When the War Between the States broke out, he joined Union forces and often led the soldiers in singing during chapel services.

He took time in the middle of the Civil War to marry Fanny Edwards, daughter of a Pennsylvania state senator, and after the war the couple settled down in Newcastle, Pennsylvania. Ira found a job with the Internal Revenue Service. The couple had two sons, and joined the Methodist Episcopal Church where Ira led the singing.

It was in Indianapolis, Indiana, in June of 1870, while attending a YMCA convention, that Ira Sankey met D. L. Moody. Moody, hearing Sankey lead the singing, began peppering him with questions: "Where are you from? Are you married? What is your business?"

Moody, with his usual directness, told Sankey he'd have to give up his job with the IRS to become the song leader for his campaigns. "I have been looking for you for the last eight years," said Moody.

For the next thirty years, the names of Moody and Sankey would be linked in the world's greatest evangelistic undertakings. As the nineteenth century wore to a close, Sankey's beautiful voice became raspy due to overuse in the great halls and arenas where Moody preached, and his eyesight failed due to glaucoma. His years of notes and research on gospel music as well as the only manuscript of his autobiography were lost in a fire. But his work lives on. He composed the music to about twelve hundred songs during his lifetime, including "Faith Is the Victory," "The Ninety and Nine," "A Shelter in the Time of Storm," "Under His Wings," and this one—"Trusting Jesus."

I Am His, and He Is Mine

George Robinson   James Mountain

1. Loved with ev - er - last - ing love, Led by grace that love to know,
2. Heav'n a - bove is soft - er blue, Earth a - round is sweet - er green;
3. Things that once were wild a - larms Can - not now dis - turb my rest;
4. His for - ev - er, on - ly His, Who the Lord and me shall part?

Spir - it breath - ing from a - bove, Thou hast taught me it is so!
Some - thing lives in ev - ery hue Christ - less eyes have nev - er seen!
Closed in ev - er - last - ing arms, Pil - lowed on the lov - ing breast!
Ah, with what a rest of bliss Christ can fill the lov - ing heart!

O this full and per - fect peace From His pres - ence all di - vine-
Birds with glad - der songs o'er - flow, Flow'rs with deep - er beau - ties shine,
O to lie for - ev - er here, Doubt and care and self re - sign,
Heav'n and earth may fade and flee, First - born light in gloom de - cline,

In a love which can - not cease, I am His and He is mine; mine.
Since I know, as I now know, I am His and He is mine; mine.
While He whis - pers in my ear, I am His and He is mine; mine.
But while God and I shall be, I am His and He is mine; mine.

I Am His, and He Is Mine

1876

... The birds of the heavens have their home; They sing among the branches. Psalm 104:12 (NKJV)

S ome hymnals list this as "Loved with Everlasting Love." It's a wonderful hymn of assurance, written by an Irish pastor named George Wade Robinson. Born in Cork, Ireland, in 1838, Robinson attended college in Dublin, then in London; and he later pastored in both Dublin and London, then in the seacoast community of Brighton. He enjoyed writing poetry, and three volumes were published: *Iona and Other Sonnets, Loveland,* and *Songs in God's World.* This poem is the only one that has endured the generations.

I especially like the second verse, for it reminds us of the freshness that fills our hearts when we trust Christ as our Savior. The words say:

> *Heav'n above is softer blue, Earth around is sweeter green!*
> *Something lives in every hue Christless eyes have never seen;*
> *Birds with gladder songs o'erflow, flowers with deeper beauties shine,*
> *Since I know, as I now know, I am His, and He is mine.*

I have no way of proving this, but I believe Robinson's words were inspired by Moody's testimony. D. L. Moody and Ira Sankey were setting Great Britain on fire. Their first evangelistic campaign to England and Ireland occurred in 1873, and Moody must have given his testimony many times and in many places. Robinson must have listened in rapt attention. Compare his verse to what Moody later wrote about the time he came to Jesus Christ as a teenager in Boston:

> *I remember the morning on which I came out of my room after I had first trusted Christ. I thought the old sun shone a good deal brighter than it ever had before—I thought it was just smiling upon me; and as I walked out upon Boston Common and heard the birds singing in the trees I thought they were all singing a song to me. Do you know, I fell in love with the birds? I had never cared for them before. It seemed to me that I was in love with all creation. I had not a bitter feeling against any man.*

The presence of Christ in our hearts makes the sun brighter, the sky bluer, the grass greener, the birds sweeter, and the flowers lovelier—since we know, as now we know, that "I am His, and He is mine."

Nothing but the Blood

Robert Lowry   Robert Lowry

1. What can wash a - way my sin? Noth-ing but the blood of Je - sus;
2. For my par-don, this I see, Noth-ing but the blood of Je - sus;
3. Noth-ing can for sin a - tone, Noth-ing but the blood of Je - sus;
4. This is all my hope and peace, Noth-ing but the blood of Je - sus;

What can make me whole a - gain? Noth-ing but the blood of Je - sus.
For my cleans-ing, this my plea, Noth-ing but the blood of Je - sus.
Naught of good that I have done, Noth-ing but the blood of Je - sus.
This is all my righ - teous-ness, Noth-ing but the blood of Je - sus.

O! pre-cious is the flow That makes me white as snow;

No oth - er fount I know; Nothing but the blood of Je - sus.

Nothing but the Blood

1876

. . . almost all things are purified with blood, and without shedding of blood there is no remission. Hebrews 9:22 (NKJV)

 s we thumb through our Bibles, we run across beloved and deeply underlined verses like these:

And when I see the blood, I will pass over you . . . It is the blood that makes atonement for the soul . . . For this is My blood of the new covenant, which is shed for many for the remission of sins . . . The church of God which He purchased with His own blood . . . Christ Jesus whom God set forth as propitiation by His blood . . . In Him we have redemption through His blood, the forgiveness of sins, according to the riches of His grace . . . With His own blood He entered the Most Holy Place once for all, having obtained eternal redemption . . . The precious blood of Christ, as of a lamb . . . The blood of Jesus Christ His Son cleanses us from all sin.*

We shouldn't be surprised, then, as we study the great hymnists of history, to find their souls thrilled and their songs filled with this theme.

In 1739, Count Zinzendorf wrote his great "Jesus, Thy Blood and Righteousness." That same year, Charles Wesley penned, "His blood can make the foulest clean, / His blood availed for me."

The melancholy William Cowper wrote, "There is a fountain filled with blood / drawn from Emmanuel's veins / And sinners plunged beneath that flood / Lose all their guilty stains."

Perhaps the most popular hymn about the blood is this one, written by two men who came to Christ as teenagers. Robert Lowry, author of the words, came to Christ at age seventeen. William Doane confessed Christ as His Savior while in high school. Together they wrote hymns and published gospel songbooks.

When "Nothing but the Blood" was published in 1876, the attached Scripture was from Hebrews 9:22: "Without shedding of blood there is no remission." Most of our hymnals omit Lowry's original final two stanzas:

Now by this I'll overcome—Nothing but the blood of Jesus,
Now by this I'll reach my home—Nothing but the blood of Jesus.

Glory! Glory! This I sing—Nothing but the blood of Jesus,
All my praise for this I bring—Nothing but the blood of Jesus.

---

*Exodus 12:13, Leviticus 17:11; Matthew 26:28; Acts 20:28; Romans 3:24–25; Ephesians 1:7; Hebrews 9:12; 1 Peter 1:18; 1 John 1:7

God of Our Fathers

Daniel C. Roberts

George W. Warren

*Trumpets before
each stanza*

1. God of our fa - thers, whose Al - might - y hand
2. Thy love di - vine hath led us in the past,
3. From war's a - larms, from dead - ly pes - ti - lence,
4. Re - fresh Thy peo - ple on their toil - some way,

Leads forth in beau - ty all the star - ry band
In this free land by Thee our lot is cast;
Be Thy strong arm our ev - er sure de - fense;
Lead us from night to nev - er end - ing day;

Of shin - ing worlds in splen - dor through the skies,
Be Thou our Rul - er, Guard - ian, Guide, and Stay,
Thy true re - li - gion in our hearts in - crease,
Fill all our lives with love and grace di - vine,

Our grate - ful songs be - fore Thy throne a - rise.
Thy word our law, Thy paths our cho - sen way.
Thy boun - teous good - ness nour - ish us in peace.
And glo - ry, laud, and praise be ev - er Thine!

God of Our Fathers

1876

The God of our fathers has chosen you that you should know His will, and see the Just One, and hear the voice of His mouth. Acts 22:14 (NKJV)

This patriotic hymn represents a double celebration of America's one hundredth birthday. The words were written in 1876 by a New England pastor in honor of the one hundredth anniversary of the signing of the Declaration of Independence. The music was written twelve years later in celebration of the one hundredth anniversary of the adoption of the United States Constitution.

Daniel Crain Roberts, a thirty-four-year-old veteran of the Civil War, authored the words. Born on Long Island in New York in 1841, Daniel attended college in Ohio and served as a private with the 84th Ohio Volunteers during the War Between the States. As the war ended, he was ordained as a deacon in the Presbyterian Episcopalian church, and shortly afterward as a priest. He served for the next thirty years pastoring Episcopalian churches in New England, including a decades-long pastorate of St. Paul's Church in Concord, New Hampshire.*

It was while serving as rector of St. Thomas Episcopal Church in Brandon, Vermont, as the nation celebrated its one hundredth birthday, that Daniel wrote this hymn. He later submitted it anonymously to the committee for the Episcopal hymnal, and it was accepted. It is the only hymn for which he is remembered.

The majestic melody is not the one to which it was originally sung. When Daniel wrote "God of Our Fathers," he set the words to the tune of the Russian national anthem! It was twelve years later that George William Warren, a self-taught organist, composed the stately tune with its trumpet fanfares. It was called NATIONAL HYMN, written to commemorate the one hundredth anniversary of the U.S. Constitution.

George Warren, lacking formal training, had originally pursued a business career. But his natural talent soon shoved him into music, and he eventually became one of America's premier organists. During his career, he served various congregations in New York City, and he also composed anthems and edited *Warren's Hymns and Tunes as Sung at St. Thomas' Church*, in 1888. He also wrote GUIDE ME for the words of the great Welsh hymn, "Guide Me, O Thou Great Jehovah."

When George Warren died in 1902, there was a feeling that no organist could play as well as he could, so not a single note of music was played at his funeral, which was attended by thousands.

---

*Interestingly, this is the same church in which, in 2003, the controversial Rev. Gene Robinson was ordained as Episcopalians' first openly homosexual bishop.

165

Immortal, Invisible, God Only Wise

Walter Chalmers Smith

Welsh Hymn Melody

1. Im - mor - tal, in - vis - i - ble, God on - ly wise,
2. Un - rest - ing, un - hast - ing, and si - lent as light;
3. To all, life Thou giv - est, to both great and small;
4. Great Fa - ther of glo - ry, pure Fa - ther of light;

In light in - ac - ces - si - ble hid from our eyes;
Nor want - ing, nor wast - ing, Thou rul - est in might.
In all life Thou liv - est, the true life of all;
Thine an - gels a - dore Thee, all veil - ing their sight;

Most bless - ed, most glo - rious, the An - cient of Days;
Thy jus - tice, like moun - tains, high soar - ing a - bove
We blos - som and flour - ish as leaves on the tree,
All praise we would ren - der: O help us to see

Al - might - y, vic - to - rious, Thy great name we praise.
Thy clouds, which are foun - tains of good - ness and love.
And with - er and per - ish, but naught chang - eth Thee.
'Tis on - ly the splen - dor of light hid - eth Thee.

Immortal, Invisible, God Only Wise

1876

Now to the King eternal, immortal, invisible, to God who alone is wise, be honor and glory forever and ever. Amen. 1 Timothy 1:17 (NKJV)

The city of Edinburgh, Scotland, with its Royal Mile and rugged hilltop castle, has produced some of Christianity's greatest hymnists: George Matheson ("O Love That Wilt Not Let Me Go"), Horatius Bonar ("I Heard the Voice of Jesus Say"), Elizabeth Celphane ("Beneath the Cross of Jesus"), and William MacKay ("Revive Us Again"), to name a few. And who but the sturdy Scotch Presbyterians could produce such a powerful hymn on the sovereign, eternal power of God as "Immortal, Invisible, God Only Wise"?

The author, Walter Chalmers Smith, was born in Aberdeen on December 5, 1824. After attending grammar school at the University of Aberdeen, he enrolled in New College, Edinburgh, and was ordained as a minister in the Free Church of Scotland in 1850. He pastored churches in several places, including the lovely Scottish village of Milnathort from 1853 to 1858.

In 1874, he became pastor of the Free High Church (Presbyterian) of Edinburgh, a charge he kept until his retirement in 1894.* Two years into his pastorate, he published a collection of hymns titled *Hymns of Christ and the Christian Life*. It was here that "Immortal, Invisible, God Only Wise" was introduced to the world.

Walter Smith was blessed with two other honors. In 1893, he was elected Moderator of the Free Church of Scotland. And in 1902, a collection of his poetry was published. His poems reflect his Scottish nature and remind us of Robert Burns. A number of them had appeared in various publications over the years, published under the pseudonyms "Orwell" and "Herman Knott." One of his best-known poems, "Glenaradale," begins:

There is no fire of the crackling boughs / On the hearth of our fathers,
There is no lowing of brown-eyed cows / On the green meadows,
Nor do the maidens whisper vows / In the still gloaming,
Glenaradale.

"Immortal, Invisible, God Only Wise" was based on 1 Timothy 1:17. It was originally published in six stanzas. When the hymn was republished in 1884, Smith made a few alterations. Today's version uses Smith's first three stanzas, and the fourth stanza is pieced together from lines in the now-discarded verses.

The powerful melody is called ST. DENIO based on a Welsh folk song.

---

*The beautiful building of Edinburgh's Free High Church was vacated by its members in 1934, and now serves as the Library for the University of Edinburgh. It is obvious to anyone who enters the library that it was originally a church.

A Child of the King

Harriet E. Buell

John B. Sumner

1. My Father is rich in hous - es and lands, He hold - eth the
2. I once was an out - cast stran - ger on earth, A sin - ner by
3. A tent or a cot - tage, why should I care? They're build - ing a

wealth of the world in His hands! Of ru - bies and dia - monds, of
choice, and an al - ien by birth; But I've been a - dopt - ed, my
pal - ace for me o - ver there; Though ex - iled from home, yet

sil - ver and gold, His cof - fers are full, He has rich - es un - told.
name's writ - ten down, An heir to a man - sion, a robe, and a crown.
still I may sing: All glo - ry to God, I'm a child of the King.

I'm a child of the King, A child of the King,

With Je - sus my Sav - ior I'm a child of the King.

A Child of the King

1877

But God demonstrates His own love toward us, in that while we were still sinners,
Christ died for us. Romans 5:8 (NKJV)

As I left my hometown of Cazenovia, New York," wrote the author of this hymn, Harriet (Hattie) Buell, "bound for the 1876 camp meeting held at the Thousand Island Park in upper New York State, my heart was hungering for the spiritual food I knew would be awaiting me there. It was an occasion I looked forward to each year, for God seemed to speak to people's hearts and especially to mine in an unusual way at that hallowed spot.

"I will never forget the opening Sunday morning service. Beginning with the doxology and through each hymn and Scripture, it all served to remind me of the greatness of a God who had made the earth, the skies, and the great universe, yet loved and cared for us, His children.

"The speaker that morning chose as his topic our relationship to God through His Son, Jesus Christ. How man, as a sinner, was alienated and far from God; but how he became an heir of God and a joint heir with Jesus Christ through faith in His finished work on the Cross. In the course of the message, the speaker could control himself no longer and shouted, 'Christian friends, we are the children of a King! Our Heavenly Father's a King! Poor ones, take heart, you'll have a palace someday built for you by Jesus Himself!'

"I don't have to tell you that I felt as if I were walking on air as I left that service and as I walked toward my cottage. The complete set of words had come to me, and I entitled them, 'The Child of a King.'"*

Meanwhile the Lord was preparing John Sumner to compose the music for Hattie's poem. Sumner, a young pastor in Pennsylvania, had traveled with his family throughout the Susquehanna Valley, teaching singing schools. One of his greatest joys had been meeting hymnist Philip Bliss. When the stunning news came of the terrible train wreck that took Bliss's life, Sumner knelt and prayed that in some way he might continue and complete Bliss's work.

The following February, while reading a Methodist revival magazine, *The Northern Christian Advocate*, he found Hattie's poem and set it to music. Gaining quick popularity, it soon found its place beside Bliss's songs in the gospel hymnbooks of the day.

---

*I'm indebted to the "Dean of Gospel Music," Alfred B. Smith, for this account which he preserved in his *Treasury of Hymn Histories.*

169

Break Thou the Bread of Life

Mary A. Lathbury, stanzas 1 & 2
Alexander Groves, stanzas 3 & 4

William F. Sherwin

1. Break Thou the bread of life, Dear Lord, to me,
2. Bless Thou the truth, dear Lord, To me, to me,
3. Thou art the Bread of Life, O Lord, to me,
4. O send Thy Spir - it, Lord, Now un - to me,

As Thou didst break the loaves be - side the sea;
As Thou didst bless the bread By Gal - i - lee;
Thy ho - ly Word the truth That sav - eth me;
That He may touch my eyes And make me see;

Be - yond the sa - cred page I seek Thee, Lord;
Then shall all bon - dage cease, All fet - ters fall;
Give me to eat and live With Thee a - bove;
Show me the truth con - cealed with - in Thy Word,

My spir - it pants for Thee, O liv - ing Word.
And I shall find my peace, My All in all.
Teach me to love Thy truth, For Thou art love.
For in Thy book re - vealed I see Thee, Lord.

Break Thou the Bread of Life

1877

And Jesus said to them, "I am the bread of life. He who comes to Me shall never hunger, and he who believes in Me shall never thirst." John 6:35 (NKJV)

On August 4, 1874, Methodist ministers John Vincent and Lewis Miller organized a Sunday school training camp beside Lake Chautauqua in New York. It was a hit. Families arrived in large numbers, paid the entrance fees, and moved into tents or cottages near an outdoor amphitheater.

Wanting national exposure, Vincent and Miller plotted to get President U. S. Grant to visit. "It would be a positive gain for the Bible, the Sunday school, and the Christian church if the President of the United States should come," wrote Vincent.

Somehow they pulled it off. On August 14, 1875, Grant's special train pulled into the station as cannons boomed and local bands played "Hail to the Chief." After an elaborate twelve-course lunch in a local home, Grant's party boarded a procession of steamboats and proceeded to the Chautauqua Camp Grounds where twenty thousand cheering people greeted the president.

Among them was Mary A. Lathbury, a local Christian who had been informally designated the "Poet Laureate of Chautauqua." She had written a "Song of Welcome" with which to greet the Commander-in-Chief on his arrival. The chorus:

Greet him! Let the air around him benedictions bear!
Let the hearts of all the people circle him with prayer!

This was one of the high points in the simple life of Mary Artemesia Lathbury. The daughter of a Methodist preacher, Mary was a native New Yorker who served as general editor of publications for the children/youth division of the Methodist Sunday School Union. She was also involved in the temperance movement and in the Chautauqua training programs.

Her hymns, however, have been her most enduring legacy, including the popular "Day Is Dying in the West," written on the shore of Lake Chautauqua.

In 1877, John Vincent asked Mary to write a hymn for the Chautauqua Bible Study Hour. Its focus was on studying Jesus Christ, the "Bread of Life" (John 6:35). In response, Mary wrote a two-stanza hymn entitled, "Break Thou the Bread of Life." (The final two stanzas were added later by Alexander Groves.)

Regarding her gift for art and verse, Mary Lathbury said that God had once told her: "Remember, my child, that you have a gift of weaving fancies into verse and a gift with the pencil of producing visions that come to your heart; consecrate these to Me as thoroughly as you do your inmost spirit."

Who Is on the Lord's Side?

Frances R. Havergal

C. Luise Reichardt

1. Who is on the Lord's side? Who will serve the King? Who will be His help-ers, Oth-er lives to bring? Who will leave the world's side? Who will face the foe? Who is on the Lord's side? Who for Him will go? By Thy call of mer-cy, By Thy grace di-vine, We are on the Lord's side— Sav-ior, we are Thine.

2. Not for weight of glo-ry, Not for crown and palm, En-ter we the ar-my, Raise the war-rior psalm; But for love that claim-eth Lives for whom He died; He whom Je-sus nam-eth Must be on His side. By Thy love con-strain-ing, By Thy grace di-vine, We are on the Lord's side— Sav-ior, we are Thine.

3. Fierce may be the con-flict, Strong may be the foe, But the King's own ar-my None can o-ver-throw. 'Round His stan-dard rang-ing, Vic-tory to se-cure, For His truth un-chang-ing Makes the tri-umph sure. Joy-ful-ly en-list-ing By Thy grace di-vine, We are on the Lord's side— Sav-ior, we are Thine.

Who Is on the Lord's Side?

1877

Then Moses stood in the entrance of the camp, and said, "Whoever is on the LORD's side—come to me!" Exodus 32:26 (NKJV)

 hen people ask me my favorite hymn, I thrash about for an answer, but when I'm asked for my favorite hymn writer, I respond quickly: Frances Ridley Havergal, author of such hymns as "Take My Life and Let It Be" and "Like a River Glorious."

Frances was born just before Christmas in 1846 in Astley, Worcestershire, England. Her father, Rev. William Henry Havergal, was a humble but influential pastor who passionately worked to improve the hymnody of the Anglican Church. He is the composer of the tune ZOAN ("I Sing the Mighty Power of God"), and the author of one hundred hymns.

As a child, Frances worried that she was not among the "Elect." As her mother was dying, she called Frances, eleven, to her bedside and said, "You are my youngest little girl, and I feel more anxious about you than the rest. I do pray for the Holy Spirit to lead and guide you. And remember, nothing but the precious blood of Christ can make you clean and lovely in God's sight."

It wasn't until Frances was fifteen that she found assurance of salvation in Christ. Soon she was writing poems and hymns to the Lord. Frances had a quick mind, a clarion voice, and a radiant personality that drew people like a magnet. During her thirties she began writing devotional books, and the combination of her hymns, poetry, and books made her one of the most popular Christian authors in England.

The year 1877 was very busy for Frances. To a friend, she wrote "What shall I do? Your letter would take two hours to answer, and I have not ten minutes; fifteen to twenty letters to write every morning, proofs to correct, editors waiting for articles, poems and music I cannot touch, American publishers clamoring for poems or any manuscripts, Bible readings or classes weekly, many anxious ones waiting for help, a mission week coming and other work after that. And my doctor says my physique is too weak to balance the nerves and brain, and that I ought not to touch a pen."

But she did touch a pen that year. After studying Exodus 32:26, she wrote this great hymn, "Who Is on the Lord's Side?" with its resounding answer:

By Thy call of mercy, by Thy grace divine,
We are on the Lord's side—Savior, we are Thine!

Truehearted, Wholehearted

Frances R. Havergal

George C. Stebbins

1. True - heart - ed, whole - heart - ed, faith - ful and loy - al,
2. True - heart - ed, whole - heart - ed, Full - est al - le - giance
3. True - heart - ed, whole - heart - ed, Sav - ior all - glo - rious!

King of our lives, by Thy grace we will be;
Yield - ing hence - forth to our glo - ri - ous King;
Take Thy great pow - er and reign there a - lone,

Un - der the stan - dard ex - alt - ed and roy - al,
Val - iant en - deav - or and lov - ing o - be - dience,
O - ver our wills and af - fec - tions vic - to - rious,

Strong in Thy strength we will bat - tle for Thee.
Free - ly and joy - ous - ly now we would bring.
Free - ly sur - ren - dered and whol - ly Thine own.

Truehearted, Wholehearted

1878

And he commanded them, saying, "Thus you shall act in the fear of the LORD, faithfully and with a loyal heart." 2 Chronicles 19:9 (NKJV)

I treasure my small collection of Frances Havergal's old devotional books. Many of them are based on her favorite theme—the joy of trusting and serving Jesus the King. "How glad we are that He Himself is our King," she wrote. "We are so sure He is able to subdue all things unto Himself in this inner kingdom which we cannot govern at all. We are so glad to take Him at His word and give up the government into His hands, asking Him to be our King in very deed, and to set up His throne of peace in the long-disturbed and divided citadel (of our minds), praying that He would bring every thought into captivity of His gentle obedience."

It was along these lines in 1878 that she wrote "Truehearted, Wholehearted, Faithful, and Loyal, / King of our Lives, by Thy grace, we will be."

Unknown to Frances, her time of earthly service to the King was ending. The next year, her health failed alarmingly. She was only forty-two, and very busy. Not only was her writing ministry in full bloom, but she was traveling widely promoting Christian and missionary causes.

She was aware of her decline, however; and one Sunday in April 1878, while walking to church, Frances turned to her sister, saying, "Marie, I've come to the conclusion it would be very nice to go to heaven."

A month later, her strength collapsed. When the doctor called on her, she startled him by asking, "Do you think I've a chance of going?" As her loved ones gathered at her bedside, they were astonished by her attitude. "If I am going, it is too good to be true," she told them. A little later, she looked up smiling and said, "Splendid to be so near the gates of heaven! I am lost in amazement! There has not failed one word of all His good promises!"

Shortly afterward, Frances looked up steadfastly as if seeing the Lord. "For ten minutes we watched that almost visible meeting with her King," wrote Maria, "and her countenance was so glad, as if she were already talking to Him! Then she tried to sing, but after one sweet, high note—'He . . .'—her voice failed and her brother commended her soul into the Redeemer's hand, and she passed away."

Follow On

William O. Cushing

Robert Lowry

1. Down in the val - ley, with my Sav - ior I would go,
2. Down in the val - ley with my Sav - ior I would go,
3. Down in the val - ley or up - on the moun - tain steep,

Where the flowers are bloom - ing and the sweet wa - ters flow;
Where the storms are sweep - ing and the dark wa - ters flow;
Close be - side my Sav - ior would my soul ev - er keep;

Ev - ery - where He leads me I would fol - low, fol - low on,
With His hand to lead me I will nev - er, nev - er fear,
He will lead me safe - ly in the path that He has trod,

Walk - ing in His foot - steps till the crown be won.
Dan - ger can - not fright me If my Lord is near.
Up to where they gath - er on the hills of God.

Follow On

<u>1878</u>

Then Jesus spoke to them again, saying, "I am the light of the world. He who follows Me shall not walk in darkness, but have the light of life." John 8:12 (NKJV)

Someone said that when God closes a door He always opens a window. What we don't realize is that the window is often much bigger than the door.

William Cushing (the man who converted George Root's Civil War song into the gospel hymn "Ring the Bells of Heaven") was born on the last day of 1823 into a Unitarian home in Massachusetts. He was converted as a child. Entering the ministry with the Disciples of Christ, he served twenty years as a faithful pastor in several New York cities and towns.

In 1870, William's wife died and his own health broke. Though only forty-seven, he suffered a paralysis that affected his voice and made it nearly impossible for him to preach. He fell into depression, but finally offered this prayer of resignation: "Lord, give me something to do for Thee."

Shortly thereafter he began writing hymns, especially for children. His little song, "Jewels," for example, became one of the most popular children's hymns of the late nineteenth century. The words said:

> *When He cometh, when He cometh / To make up His jewels,*
> *All His jewels, precious jewels, / His loved and His own.*
> *Like the stars of the morning, / His brightness adorning,*
> *They shall shine in their beauty, / Bright gems for His crown.*

In subsequent years, William produced more than three hundred hymns, including the favorite "Under His Wings."

About "Follow On," William later told Ira Sankey:

> *I wrote this hymn in 1878. Longing to give up all for Christ who had given his life for me, I wanted to be willing to lay everything at his feet, with no wish but to do his will, to live henceforth only for his glory. Out of this feeling came the hymn, "Follow On." It was written with the prayer and the hope that some heart might by it be led to give up all for Christ. Much of the power and usefulness of the hymn, however, are due to Mr. Lowry, who put it into song.*

Sankey added that William's work as a hymnist has "blessed tens of thousands throughout the world, whom his voice as a preacher could never have reached."

177

Are You Washed in the Blood?

Elisha A. Hoffman

Elisha A. Hoffman

1. Have you been to Je - sus for the cleans - ing power? Are you
2. Are you walk - ing dai - ly by the Sav - ior's side? Are you
3. Lay a - side the gar - ments that are stained with sin And be

washed in the blood of the Lamb? Are you ful - ly trust - ing in His
washed in the blood of the Lamb? Do you rest each mo - ment in the
washed in the blood of the Lamb. There's a foun - tain flow - ing for the

grace this hour? Are you washed in the blood of the Lamb?
Cru - ci - fied? Are you washed in the blood of the Lamb? Are you
soul un - clean, O be washed in the blood of the Lamb!

washed in the blood, in the soul-cleans-ing blood of the Lamb? Are your

gar-ments spot-less? Are they white as snow? Are you washed in the blood of the Lamb?

Are You Washed in the Blood?

1878

To Him who loved us and washed us from our sins in His own blood . . . to Him be glory and dominion forever and ever. Amen. Revelation 1:5, 6 (NKJV)

A s a preacher, Elisha Hoffman was of average ability, but as a minister who cared for the poor and downtrodden, he excelled. He also stands among the giants of the gospel song era, the author of such favorites as: "I Must Tell Jesus," "Down at the Cross," and "Leaning on the Everlasting Arms."

Elisha was born on May 7, 1839, in Orwigsburg, Pennsylvania, and died ninety years later, in 1929, in Chicago. His parents, Rev. Francis A. and Rebecca Ann Hoffman, were devoted to Christ and devoted to a denomination called the Evangelical Association. They gave their son the middle name of Albright in honor of Jacob Albright, the denomination's founder.

Elisha attended public school in Philadelphia, then enrolled in Union Bible Seminary at New Berlin, Pennsylvania, planning to follow his father's footsteps into the ministry. When the Civil War erupted, Elisha served with the 47th Pennsylvania Infantry Division. Near the war's end, he married Susan Orwig, the daughter of one of the bishops of the Evangelical Association. The couple moved to Cleveland, Ohio, where Elisha was hired as the publishing agent for the Board of Publications of the Evangelical Association. He later pastored churches in Ohio, Illinois, and Michigan.

In 1894, Elisha became the first music editor for the Hope Publishing Company of Chicago. He remained in that post until 1912. Through his years at Hope, he published fifty songbooks and hymnals and wrote the words or music to at least one thousand gospel and Sunday school songs. Some sources put the number at two thousand.

"Are You Washed in the Blood?" first appeared in *Spiritual Songs for Gospel Meetings and Sunday School,* published in 1878. Three years later, it was included in Ira Sankey's *Sacred Songs and Solos,* published in England.

Elisha Hoffman is credited for popularizing the element of "altar" into hymnology of his day. Consider this well-known hymn that came from his pen:

You have longed for sweet peace, | And for faith to increase,
And have earnestly, fervently prayed; | But you cannot have rest, or be perfectly blest,
Until all on the altar is laid.

Is your all on the altar of sacrifice laid? | Your heart does the Spirit control?
You can only be blest, and have peace and sweet rest,
As you yield Him your body and soul.

Breathe on Me

Edwin Hatch   B.B. McKinney

1. Ho - ly Spir-it, breathe on me, Un - til my heart is clean;
2. Ho - ly Spir-it, breathe on me, My stub-born will sub - due.
3. Ho - ly Spir-it, breathe on me, Fill me with pow'r di - vine;
4. Ho - ly Spir-it, breathe on me, Till I am all Thine own,

Let sun - shine fill its in - most part, With not a cloud be - tween.
Teach me in words of liv - ing flame What Christ would have me do.
Kin - dle a flame of love and zeal With - in this heart of mine.
Un - til my will is lost in Thine, To live for Thee a - lone.

Breathe on me, breathe on me, Ho - ly Spir-it, breathe on me;

Take Thou my heart, cleanse ev - 'ry part, Ho - ly Spir - it, breathe on me.

Breathe on Me

1878

And when He had said this, He breathed on them, and said to them, "Receive the Holy Spirit." John 20:22 (NKJV)

John 20:22 has inspired several great hymns of aspiration. This one, "Breathe on Me," was written in 1878 by an Anglican priest named Edwin Hatch, who, deeply impressed with the words of John 20:22, wanted to be included in our Lord's blessing to His disciples. Hatch published his hymn in a privately printed leaflet entitled *Between Doubt and Prayer.*

During his lifetime, Hatch was one of England's greatest theologians. He became a scholar of Pembroke College, Oxford, and won the Ellerton prize in 1858. He was professor of classics in Trinity College, Toronto, from 1859 to 1862, when he became rector of the high school at Quebec. Returning to England in 1867, he was appointed vice-principal of St. Mary Hall at Oxford. He gave the famous Bampton Lectures in 1880 and the Hibbert Lectures in 1888. One commentator remarked that Hatch's religious poems were "a beautiful supplement to his theology and reveal the depth and tenderness of his religious life."

In 1937, inspired by Hatch's hymn, the Southern Baptist hymnist, B. B. McKinney, wrote an "updated version" which he titled, "Holy Spirit, Breathe on Me." It is essentially a "paraphrase" of Hatch's hymn. McKinney was a Southern Baptist pastor, educator, and songwriter who published over 500 hymns. He would have undoubtedly written many others but for his sudden death in a car accident in 1952.

Jesus' words in John 20:22 have inspired a number of similar verses. Wesley's great hymn, "Love Divine, All Loves Excelling" echoes this thought in the stanza that says: "Breathe, O breathe Thy Loving Spirit into every troubled breast! / Let us all in Thee inherit; let us find that second rest."

Alfred Vine wrote a hymn (often sung to the tune "O Master Let Me Walk with Thee") that says:

> *O breath of God, breathe on us now, / And move within us while we pray:*
> *The Spring of our new life art Thou, / The very light of our new day.*

My favorite treatment of this theme is Bessie Head's 1914 hymn, "O Breath of Life," which says:

> *O Breath of life, come sweeping through us, / Revive Thy church with life and power;*
> *O Breath of life, come, cleanse, renew us, / And fit Thy church to meet this hour.*

May our Lord answer all these prayers. Come now, Lord, and breathe on us.

Softly and Tenderly

Will L. Thompson

Will L. Thompson

1. Soft - ly and ten - der - ly Je - sus is call - ing, Call - ing for
2. Why should we tar - ry when Je - sus is plead - ing, Plead - ing for
3. O for the won - der - ful love He has prom - ised, Prom - ised for

you and for me. See, on the por - tals He's wait - ing and watch-ing,
you and for me? Why should we lin - ger and heed not His mer - cies,
you and for me! Though we have sinned, He has mer - cy and par - don,

Watch - ing for you and for me. Come home, come home,
Mer - cies for you and for me? Come home, come home,
Par - don for you and for me.

Ye who are wea - ry, come home; Ear - nest - ly,

ten - der - ly Je - sus is call-ing, Call - ing, "O sin - ner, come home!"

Softly and Tenderly

1880

When Jesus heard it, He said to them, ". . . I did not come to call the righteous, but sinners, to repentance." Mark 2:17 (NKJV)

T he author of this hymn, Will Lamartine Thompson, was born on November 7, 1847, in East Liverpool, Ohio, a small town on the Ohio River across from Kentucky. His father was a local merchant and a member of the Ohio State Legislature. Will attended Mt. Union College in nearby Alliance, Ohio. His musical abilities took him on to the Boston Conservatory of Music and to Leipzig, Germany, to study with the greats.

Will was interested in writing secular and patriotic songs; but when he traveled to Cleveland to sell his music manuscripts, he was offered only twenty-five dollars. Feeling slighted, Will rolled up his music, returned to East Liverpool, and prayed about what to do next.

When his father sent him to New York on business, Will took his songs to a printer, intent on publishing and selling them himself. "My Home on the Old Ohio," and "Gathering Shells from the Sea" were hits, and Will soon became known as the "Bard of Ohio." He became a millionaire.

The young man credited the Lord with his success, and, wanting to return thanks, he dedicated himself to writing Christian songs—and Christian songs only. He established Will L. Thompson & Co. with offices in East Liverpool and Chicago, and his quartet numbers sold two million copies.

In 1880, this hymn, "Softly and Tenderly," appeared in a book entitled *Sparkling Gems, Nos. 1 and 2 Combined*, published by Thompson & Co.

Despite his success and wealth, Will was known as a simple and sincere man. He felt concerned that while famous musicians traveled to the great cities to perform before large crowds, people in the rural areas and small towns seldom had anyone to come and minister to them in like fashion. So he loaded an upright piano on his two-horse wagon and drove into the country to sing and play his own songs in small churches throughout the Midwest.

In the late 1890s, he paid a visit to evangelist D. L. Moody, who was very ill and near death. Most visitors had been turned away, but when Moody heard that Thompson was downstairs, he called for him. "Will," he said, "I would rather have written 'Softly and Tenderly Jesus Is Calling,' than anything I have been able to do in my whole life."

183

A Shelter in the Time of Storm

Vernon J. Charlesworth

Ira D. Sankey

1. The Lord's our Rock, in Him we hide, A shel-ter in the time of storm;
2. A shade by day, de - fense by night, A shel-ter in the time of storm;
3. The rag - ing storms may round us beat, A shel-ter in the time of storm;
4. O Rock di - vine, O Ref - uge dear, A shel-ter in the time of storm;

Se - cure what - ev - er ill be - tide, A shel-ter in the time of storm.
No fears a - larm, no foes af - fright, A shel-ter in the time of storm.
We'll nev - er leave our safe re - treat, A shel-ter in the time of storm.
Be Thou our help - er ev - er near, A shel-ter in the time of storm.

O Je - sus is a Rock in a wea - ry land, A

wea - ry land, a wea - ry land; O Je - sus is a

Rock in a wea - ry land; A Shel - ter in the time of storm.

A Shelter in the Time of Storm

1880

You are my hiding place; You shall preserve me from trouble; You shall surround me with songs of deliverance. Selah. Psalm 32:7 (NKJV)

After a prolonged period of personal sorrow, I came to church one Sunday night broken in spirit. I'd asked my friend, missionary Tim Kenner, to bring the evening message. As he spoke from Colossians 3:3, a peace swept over me that has never left: "For you died, and your life is hidden with Christ in God."

Somehow I realized we must just die to our struggles, our sorrows, and our insolvable problems. We must flee to the Rock that is higher than we are (Psalm 61:2). We have to say, "Lord, if all around me collapses, my security is still in You. I'm hiding in You till the storm passes by."

The author of this hymn, Vernon John Charlesworth, was a British pastor, remembered in history for three things. First, he wrote an enduring biography of Rowland Hill, the British nonconformist preacher who used his personal wealth to build London's famous Surrey Chapel, where Vernon would later serve as co-pastor (along with Rev. Newman Hall).

Second, he left Surrey Chapel to become administrator of Charles Spurgeon's orphanage. Spurgeon's early biographer, W. Y. Fullerton, wrote, "The coming as headmaster of the orphanage of the Rev. Vernon J. Charlesworth, who up to then had been assistant to Newman Hall at Surrey Chapel, was an event of first importance. His influence on the boys, his advocacy of the orphanage, and his guidance of affairs were a great asset for many years, until in 1914 he finished his course."

Third, he wrote "A Shelter in the Time of Storm," based, it is said, on his study of Psalm 32:7: "You are my hiding place; You shall preserve me from trouble; You shall surround me with songs of deliverance."

Someone apparently set it to music, and it became popular along the coast of England. Ira Sankey, in his autobiography, wrote, "I found this hymn in a small paper published in London called *The Postman*. It was said to be a favorite song of the fishermen on the north coast of England, and they were often heard singing it as they approached their harbors in the time of storm. As the hymn was set to a weird minor tune, I decided to compose one that would be more practical, one that could be more easily sung by the people."

The Lily of the Valley

Charles W. Fry

William S. Mays

1. I have found a friend in Je - sus, He's ev - 'ry-thing to me, He's the
2. He all my grief has tak - en and all my sor - rows borne, In temp-
3. He will nev - er, nev - er leave me nor yet for-sake me here, While I

fair - est of ten thou-sand to my soul; The Lil - y of the Val - ley, in
ta - tion He's my strong and might - y tow'r; I have all for Him for-sak - en and
live by faith and do His bless - ed will; A wall of fire a - bout me, I've

Lil - y of the Val - ley, the
Fine

Him a - lone I see All I need to cleanse and make me ful - ly whole.
all my i - dols torn From my heart, and now He keeps me by His pow'r.
noth - ing now to fear, From His man - na He my hun - gry soul shall fill.

Bright and Morn-ing Star, He's the fair - est of ten thou - sand to my soul.

In sor - row He's my com - fort, in trou - ble He's my stay, He
Though all the world for - sake me and Sa - tan tempt me sore, Through
Then sweep - ing up to glo - ry I'll see His bless - ed face, Where

D.S. al Fine

tells me ev - 'ry care on Him to roll; He's the
Je - sus I shall safe - ly reach the goal; He's the
riv - ers of de - light shall ev - er roll; He's the

Hal - le - lu - jah!

The Lily of the Valley

1881

I am the rose of Sharon, And the lily of the valleys. Song of Solomon 2:1 (NKJV)

s Christianity flourished during England's Victorian Era, great concern emerged for the orphans, the poor, the homeless, and the great masses battered by the rising Industrial Revolution. One man determined to make a difference.

William Booth, born in Nottingham in 1829, became a Christian as a teenager and instantly began winning others to Christ. He moved to London to open a pawnbroker's shop, but soon left his business to travel around as a Methodist evangelist. By 1865, his ministry was primarily focused among the poor of London's East End. Some evenings, he stumbled home, haggard with fatigue, his clothes torn, and bloody bandages swathing his head where a stone had struck him.

In 1878 Booth began calling his ministry "The Salvation Army," and something about that name captured people's imagination. Men, women, and children saw their conversion as leaving their old lives behind to enlist in a new army—the Lord's army. The movement spread throughout England and around the world.

That very year, 1878, a group of Salvation Army workers sought to establish a ministry in Salisbury, about ninety miles west of London. They were treated badly, bricks and eggs flying in their direction whenever they tried to preach on the streets.

There lived in Salisbury a local builder and amateur musician named Charles Fry, an active layman in the Methodist Church. Seeing the abuse hurled at the Salvation Army workers, Charles offered, along with his three strapping sons—musicians all— to serve as bodyguards.

The next day the four Frys showed up bearing their weapons—two cornets, a trombone, and a small tuba. Between fighting off hooligans, the four drew crowds for the preachers with their music. Thus was born the first of the now-famous Salvation Army Brass Bands.

In 1881, Charles Fry wrote "The Lily of the Valley." It was published that year in the December 29th issue of the Salvation Army magazine, *The War Cry*.

The next August, Charles passed away. Another verse he had written was inscribed on his grave:

> *The former things are past, and ended is the strife,*
> *I'm safe home at last! I live an endless life!*

Jesus Saves

Priscilla J. Owens

William J. Kirkpatrick

1. We have heard the joy-ful sound: Je-sus saves! Je-sus saves!
2. Waft it on the roll-ing tide: Je-sus saves! Je-sus saves!
3. Sing a-bove the bat-tle strife: Je-sus saves! Je-sus saves!
4. Give the winds a might-y voice: Je-sus saves! Je-sus saves!

Spread the tid-ings all a-round: Je-sus saves! Je-sus saves!
Tell to sin-ners far and wide: Je-sus saves! Je-sus saves!
By His death and end-less life: Je-sus saves! Je-sus saves!
Let the na-tions now re-joice: Je-sus saves! Je-sus saves!

Bear the news to ev-'ry land, Climb the steeps and cross the waves;
Sing ye is-lands of the sea; Ech-o back, ye o-cean caves;
Sing it bright-ly through the gloom, When the heart for mer-cy craves;
Shout sal-va-tion full and free, High-est hills and deep-est caves;

On-ward! 'tis our Lord's com-mand; Je-sus saves! Je-sus saves!
Earth shall keep her ju-bi-lee: Je-sus saves! Je-sus saves!
Sing in tri-umph o'er the tomb: Je-sus saves! Je-sus saves!
This our song of vic-to-ry: Je-sus saves! Je-sus saves!

Jesus Saves

1882

Believe in the Lord Jesus, and you will be saved—you and your household. Acts 16:31 (NIV)

T his hymn came from the pen of a public school teacher named Priscilla Owens, a lifelong native of Baltimore, Maryland. For forty-nine years she taught school in Baltimore, devoting her spare time to her local Methodist Episcopal Church. In addition, Priscilla wrote prose and poetry, much of it being published in the *Methodist Protestant* and the *Christian Standard*. Priscilla wrote this hymn in 1882 for the anniversary of the Union Square Methodist Sunday School in Baltimore. Her original version said, "We have heard a joyful sound," but in later editions it was changed to *"the* joyful sound."

You might be familiar with another of Priscilla's poems, "Will Your Anchor Hold?"—a rousing hymn based on Hebrews 6:19: "This hope we have as an anchor of the soul, both sure and steadfast . . ." Most hymnals omit several of these verses, but they're too picturesque and perfect to be missed:

Will your anchor hold in the storms of life, / When the clouds unfold their wings of strife?
When the strong tides lift and the cables strain, / Will your anchor drift, or firm remain?

It is safely moored, 'twill the storm withstand, / For 'tis well secured by the Savior's hand;
And the cables, passed from His heart to mine, / Can defy that blast, thro' strength divine.

It will surely hold in the Straits of Fear— / When the breakers have told that the reef is near;
Though the tempest rave and the wild winds blow, / Not an angry wave shall our bark (boat) o'erflow.

It will firmly hold in the Floods of Death— / When the waters cold chill our latest breath,
On the rising tide it can never fail, / While our hopes abide within the Veil.

When our eyes behold through the gath'ring night / The city of gold, our harbor bright,
We shall anchor fast by the heav'nly shore, / With the storms all past forevermore.

CHORUS:
We have an anchor that keeps the soul / Steadfast and sure while the billows roll,
Fastened to the Rock which cannot move, / Grounded firm and deep in the Savior's love.

I Know Whom I Have Believed

Daniel W. Whittle

James McGranahan

1. I know not why God's won-drous grace To me He hath made known;
2. I know not how this sav-ing faith To me He did im - part,
3. I know not how the Spir - it moves, Con-vinc-ing men of sin,
4. I know not what of good or ill May be re-served for me.
5. I know not when my Lord may come, At night or noon - day fair,

Nor why, un - wor - thy, Christ in love Re - deemed me for His own.
Nor how be - liev - ing in His Word Wrought peace with - in my heart.
Re - veal-ing Je - sus through the Word, Cre - at - ing faith in Him.
Of wea - ry ways or gold - en days, Be - fore His face I see.
Nor if I'll walk the vale with Him, Or meet Him in the air.

But "I know whom I have be - liev - ed, And am per - suad - ed that He is

a - ble To keep that which I've com - mit - ted, Un - to Him a - gainst that day."

I Know Whom
I Have Believed

__1883__

I know whom I have believed and am persuaded that He is able to keep what I have committed to Him until that Day. 2 Timothy 1:12 (NKJV)

The golden era of English hymnody gave us names like Watts, Wesley, Newton, and Cowper. The lighter, more emotional age of American gospel music gave us a new set of names: Sankey, Crosby, Bliss, and the author of this hymn—Major Daniel Webster Whittle.

Whittle entered the world in Chicopee Falls, Massachusetts, about ninety miles west of Boston, on November 22, 1840. He left home as a teenager and moved to Chicago, where he secured a job as cashier at the Wells Fargo Bank.

When the Civil War broke out, Whittle enlisted in the 72nd Illinois Infantry. He had fallen deeply in love at the time, and on the day prior to his departure, he married his sweetheart, Abbie Hanson. With trembling heart, Abbie watched her new groom leave with Company B, heading into the bloodiest conflict in American history. Imagine her alarm when news came that he had been badly wounded in the Battle of Vicksburg and taken prisoner by the Confederates. His injuries were serious. He had lost his right arm.

But the Lord was in it, for while in the hospital recovering from his wounds, the young POW grew bored. Looking around for something to read, Whittle grabbed a spare New Testament. As he read its words, his heart was moved and he felt a need to accept Christ as his Savior. He wasn't ready to do that, however, and he drifted into sleep.

Shortly, a hospital orderly awakened him, saying that another POW was dying and wanted someone to pray with him. Whittle replied that he was unable, that someone else should be called. The orderly said, "But I thought you were a Christian; I have seen you reading your Bible."

Whittle later wrote, "I dropped on my knees and held the boy's hand in mine. In a few broken words, I confessed my sins and asked Christ to forgive me. I believed right there that He did forgive me. I then prayed and pleaded God's promises. When I arose from my knees, he was dead. A look of peace had come over his troubled face, and I cannot but believe that God who used him to bring me to the Savior used me to lead him to trust Christ's precious blood and find pardon."

Daniel Whittle later wrote this hymn—"I Know Whom I Have Believed"—as an expression of his testimony of faith in Jesus Christ.

There Shall Be Showers of Blessing

Daniel W. Whittle

James McGranahan

1. There shall be show-ers of bless-ing: This is the prom-ise of love;
2. There shall be show-ers of bless-ing: Pre-cious re-viv-ing a - gain;
3. There shall be show-ers of bless-ing: Send them up-on us, O Lord;
4. There shall be show-ers of bless-ing: O, that to-day they might fall,

There shall be sea-sons re - fresh-ing, Sent from the Sav-ior a - bove.
O - ver the hills and the val - leys, Sound of a-bun-dance of rain.
Grant to us now a re-fresh-ing, Come, and now hon-or Thy Word.
Now as to God we're con - fess-ing, Now, as on Je-sus we call!

Show - ers of bless - ing, Show-ers of bless-ing we need:
Show - ers, show-ers of bless - ing,

Mer-cy drops 'round us are fall - ing, But for the show-ers we plead.

There Shall Be Showers of Blessing

1883

I will cause showers to come down in their season; there shall be showers of blessing. Ezekiel 34:26 (NKJV)

T here Shall Be Showers of Blessing" by Major Daniel Whittle is one of those songs which, if learned in childhood, is never forgotten. Based on Ezekiel 34:26, it uplifts us with the happy assurance of God's unceasing blessing on our lives, even during our worst days.

When Howard Rutledge's plane was shot down over Vietnam, he parachuted into a little village and was immediately attacked and imprisoned. For the next seven years he endured brutal treatment. His food was little more than a bowl of pig fat. He was frequently cold, alone, and often tortured. How did he keep his sanity?

In his book, *In the Presence of Mine Enemies*, Rutledge wrote, "I wanted to talk about God and Christ and the church. But in Heartbreak (his concentration camp), there was no pastor, no Sunday school teacher, no Bible, no hymnbook. . . . I had completely neglected the spiritual dimension of my life. It took prison to show me how empty life is without God, and so I had to go back in my memory to those Sunday school days in Tulsa, Oklahoma. If I couldn't have a Bible and hymnbook, I would try to rebuild them in my mind.

"I tried desperately to recall . . . gospel choruses from childhood, and hymns we sang in church. The first three dozen songs were relatively easy. Every day I'd try to recall another verse or a new song. One night there was a huge thunderstorm—it was the season of the monsoon rains—and a bolt of lightning knocked out the lights and plunged the entire prison into darkness. I had been going over hymn tunes in my mind and stopped to lie down and sleep when the rains began to fall. The darkened prison echoed with wave after wave of water. Suddenly, I was humming my thirty-seventh song, one I had entirely forgotten since childhood.

> *Showers of blessing, showers of blessing we need!*
> *Mercy drops round us are falling, but for the showers we plead.*

"The enemy knew that the best way to break a man's resistance was to crush his spirit in a lonely cell," Howard wrote. "In other words, some of our POWs after solitary confinement lay down in a fetal position and died. All this talk of Scripture and hymns may seem boring to some, but it was the way we conquered our enemy and overcame the power of death around us."*

---

*Howard and Phyllis Rutledge with Mel and Lyla White, *In the Presence of Mine Enemies* (Old Tappan, NJ: Fleming H. Revell Co., 1973), excerpts taken from chapter 5.

The Banner of the Cross

Daniel W. Whittle   James McGranahan

1. There's a roy - al ban - ner giv - en for dis - play To the sol - diers
2. Though the foe may rage and gath - er as the flood, Let the stan - dard
3. O - ver land and sea, wher - ev - er man may dwell, Make the glo - rious
4. When the glo - ry dawns, 'tis draw - ing ver - y near, It is has - tening

of the King; As an en - sign fair we lift it up to - day,
be dis - played; And be - neath its folds, as sol - diers of the Lord,
tid - ings known; Of the crim - son ban - ner now the sto - ry tell,
day by day; Then be - fore our King the foe shall dis - ap - pear,

While as ran - somed ones we sing.
For the truth be not dis - mayed! March - ing on, march - ing
While the Lord shall claim His own!   on, on
And the cross the world shall sway!

on,   For Christ count ev - ery - thing but loss!   And to
    on, on,   ev - ery - thing,   ev - ery - thing but loss!

crown Him King,   toil and sing   'Neath the ban - ner of the cross!
            we'll   Be - neath

The Banner of the Cross

1885

You have given a banner to those who fear You, that it may be displayed because of the truth. Selah. Psalm 60:4 (NKJV)

While recovering from wounds sustained in the Civil War, Daniel Whittle became a Christian; and after the War, he returned to his new bride in Chicago. He had lost his right arm, but had found eternal life. He also had a new title. He had reached the rank of Major in the Union Army, and henceforth he was known as "Major Whittle."

Back in Chicago, he became treasurer of the Elgin Watch Company. But his newfound faith in Christ burned in his heart, and he was drawn into the ministry of the Chicago-based evangelist, D. L. Moody.* Whittle served as superintendent of one of the largest mission Sunday schools in Chicago, and often preached to the children, using blackboard illustrations and chemical experiments to keep their attention.

In 1873, at Moody's urging, Whittle resigned his work to enter fulltime evangelism. He proved to be a powerful preacher, eventually becoming one of the greatest evangelists of his time.

In about 1877, Whittle also began writing gospel songs, usually publishing them under the penname "El Nathan." He's the author of such favorites as "Moment by Moment," "I Know Whom I Have Believed," and "Showers of Blessing."

The lowest point in the Major's life came in 1894. While preaching in Pennsylvania, Major Whittle received news that his son had been killed in an accident. Hurrying home, he comforted his family as best he could before, at length, returning to his Pennsylvania campaign. He assuaged his grief by writing a poem that begins: *Be still, my heart! Thy Savior knows full well / The burden on thee laid; / And to thy side He comes, with love to heal / The wound His love hath made.*

One of Whittle's last efforts was with the soldiers in the Spanish-American War. Remembering how he had come to Christ while in the army, he joined the men at their camp, eating with them, sleeping with them, traveling with them, and preaching to them. The effort overtaxed him, and afterward Whittle returned home to live with his daughter in Northfield, Massachusetts. He passed away on March 4, 1901, after years of faithful service under the banner of the Cross.

Marching on, marching on, for Christ count everything but loss!
And to crown Him King, we'll toil and sing, 'neath the banner of the cross!

---

*Whittle's daughter, May, later married Moody's son, Will.

195

I Will Sing the Wondrous Story

Francis H. Rowley

Peter P. Billhorn

1. I will sing the won-drous sto-ry Of the Christ Who died for me,
2. I was lost but Je-sus found me, Found the sheep that went a-stray,
3. I was bruised but Je-sus healed me, Faint was I from man-y a fall.
4. He will keep me till the riv-er Rolls its wat-ers at my feet.

How He left His home in glo-ry For the cross of Cal-va-ry.
Threw His lov-ing arms a-round me, Drew me back in-to His way.
Sight was gone and fears pos-sessed me, But He freed me from them all.
Then He'll bear me safe-ly o-ver, Where the loved ones I shall meet.

Yes, I'll sing the won-drous sto-ry Of the Christ Who died for

me, Sing it with the saints in glo-ry Gath-ered by the crys-tal sea.

I Will Sing the
Wondrous Story
1886

Aren't two sparrows sold for only a penny? But your Father knows when any one of them falls to the ground. Matthew 10:29 (CEV)

T he Lord of Creation is an animal lover. He made them, saved them during the flood, and often used them in the Bible. Remember Balaam's donkey? Peter's rooster? Jonah's whale? Elijah's ravens? The Lord expressed concern for the cattle of Nineveh (Jonah 4:11), and Jesus said that the heavenly Father notes the flight and fall of the smallest sparrow (Matthew 10:29). There's even a special verse in the Bible for pet owners—Proverbs 12:10: "A wise man cares for the needs of his animal" (NIV).

What does that have to do with singing this hymn?

Dr. Francis Rowley, dentist's son and star student, was born during the summer of 1854, in Hilton, New York. As a young man, he felt God's call into the ministry, and he was ordained in 1878. He pastored churches in Pennsylvania, Massachusetts, and Illinois.

Dr. Rowley later said, "We were having a revival at the First Baptist Church at North Adams, Massachusetts, in 1886, the third year of my pastorate there, which was one of the richest and most blessed experiences of my entire ministry. I was assisted by a young Swiss musician named Peter Bilhorn who suggested I write a hymn for which he would compose the music. The following night this hymn ["I Will Sing the Wondrous Story"] came to me without any particular effort on my part."

In 1910, Rowley left the pastorate and became president of the Massachusetts Society for the Prevention of Cruelty to Animals. He served in that position until the age of ninety-one, when he was made chairman of the board. Under his tenure, the first motorized horse ambulance was purchased and the Angell Memorial Animal Hospital opened in Boston. Rowley was also instrumental in drafting a resolution that led to the first national "Be Kind to Animals Week." In 1917, he helped establish a permanent animal shelter designed to care for retired police horses, and in 1918, he led in the formation of the Jack London Club to enlist young people in the protection of animals. In 1922, the first Christmas Dinner for Horses was conducted, and in 1929, the Springfield Animal Hospital was opened, later renamed the Rowley Memorial Animal Hospital.

The Rowley School of Humanities at Oglethorpe University in Atlanta is also named for this hymnist whose watchword was: "Sing of your Redeemer—and be kind to His creatures!"

Away in a Manger

Anonymous

James R. Murray

1. A - way in a man - ger, no crib for a bed,
2. The cat - tle are low - ing, the ba - by a - wakes,
3. Be near me, Lord Je - sus; I ask Thee to stay

The lit - tle Lord Je - sus laid down His sweet head.
But lit - tle Lord Je - sus, no cry - ing He makes.
Close by me for - ev - er, and love me, I pray.

The stars in the sky look down where He lay,
I love Thee, Lord Je - sus, look down from the sky,
Bless all the dear chil - dren in Thy ten - der care,

The lit - tle Lord Je - sus, a - sleep on the hay.
And stay by my cra - dle till morn - ing is nigh.
And take us to heav - en to live with Thee there.

Away in a Manger

<u>1887</u>

And she brought forth her firstborn Son, and wrapped Him in swaddling cloths, and laid Him in a manger, because there was no room for them in the inn. Luke 2:7 (NKJV)

This is commonly known as "Luther's Cradle Hymn." But did the great German Reformer, Martin Luther, really write the words? Did he sing them by the cradle of his little son, Hans? This is a great mystery in hymnology.

In 1887, "Away in a Manger" appeared in a little book of songs entitled *Dainty Songs for Little Lads and Lasses,* published in Cincinnati by the John Church Company. The songbook was compiled by James R. Murray. A notation beneath "Away in a Manger" said: *Luther's Cradle Hymn (Composed by Martin Luther for his children and still sung by German mothers to their little ones.)* Only stanzas one and two were given.

"Away in a Manger" quickly became America's favorite children's carol, the words being sung to forty-one different tunes! Everyone assumed the poem had been written by the great Reformer, Martin Luther.

Then in 1945, Richard Hill published a fascinating article entitled "Not So Far Away in a Manger" in which he announced he had discovered the first two stanzas of "Away in a Manger," in an 1885 songbook entitled *Little Children's Book,* published by German Lutherans in Pennsylvania. No authorship was given. Nor could Hill find any appearance of this carol in German church history or in Luther's works.

After extensive research, Hill concluded: "It seems essential to lay [aside] once for all the legend that Luther wrote a carol for his children, which no one else knew anything about, until it suddenly turned up in English dress 400 years later in Philadelphia. Luther can well afford to spare the honor." But he adds, "Although Luther himself had nothing to do with the carol, the colonies of German Lutherans in Pennsylvania almost certainly did."

So the mystery endures. Who wrote "Away in a Manger"? There were apparently two unknown writers: A German Lutheran in Pennsylvania who wrote the first two stanzas, with another unknown author adding a third verse which first appeared in an 1892 songbook published by Charles H. Gabriel.

Well, who cares? Certainly not the generations of children around the world who have come to love and know the little Jesus through this sweet carol, and who have gone to sleep praying:

*I love Thee, Lord Jesus; look down from the sky
And stay by my cradle till morning is nigh.*

Jesus, I Come

William T. Sleeper   George C. Stebbins

1. Out of my bond-age, sor-row, and night, Je-sus, I come; Je-sus I come.
2. Out of my shame-ful fail-ure and loss, Je-sus, I come; Je-sus, I come.
3. Out of un-rest and ar-ro-gant pride, Je-sus, I come; Je-sus, I come.
4. Out of the fear and dread of the tomb, Je-sus, I come; Je-sus I come.

In-to Thy free-dom, glad-ness, and light, Je-sus, I come to Thee.
In-to the glo-rious gain of Thy cross, Je-sus, I come to Thee.
In-to Thy bless-ed will to a-bide, Je-sus, I come to Thee.
In-to the joy and light of Thy home, Je-sus, I come to Thee.

Out of my sick-ness, in-to Thy health, Out of my want and in-to Thy wealth.
Out of earth's sor-rows in-to Thy balm, Out of life's storms and in-to Thy calm.
Out of my-self to dwell in Thy love, Out of de-spair to rap-tures a-bove,
Out of the depths of ru-in un-told, In-to the peace-ful, shel-ter-ing fold,

Out of my sin and in-to Thy-self, Je-sus, I come to Thee.
Out of dis-tress to ju-bi-lant psalm, Je-sus, I come to Thee.
Up-ward I rise on wings like a dove, Je-sus, I come to Thee.
Ev-er Thy glo-rious face to be-hold, Je-sus, I come to Thee.

Jesus, I Come

1887

I will exalt you, O LORD, for you lifted me out of the depths . . . Psalm 30:1 (NIV)

O ne of the best histories of the gospel song era is George Stebbins' autobiography, *Reminiscences and Gospel Hymn Stories*. Stebbins was born in the mid-1800s in New York and showed early musical prowess. At age twenty-three, he moved to Chicago where he worked in churches and became acquainted with some of the "greats" of gospel music, such as Sankey and Bliss. In the late 1870s, D. L. Moody got hold of him, sending him into a lifetime of music evangelism.

Stebbins' first impressions of Moody are fascinating. Major Daniel Whittle had invited him to Northfield, Massachusetts, to meet Moody. That Sunday, Moody preached at the village church, asking Stebbins to lead the singing. Stebbins, a bit nervous, sat at the little organ in front of the pulpit.

As he played the organ and led the congregation, he was discomposed by a terrible wheezing noise. He described it as ". . . a discordant sound I kept hearing during the singing, which I at first thought was caused by something wrong with the organ. I determined to ascertain if my suspicions were well founded, so when there was an interval between verses, I listened to see if there might be one of the notes of the organ sounding when it ought to be silent, and found the discords were not from that source."

"I was not long in doubt, however, for I soon heard the voice of Mr. Moody singing away as heartily as you please, with no more idea of tune or time than a child. I then learned for the first time that he was one of the unfortunates who have no sense of pitch or harmony."

Stebbins went on to work for years alongside Moody, in the process composing several of our favorite hymn tunes. Included among them are the invitation hymns: "Have Thine Own Way, Lord," "Jesus Is Tenderly Calling You Home," "What Will Ye Do with Jesus?" and this one, "Jesus, I Come."

Stebbins' friend, William Sleeper, a New England home missionary and pastor, wrote the words to "Jesus, I Come." The two had previously collaborated on the hymn, "Ye Must Be Born Again." Sleeper developed the words to "Jesus, I Come" and sent them to Stebbins who put them to music. It first appeared in 1887 in *Gospel Hymns, No. 5.* with this Bible verse as a subtitle: "Deliver me, O my God" (Psalm 71:4).

Lead On, O King Eternal

Ernest W. Shurtleff

Henry T. Smart

1. Lead on, O King e - ter - nal, The day of march has come;
2. Lead on, O King e - ter - nal, Till sin's fierce war shall cease,
3. Lead on, O King e - ter - nal, We fol - low not with fears,

Hence - forth in fields of con - quest Thy tents shall be our home.
And ho - li - ness shall whis - per The sweet A - men of peace.
For glad - ness breaks like morn - ing Wher - e'er Thy face ap - pears.

Thro' days of prep - a - ra - tion Thy grace has made us strong, And
For not with swords loud clash - ing, Nor roll of stir - ring drums, With
Thy cross is lift - ed o'er us, We jour - ney in its light; The

now, O King e - ter - nal, We lift our bat - tle song.
deeds of love and mer - cy The heav'n - ly king - dom comes.
crown a - waits the con - quest: Lead on, O God of might.

Lead On, O King Eternal

1887

Now to the King eternal, immortal, invisible, the only God, be honor and glory for ever and ever. Amen. 1 Timothy 1:17 (NIV)

T his regal prayer has been sung at graduations around the world every year since 1887, when Ernest W. Shurtleff wrote it for his own graduation. A native of Boston and a graduate at Harvard, Ernest, twenty-six, was a student at Andover Theological Seminary when he envisioned his fellow seminarians marching for their diplomas singing a great prayer for God's guidance on the rest of life. Selecting a tune called LANCASHIRE, Ernest wrote words as regal as the music, and thus a great tradition was born.

Ernest went on to be ordained a Congregational minister and to hold pastorates in Massachusetts, Minnesota, and California. In 1905, he organized a church in Frankfort, Germany. He and his wife also worked tirelessly with European students. When World War I broke out, Ernest labored to exhaustion in relief ministries, feeding the poor and displaced. He died in Paris in 1917, during the war. His life was the embodiment of his hymn; yet nothing he did was as enduring to history as that hymn, written at age twenty-six.

Likewise, nothing that composer Henry Smart did was more enduring than this tune, LANCASHIRE, penned at age twenty-two. Henry had grown up surrounded by music, for his father was a piano and organ builder. As a young man, Henry enrolled in the university to study law; but, unable to get music out of his heart, he switched professions and became a self-taught organist and composer. He wrote LANCASHIRE for a music festival at Blackburn, England, on October 4, 1835, to commemorate the three hundredth anniversary of the English Reformation. Unfortunately, Henry worked so hard at his music that he damaged his eyesight beyond repair.

For nearly fifty years Henry Smart served as organist at various churches in England. He also edited the hymnbook of the United Presbyterian Church of Scotland, and he was often consulted for new organ installations throughout Great Britain. He became one of nineteenth-century England's favorite musicians.

In his final years, Henry was totally blind, yet he continued composing by dictating his pieces to his daughter, and he continued playing the organ by memory until his death at age sixty-three in 1879. Henry Smart wrote over two hundred fifty secular works and several religious compositions, including the beautiful REGENT SQUARE, the melody of "Angels from the Realms of Glory."

Look and Live

William A. Ogden   William A. Ogden

1. I've a mes-sage from the Lord, Hal-le - lu - jah! The mes-sage un - to you I'll give.
2. I've a mes-sage full of love, Hal-le - lu - jah! A mes-sage, O my friend, for you.
3. Life is of - fered un - to you, Hal-le - lu - jah! E - ter-nal life your soul shall have
4. I will tell you how I came, Hal-le - lu - jah! To Je-sus when He made me whole:

'Tis re-cord-ed in His Word, Hal-le - lu - jah! It is on-ly that you "look and live."
'Tis a mes-sage from a-bove, Hal-le - lu - jah! Je-sus said it, and I know 'tis true.
If you'll on - ly look to Him, Hal-le - lu - jah! Look to Je-sus, who a - lone can save.
'Twas be - liev-ing on His name, Hal-le - lu - jah! I trust-ed and He saved my soul.

"Look and live," my broth-er, live. Look to Je - sus now and live.
"Look and live," "look and live,"

'Tis re - cord-ed in His Word, Hal-le - lu - jah! It is on-ly that you "look and live."

Look and Live

1888

Then the L<small>ORD</small> said to Moses, "Make a fiery serpent, and set it on a pole; and it shall be that everyone who is bitten, when he looks at it, shall live. Numbers 21:8 (N<small>KJV</small>)

This hymn was written by William Ogden, who also wrote the words to "Where He Leads, I'll Follow" and the music to the popular gospel song "Bring Them In."

William was born in Ohio in 1841. He had an inborn love for music, but the Civil War interrupted his studies, and he spent four years serving in the 30th Indiana Volunteer Infantry. After the war, he continued his pursuit of music, studying under Lowell Mason. William went on to become a personable and popular schoolteacher and a featured leader at music conventions. In 1887, he became supervisor for music in the Toledo public schools, a position he retained until his death ten years later.

This hymn was based on the remarkable incident recorded in Numbers 21, when Moses crafted a bronze serpent and raised it among the Israelites. Because of their sin, an infestation of poisonous snakes had left many of them dying, but all who looked at the serpent on the pole lived. Jesus later used the incident as an illustration of His work on the Cross. This strange analogy paved the way for the most famous verse in the Bible—John 3:16:

And as Moses lifted up the serpent in the wilderness, even so must the Son of Man be lifted up, that whoever believes in Him should not perish but have eternal life. For God so loved the world that He gave His only begotten Son, that whoever believes in Him should not perish but have everlasting life" (John 3:14–16).

William Ogden wrote a number of other hymns, many of which have been forgotten with the passing of time. As I surveyed his songs, one stood out in particular, for I remember singing it often as I grew up attending church in the Tennessee mountains. It's unusual in that in the chorus, the melody is in the bass line.

Seeking the lost, yes, kindly entreating | Wanderers on the mountain astray;
"Come unto Me," His message repeating, | Words of the Master speaking today.

C<small>HORUS</small>:
Going afar (going afar) | Upon the mountain (upon the mountain)
Bringing the wanderer back again (back again), | Into the fold (into the fold)
Of my Redeemer (of my Redeemer) | Jesus the Lamb for sinners slain, for sinners slain.

The Haven of Rest

Henry L. Gilmour

George D. Moore

1. My soul, in sad ex - ile, was out on life's sea. So bur-dened with
2. I yield-ed my-self to His ten - der em - brace, And, faith tak - ing
3. The song of my soul, since the Lord made me whole, Has been the old

sin and dis - tressed, 'Til I heard a sweet voice say-ing, "Make Me your choice,"
hold of the Word, My fet - ters fell off, and I an - chored my soul,
sto - ry so blest Of Je - sus, who'll save who-so - ev - er will have

And I en-tered the ha - ven of rest. I've an-chored my soul in the
The ha - ven of rest is my Lord.
A home in the ha - ven of rest.

Ha-ven of Rest, I'll sail the wide seas no more; The tem - pest may

sweep o'er the wild, storm - y deep, In Je - sus I'm safe ev - er - more.

The Haven of Rest

1890

He calms the storm, so that its waves are still. Then they are glad because they are quiet; so He guides them to their desired haven. Psalm 107:29–30 (NKJV)

Henry Gilmour was always working on people's mouths. Eight months out of the year, he earned his keep as a New Jersey dentist. The remaining months, he filled his audiences' mouths with song. He was a singing evangelist, a camp meeting music director, a Methodist hymnist, and the author of such classics as "The Haven of Rest" and "He Brought Me Out of the Miry Clay" (music and chorus).

Gilmour had emigrated from Ireland as a teen. Arriving in America, he found work as a painter, but was soon caught in the grip of the Civil War where he wore the Union uniform. Captured by Confederate forces, he was marched to Libbey Prison, alongside the cold James River in Richmond, Virginia.

One of Gilmour's fellow prisoners later wrote that they were "taken to Richmond and placed in the old tobacco warehouse commonly known as Libbey Prison. There we received a small loaf of baker's bread and a small piece of meat for 24 hours ration. We had city water for coffee. . . ."

Another POW spoke of suffering paralysis from the bitter cold of the unheated warehouse. Others used words like "dreaded" and "miserable" and "the horrors of Libbey" to describe its discomforts, and some inmates spoke of being stripped naked and deprived of the necessities of life. The young Irishman must have wondered what had possessed him to sail to America.

Many POWs died at Libbey, but Henry survived; and after the war, he became a dentist and moved to Wenonah, New Jersey, where he became active in the Methodist Holiness movement. For over forty years, he worked in Methodist camp meetings, especially in Mountain Lake Park, Maryland, and Ridgeview Park, Pennsylvania. As his popularity grew, he had the opportunity of publishing gospel songbooks and encouraging new hymnists. It was largely through his efforts that Lelia Morris began writing hymns.*

We aren't sure what inspired Gilmour's greatest song, "The Haven of Rest." Was it his POW experiences, or perhaps the memories of his long voyage to America? Whatever it was, he's one dentist who filled the mouths of future generations with one of our greatest gospel songs.

I've anchored my soul in the "Haven of Rest," / I'll sail the wide seas no more; / The tempest may sweep over wild, stormy, deep, / In Jesus I'm safe evermore.

---

*See the stories for "Nearer, Still Nearer" and "Jesus Is Coming to Earth Again."

He Hideth My Soul

Fanny J. Crosby

William J. Kirkpatrick

1. A won - der - ful Sav - ior is Je - sus my Lord, A
2. When clothed in His bright - ness trans - port - ed I rise To

won - der - ful Sav - ior to me; He hid - eth my soul in the
meet Him in clouds of the sky, His per - fect sal - va - tion, His

cleft of the rock, Where riv - ers of pleas - ure I see.
won - der - ful love, I'll shout with the mil - lions on high.

He hid - eth my soul in the cleft of the rock That shad - ows a

dry, thirst - y land. He hid - eth my life in the depths of His love,

And cov - ers me there with His hand, And cov - ers me there with His hand.

He Hideth My Soul

1890

So it shall be, while My glory passes by, that I will put you in the cleft of the rock, and will cover you with My hand while I pass by. Exodus 33:22 (NKJV)

Bouncing back—that's a quality to be cultivated, because life is full of struggles. How do we become resilient? Unsinkable? Joyful amid the blows and burdens of life? This hymn tells us:

A wonderful Savior is Jesus my Lord, He taketh my burden away;
He holdeth me up, and I shall not be moved, He giveth me strength as my day.

This hymn by Fanny Crosby explains the author's life, for Fanny faced three incredible hardships during her ninety-five years. The first was her blindness, caused by a careless doctor when she was only six weeks of age.

The second was a less-than-ideal marriage. Fanny was teaching at the New York Institution for the Blind when a young musician named Alexander Van Alstyne joined the faculty. Fanny later recalled, "After hearing several of my poems he became deeply interested in my work; and I after listening to his sweet strains of music became interested in him. Thus we soon grew to be very much concerned for each other . . . Love met love, and all the world was changed. We were no longer blind, for the light of love showed us where the lilies bloomed." The two were married on March 5, 1858. No one knows what happened, but years later the two drifted apart and in the end occupied separate addresses.

Fanny's deepest blow was the loss of her child. To this day, no one knows if it was a boy or a girl. Fanny seldom spoke of the infant. The child's death seems to have devastated her, and she privately bore the sadness all her life.

Yet all who knew Fanny Crosby spoke of her energy, her zest for life, her joy. One biographer said, "Even in extreme old age, she would tire out people twenty or thirty years her junior."

She said, "How long am I going to travel and lecture? Always! There is nothing that could induce me to abandon my work. It means nothing to be eighty-four years of age, because I am still young! What is the use of growing old? People grow old because they are not cheerful, and cheerfulness is one of the greatest accomplishments in the world!"

Fanny Crosby lived out her song every day of her life: "He hideth my soul in the depths of His love, and covers me there with His hand."

Make Me a Captive, Lord

George Matheson

George J. Elvey

1. Make me a cap-tive, Lord, And then I shall be free; Force me to ren-der up my sword, And I shall con-queror be. I sink in life's a-larms When by my-self I stand; Im-pris-on me with-in Thine arms, And strong shall be my hand.

2. My heart is weak and poor Un-til its Mas-ter find; It has no spring of ac-tion sure, It var-ies with the wind. It can-not free-ly move Till Thou hast wrought its chain; En-slave it with Thy match-less love, And death-less it shall reign.

3. My power is faint and low Till I have learned to serve; It wants the need-ed fire to glow, It wants the breeze to nerve; It can-not drive the world, Un-til it-self be driv'n; Its flag can on-ly be un-furled When Thou shalt breathe from heav'n.

4. My will is not my own Till Thou hast made it Thine; If it would reach a mon-arch's throne, It must its crown re-sign; It on-ly stands un-bent, A-mid the clash-ing strife, When on Thy bos-om it has leant And found in Thee its life.

Make Me a Captive, Lord

__1890__

The Spirit of the LORD is upon Me, because He has anointed Me to preach the gospel to the poor; . . . to proclaim liberty to the captives. Luke 4:18 (NKJV)

*I*t was a dark and stormy night—August 16, 1809. Crowds returning from the market crammed onto a ferryboat in Scotland. As the overloaded ferry reached the middle of the Firth, it began tipping in the waves and filling with water. Despite desperate attempts to return to shore, the boat sank, drowning almost all on board—forty-three men and fifty-six women. Among them was George Matheson, who left behind a pregnant wife and two children.

One of the surviving sons was named for his father. It's said that as a young man, this George Matheson considered going into the ministry but was persuaded by a friend to form a business partnership. In time, George became a wealthy merchant and the father of eight children.

One of these children was named George—and he is the author of our hymn. George Matheson III later explained that he inherited a mind for business from his father, and from his mother the gift of song. From both parents, he received a rich and traditional theology and a love for the Lord.

George attended Glasgow University, graduating with a bachelor's degree in 1891, and with a master's in 1892. But he struggled with poor vision. Even in childhood, he used powerful glasses and sat near a window. During his university days, he was declared blind, and only the help of his loyal sister enabled him to finish school and enter the ministry.

Like Fanny Crosby, George was never totally blind; he could vaguely distinguish light and darkness. But also like Fanny Crosby, he was known for his phenomenal memory, optimism, buoyant spirit, and inspiring personality. In fact, many of the people flocking to hear him preach at St. Bernard's in Edinburgh didn't realize he was blind.

Matheson was a prolific student and author. With the help of secretaries and, later, by using a Braille typewriter, he wrote many articles and books. As a preacher, he was among the most popular in Britain. Queen Victoria came to hear him. As a hymnist, he is remembered for "O Love That Wilt Not Let Me Go," and this hymn— "Make Me a Captive, Lord," which speaks of the paradox of Christianity—that surrender to Christ brings victory in life.

Matheson suffered a stroke and died suddenly on August 28, 1906, in Edinburgh, but his songs, sermons, and influence will continue until Christ returns.

Send the Light

Charles H. Gabriel

Charles H. Gabriel

1. There's a call comes ring - ing o'er the rest - less wave, "Send the light!
2. We have heard the Mac - e - do - nian call to - day, "Send the light!
3. Let us pray that grace may ev - ery - where a - bound, "Send the light!
4. Let us not grow wea - ry in the work of love, "Send the light!

Send the light!" There are souls to res - cue, There are souls to save,
Send the light!" And a gold - en off - 'ring at the cross we lay,
Send the light!" And a Christ - like spir - it ev - 'ry - where be found,
Send the light!" Let us gath - er jew - els for a crown a - bove,

Send the light! Send the light! Send the light, The bless - ed gos - pel light;

Let it shine from shore to shore! Send the shine for - ev - er - more!

Send the Light

1890

Send forth your light and your truth, let them guide me . . . Psalm 43:3 (NIV)

C harles Gabriel grew up in Iowa, living on a farm until age seventeen. Even in childhood, he was drawn toward music; and when his Methodist family purchased a small reed organ, he taught himself to play it. With his parents' encouragement, he was leading singing schools by age sixteen.

He married, but because of his frantic schedule of traveling and teaching music, his marriage failed. In 1887, he moved to California to get a new start, and soon he remarried. In 1890, he began working at Grace Methodist Episcopal Church in San Francisco. When the Sunday school superintendent came to him asking for a missionary hymn for Easter Sunday to highlight a Golden Offering, Gabriel wrote "Send the Light." It was sung with enthusiasm that day, March 6, 1890, and a visiting missionary representative who liked the words carried the hymn back to the East.

The immediate popularity of "Send the Light" propelled Gabriel to prominence in the hymn-writing community. Once before he tried supporting himself by writing hymns, but failed. Now, he tried again. Within two years, he was in Chicago, devoting his life full time to writing and publishing hymns.

In all, Gabriel edited thirty-five gospel songbooks, eight Sunday school songbooks, seven books for men's chorus, six for women, ten for children, nineteen collections of anthems, and twenty-three cantatas. He's best known, however, for his amazing output of seven thousand hymns, including these timeless favorites:

"His Eye Is on the Sparrow" (music)
"I Stand Amazed in the Presence" (words and music)
"Brighten the Corner Where You Are" (music)
"What a Savior" (words and music)
"Just When I Need Him" (music)
"He Is So Precious to Me" (words and music)
"That Will Be Glory for Me" (words and music)
"More Like the Master" (words and music)
"Higher Ground" (music)
"In Lovingkindness Jesus Came" (words and music)
"Awakening Chorus" (music)
"Will the Circle Be Unbroken?" (music)
"Since Jesus Came into My Heart" (music)
"The Way of the Cross" (music)

But then, what else would you expect from a man named Gabriel?

213

Saved by Grace

Fanny J. Crosby

George C. Stebbins

1. Some day the sil-ver cord will break, And I no more as now shall sing;
2. Some day my earth-ly house will fall, I can-not tell how soon 'twill be,
3. Some day when fades the gold-en sun Be-neath the ros-y-tint-ed west,
4. Some day till then I'll watch and wait, My lamp all trimmed and burn-ing bright,

But O the joy when I shall wake With-in the pal-ace of the King!
But this I know: my All in All Has now a place in heav'n for me.
My bless-ed Lord will say, "Well done!" And I shall en-ter in-to rest.
That when my Sav-ior ope's the gate, My soul to Him may take its flight.

And I shall see Him face to face, And tell the sto-ry— Saved by grace;

And I shall see Him face to face, And tell the sto-ry— Saved by grace;

Saved by Grace

1891

We believe it is through the grace of our Lord Jesus that we are saved . . . Acts 15:11 (NIV)

F anny Crosby continued writing hymns until the day she died, though she did slow down a bit in her eighties, reducing her quota from two hundred hymns a year to about fifty. One of her last popular songs was "Saved by Grace." She later said it was inspired by a sermon preached by Dr. Howard Crosby, a distant relative and dear friend. In his message, Dr. Crosby said that no Christian "should fear death, for if each of us was faithful to the grace given us by Christ, the same grace that teaches us how to live would also teach us how to die."

His remarks deeply moved Fanny, and she wrote "Saved by Grace" as a personal hymn for herself, not to be published.

Some time later at a Bible Conference, D. L. Moody asked Fanny to share a word of testimony. Caught off guard, Fanny used this poem, saying, "There is one hymn I have written which has never been published. I call it my soul's poem. Sometimes when I am troubled, I repeat it to myself, for it brings comfort to my heart."

Soon thereafter it was published, and became one of her "greats."

Several years later, Fanny, who reached the age of ninety-five, realized she was dying—a prospect that brought her great joy. During the last weeks of her life, her face manifested an unusual glow. Numerous people observed it, and it became a curious subject of interest. On February 11, 1915, Fanny said she didn't feel well and would stay in bed that day. "Tomorrow I shall be well," she declared. That evening, she dictated a final hymn: "In the morn of Zion's glory, / When the clouds have rolled away, / And my hope has dropped its anchor / In the vale of perfect day, / When with all the pure and holy / I shall strike my harp anew, / With a power no arm can sever, / Love will hold me fast and true."

At 3:30 in the morning, Fanny's niece, Florence Booth, heard her walking down the hall, presumably going to the bathroom. Rising to see about her, Florence reached her just as she fainted. Florence carried the tiny figure to bed, and Fanny quickly slipped into the presence of the King, fulfilling her own soul's poem:

And I shall see Him face to face
And tell the story—Saved by Grace.

Faith Is the Victory

John H. Yates

Ira D. Sankey

1. En - camped a - long the hills of light, Ye Chris - tian sol - diers, rise, And
2. His ban - ner o - ver us is love, Our sword the Word of God. We
3. To him that o - ver - comes the foe, White rai - ment shall be giv'n. Be -

press the bat - tle ere the night Shall veil the glow - ing skies. A - gainst the foe in
tread the road the saints a - bove With shouts of tri - umph trod. By faith they like a
fore the an - gels he shall know His name con - fessed in heav'n. Then on - ward from the

vales be - low, Let all our strength be hurled; Faith is the vic - to - ry, we know,
whirl-wind's breath, Swept on o'er ev - 'ry field; The faith by which they con-quer'd death
hill of light, Our hearts with love a - flame; We'll van-quish all the hosts of night,

That ov - er - comes the world.
Is still our shin - ing shield. Faith is the vic - to - ry! Faith is the
In Je - sus' con - qu'ring name.

vic - to - ry! O, glo - ri - ous vic - to - ry, That ov - er - comes the world.

Faith Is the Victory

1891

For whatever is born of God overcomes the world. And this is the victory that has overcome the world—our faith. 1 John 5:4 (NKJV)

T his hymn was written by a shoe salesman who eventually became a Freewill Baptist pastor in upstate New York.

John Henry Yates was born in Batavia, on November 21, 1837, the son of John and Elizabeth Yates who had emigrated from England. After attending Batavia Union School, John became a shoe seller, and in 1871, he became the local department manager for a hardware firm called E. L. & G. D. Kenyon Store. He worked there fifteen years before becoming editor of the local paper, a job he held for the next ten years.

In 1858, he was licensed to preach in the Methodist church, and he was later ordained. He served for seven years as pastor of the West Bethany Freewill Baptist Church.

Along the way, John Henry wrote poems, and one of them, "The Model Church," came to the attention of Ira Sankey, who, after seeing it in a newspaper wrote music for it and sang it for the first time in Atlanta, Georgia. In his memoirs, Sankey wrote, "Once, in Buffalo, I had the pleasure of meeting Mr. Yates of Batavia, New York; and I urged him to devote more of his time to writing gospel hymns. He has since written several popular songs."

In 1891, Yates sent this "Faith Is the Victory" to Sankey, who wrote the music for it. It first appeared that year in *The Christian Endeavor Handbook* and in *Gospel Hymns No. 6.*

In 1897, John published his one and only book, *Poems and Ballads.* He died three years later, in Batavia, on September 5, 1900.

His other hymns are almost forgotten now, but were quite popular in their day, including one that defended the Bible against critical attacks that were coming in waves from liberal scholars in the late nineteenth century. As with "Faith Is the Victory," it is marked by Yates' gift of imagery:

> *The old Book stands! O yes, it stands!*
> *Firm as a rock 'mid shifting sands!*
> *Billows may run high, tempests sweep the sky;*
> *Firmly the old Book stands.*

Lord, I'm Coming Home

William J. Kirkpatrick

William J. Kirkpatrick

1. I've wan-dered far a - way from God, Now I'm com-ing home;
2. I've wast-ed man - y pre - cious years, Now I'm com-ing home;
3. I'm tired of sin and stray - ing, Lord, Now I'm com-ing home;
4. My soul is sick, my heart is sore, Now I'm com-ing home;

The paths of sin too long I've trod, Lord, I'm com-ing home.
I now re - pent with bit - ter tears, Lord, I'm com-ing home.
I'll trust Thy love, be - lieve Thy Word, Lord, I'm com-ing home.
My strength re - new, my hope re - store, Lord, I'm com-ing home.

Com - ing home, com-ing home, Nev - er - more to roam,

O - pen wide Thine arms of love, Lord, I'm com - ing home.

Lord, I'm Coming Home
1892

I said, "LORD, be merciful to me; Heal my soul, for I have sinned against You."
Psalm 41:4 (NKJV)

The Methodist camp meetings of the 1800s changed the shape of Christianity in America, and their influence lingers to this day—especially in our hymnology. Large crowds often numbering in the thousands gathered for days, camping with their families around huge tents, tabernacles, or open-air arenas. The women cooked the meals, the children played together, the teenagers courted, and the men talked politics. Several times a day, they'd gather for fervent singing, emotional testifying, and firebrand preaching.

By the late 1800s, many of these camp meeting sites had become regular conference centers and retreat grounds, providing a place of ministry to the greatest preachers, soloists, and song leaders of the day.

William J. Kirkpatrick, minister of music at Grace Methodist Episcopal Church in Philadelphia, was a popular figure on the summer revival circuit.* On one occasion in the early 1890s, as Kirkpatrick led singing at a camp meeting outside Rawlinsville, Pennsylvania, he began to question the sincerity and salvation of the soloist with whom he was working. The man left the meeting as soon as he had sung, and he withdrew from fellowship times. His name has been lost to us, but we know that Kirkpatrick began earnestly praying for him.

"I became very burdened for him and the Lord led me to use an unusual plan," Kirkpatrick wrote. "[The Lord] told me to write a special song of invitation with just the singer in mind and then I was to have him sing it. This I did, and the very evening he sang it, God so spoke to his heart that he did not go out after singing but stayed to hear the message. Praise God!—he was the first to the altar letting Christ come into his heart. My new song had been the Lord's means of answering my prayer. It was 'Lord, I'm Coming Home.'"

Kirkpatrick's song first appeared in a book of camp meeting hymns in 1892, and has since been a popular hymn of invitation for over one hundred years. Untold numbers have come to Christ through its singing, but the initial convert was the man who first sang this hymn on a summer's night in a camp meeting near Rawlinsville, Pennsylvania.

> *Coming home, coming home,*
> *Nevermore to roam;*
> *Open now Thine arms of love—*
> *Lord, I'm coming home.*

---

*A summary of Kirkpatrick's interesting life is told under the story for "O to Be Like Thee."

Moment by Moment

Daniel W. Whittle

May W. Moody

1. Dy-ing with Je - sus, by death reck-oned mine, Liv-ing with Je - sus a
2. Nev-er a tri - al that He is not there, Nev-er a bur - den that
3. Nev-er a heart-ache, and nev - er a groan, Nev-er a tear-drop and
4. Nev-er a weak-ness that He doth not feel, Nev-er a sick-ness that

new life di - vine, Look-ing to Je - sus 'til glo - ry doth shine, Mo-ment by
He doth not bear, Nev - er a sor-row that He doth not share, Mo-ment by
nev - er a moan; Nev - er a dan-ger but there on the throne, Mo-ment by
He can-not heal; Mo - ment by mo-ment, in woe or in weal, Je - sus, my

mo-ment, O Lord, I am Thine.
mo-ment, I'm un - der His care.
mo-ment, He thinks of His own. Mo-ment by mo-ment I'm kept in His love,
Sav-ior, a - bides with me still.

Mo-ment by mo-ment I've life from a - bove; Look-ing to Je - sus 'til

glo-ry doth shine, Mo - ment by mo-ment, O Lord, I am Thine.

Moment by Moment

<u>1893</u>

Praise be to the Lord, to God our Savior, who daily bears our burdens. Psalm 68:19 (NIV)

Much of our information about the hymns of the gospel song era comes from *My Life and the Story of the Gospel Hymns,* by Ira Sankey, the "singing evangelist," who accompanied D. L. Moody around the world.* Here's what he said about this enduring hymn:

"While I was attending the World's Fair in Chicago, Henry Varley, a lay preacher from London, said to Major Daniel Whittle: 'I do not like the hymn, "I Need Thee Every Hour," very well, because I need Him every moment of the day.' Soon after Major Whittle wrote this sweet hymn, having the chorus:

> *Moment by moment I'm kept in His love;*
> *Moment by moment I've life from above;*
> *Looking to Jesus till glory doth shine;*
> *Moment by moment, O Lord, I am Thine.*

"Mr. Whittle brought the hymn to me in manuscript a little later, saying that he would give me the copyright of both the words and music if I would print for him five hundred copies on fine paper, for distribution among his friends. His daughter, May Whittle, who later became the wife of Will R. Moody, composed the music. I did as Mr. Whittle wished; and I sent the hymn to England, where it was copyrighted on the same day as in Washington.

"In England, the hymn became very popular. Falling into the hands of the well-known Rev. Andrew Murray, of South Africa, then visiting London, he adopted it as his favorite hymn. A year later Mr. Murray visited Northfield, and while holding a meeting for men in the church he remarked, 'If Mr. Sankey only knew a hymn which I found in London, and would sing it; he would find that it embraces my entire creed.'

"I was very anxious to know what hymn it was, and when he had recited it, I said to him, 'Doctor, that hymn was written within five hundred yards of where we are standing.'"

---

*Sankey wrote the original version of his combined autobiography and hymn history in Battle Creek, Michigan, where he was recovering from illness. Unfortunately, a fire broke out and destroyed his one and only manuscript, along with all his collected notes. Greatly depressed, Sankey, who was blind by then, dictated *My Life and the Story of Gospel Hymns* from memory, relying on scraps of information, as best he could. It is still an amazing book.

The Lord Will Provide

Mrs. A.W. Cook

Phillip Phillips

1. In some way or oth-er the Lord will pro-vide; It
2. At some time or oth-er the Lord will pro-vide; It
3. De-spond then no long-er; the Lord will pro-vide; And
4. March on then right bold-ly; the sea shall di-vide, The

may not be my way, It may not be thy way; And yet, in His
may not be my time, It may not be thy time; And yet, in His
this be the to-ken, No word He hath spo-ken Was ev-er yet
path-way made glor-ious, With shout-ings vic-tor-ious We'll join in the

own way, "The Lord will pro-vide."
own time, "The Lord will pro-vide."
bro-ken: "The Lord will pro-vide."
cho-rus, "The Lord will pro-vide."

Then, we'll trust in the Lord, And

He will pro-vide; Yes, we'll trust in the Lord, And He will pro-vide.

The Lord Will Provide

1894

So Abraham called that place The LORD Will Provide. And to this day it is said,
"On the mountain of the LORD it will be provided. Genesis 22:14 (NIV)

T his hymn is seldom sung today, and we know little of its author, Mrs. A. W. Cook, but I wanted to include it because it played a part in the conversion of the great evangelist, Rodney "Gypsy" Smith.

Rodney was born in a gypsy tent in England. His father, Cornelius, earned money playing his fiddle at local taverns, where he always got drunk. But one day, he was converted.

"In the agony of his soul," Rodney later wrote, "he fell on the floor unconscious, and lay there wallowing and foaming for half an hour. I was in great distress, and thought my father was dead . . . but presently he came to himself, stood up and, leaping joyfully, exclaimed, 'I am converted!'"

Cornelius, a truly changed man, resolved never to play in taverns again. In his autobiography, Rodney describes the incident that helped lead to his own conversion:

All this time my father was very poor, and one winter at Cambridge we were in the hardest straits. . . . I wanted to know what we were going to have for Christmas, and I asked my father. "I do not know, my dear," he said quietly. . . . Then the devil came and tempted him. His fiddle was hanging on the wall, and he looked at it desperately and thought to himself, "If I just . . . go to a public house and play to the people there, my children, too, will have a good Christmas dinner." But the temptation was very soon overcome. My father fell on his knees and began to pray. . . . When he arose from his knees he said, "I don't know quite what we shall have for Christmas, but we will sing." He began to sing with a merry heart: "In some way or other / The Lord will provide: / It may not by my way, / It may not be thy way; / But yet in His own way / The Lord will provide." Just then, while we were singing, there was a knock at the door of the van.

"Who is there?" cried my father.

It was the old Cambridge town missionary, Mr. Sykes.

"It is I, Brother Smith. God is good, is He not? I have come to tell you how the Lord will provide. In a shop in this town there are three legs of mutton and groceries waiting for you and your brothers."

A wheelbarrow was needed to bring home the store.

They Were in an Upper Chamber

Charlie D. Tillman   Charlie D. Tillman

1. They were in an up-per cham-ber, They were all with one ac-cord,
2. Yes, this pow'r from heav'n de-scend-ed, With the sound of rush-ing wind;
3. Yes, this "old-time" pow'r was giv-en To our fa-thers who were true;

When the Ho-ly Ghost de-scend-ed, As was prom-ised by our Lord.
Tongues of fire came down up-on them, As the Lord said He would send.
This is prom-ised to be-liev-ers, And we all may have it too.

O Lord, send the pow'r just now, O Lord, send the pow'r just now,

O Lord, send the pow'r just now, And bap-tize ev-'ry one.

They Were in an Upper Chamber

<u>1895</u>

And when they were come in, they went up into the upper chamber, where they were abiding. Acts 1:13 (ASV)

Until the late 1800s, most American hymnody came from the North and Midwest, from composers in states like Pennsylvania and Illinois. As the South began reconstruction efforts, a few hymnists and music publishers began appearing south of the Mason-Dixon Line. Chief among them was Charles Tillman.

Charles was born in Tallassee, Alabama, in 1861, just as the Civil War was heating up. His father, James Lafayette Tillman, was a traveling evangelist, and young Charles often accompanied him on his campaigns.

Coming of age himself, Charles first worked as a house painter, and then signed up as a traveling salesman for a music company headquartered in Raleigh, North Carolina. He traveled throughout the South during Reconstruction Days, singing comic songs on a traveling wagon that advertised Wizard Oil. He was first tenor in a male quartet.

By 1887, he was ready to launch out on his own as a singing evangelist. In time, Charles established his own publishing company in Atlanta and published about twenty volumes of gospel songs, which became quite popular in the South.

In 1891, as he and his father were ministering together in a tent revival in Lexington, South Carolina, Charles heard a group of Black musicians singing a Negro spiritual called, "Old Time Religion." Writing down the words and music, Tillman published it for the first time. Its popularity paved the way for a number of Tillman's own songs.

Based on the second chapter of Acts, "They Were in an Upper Chamber" was Tillman's prayer for a Pentecost-like revival in the current day. Another highly popular Tillman song, especially in the South, was "Life's Railway to Heaven." The source of the words is unclear, but Tillman was responsible for the music:

> *Life is like a mountain railroad, with an engineer that's brave;*
> *We must make the run successful, from the cradle to the grave;*
> *Watch the curves, the fills, the tunnels; never falter, never quail;*
> *Keep your hand upon the throttle, and your eye upon the rail.*

By the time he died in Atlanta in 1943, Charles Davis Tillman had helped establish Southern gospel music, leaving behind such beloved songs as "My Mother's Bible," and the classic "When I Get to the End of the Way."

No, Not One!

Johnson Oatman, Jr.   George C. Hugg

1. There's not a friend like the low-ly Je-sus, No, not one! No, not one!
2. No friend like Him is so high and ho-ly, No, not one! No, not one!
3. There's not an hour that He is not near us, No, not one! No, not one!
4. Did ev-er saint find this Friend for-sake Him? No, not one! No, not one!
5. Was e'er a gift like the Sav-ior giv-en? No, not one! No, not one!

None else could heal all our soul's dis-eas-es, No, not one! No, not one!
And yet no friend is so meek and low-ly, No, not one! No, not one!
No night so dark but His love can cheer us, No, not one! No, not one!
Or sin-ner find that He would not take Him? No, not one! No, not one!
Will He re-fuse us a home in heav-en? No, not one! No, not one!

Je-sus knows all a-bout our strug-gles, He will guide 'til the day is done;

There's not a friend like the low-ly Je-sus, No, not one! No, not one!

No, Not One!

1895

For He Himself has said, "I will never leave you nor forsake you." Hebrews 13:5 (NKJV)

My keenest memories of this hymn involve a story my father, John Morgan, told about two churches across the road from one another in our native Tennessee mountains. The congregations had originally been one, but a split had occurred and bad feelings lingered. One evening, a passerby paused between the churches to listen to their music. One of the churches was singing, "Will There Be Any Stars in My Crown?" From across the road came the reply: "No, Not One! No, Not One!"

Johnson Oatman, the author of "No, Not One!" was born to Christian parents near Medford, New Jersey, on April 21, 1856. He was a child during the Civil War, and after the war he joined his father in the mercantile business. He also stood beside his father in church, for both men had good voices and enjoyed singing.

Johnson was ordained a Methodist minister as a young man, but spent most of his life working in the business world rather than pastoring. After his father's death, he moved to Mount Holly, New Jersey, where he sold insurance.

In 1892, when he was in his mid-thirties, Johnson began writing gospel songs. The next year, failing health forced him to retire from business, and he began devoting himself to full-time songwriting.

Some sources say that he wrote 3,000 hymns; other sources put the number at 5,000. The usually reliable 1992 edition of *Handbook to the Baptist Hymnal* claims that Oatman wrote more than 7,000 texts. He was usually only paid a dollar or so per song, but he became one of the most important gospel songwriters of the turn of the century.

This song, "No, Not One," emphasizes friendship with Christ. The Gospels call Jesus the "Friend of Sinners" (Matt. 11:19). In John 15, He told His disciples, "Greater love has no one than this, than to lay down one's life for his friends. You are My friends. . . . I have called you friends." Jesus is a friend who "sticks closer than a brother" (Prov. 18:24). If you're feeling lonely today, could you ever find a better, closer, wiser, stronger friend?

No, not one.*

---

*Incidentally, those who complain that today's praise and worship music is too repetitious should notice that in singing Oatman's hymn, we repeat the phrase "No, Not One" thirty times!

Open My Eyes That I May See

Clara H. Scott

Clara H. Scott

1. O-pen my eyes that I may see   Glimps-es of truth Thou hast for me;
2. O-pen my ears that I may hear   Voic-es of truth Thou send-est clear;
3. O-pen my mouth and let me bear   Glad-ly the warm truth ev-ery-where.
4. O-pen my mind that I may read   More of Thy love in word and deed.

Place in my hands the won-der-ful key That shall un-clasp and set me free.
And while the wave-notes fall on my ear, Ev-ery-thing false will dis-ap-pear.
O-pen my heart and let me pre-pare Love with Thy chil-dren thus to share.
What shall I fear while yet Thou dost lead? On-ly for light from Thee I plead.

Si-lent-ly now I wait for Thee, Read-y, my God, Thy will to see.

O-pen my eyes, il-lu-mine me, Spir-it di-vine!
O-pen my ears, il-lu-mine me, Spir-it di-vine!
O-pen my heart, il-lu-mine me, Spir-it di-vine!
O-pen my mind, il-lu-mine me, Spir-it di-vine!

Open My Eyes That I May See

1895

The LORD opens the eyes of the blind; The LORD raises those who are bowed down; The LORD loves the righteous. Psalm 146:8 (NKJV)

N ext time you sit down to read your Bible, try pausing a moment, asking God to bless your time in His Word. Two great biblical prayers teach this. The first is in 1 Samuel 3:9, where the boy Samuel was taught to pray, "Speak, Lord, for Your servant hears." That simple prayer has inspired a number of hymns, such as Frances Havergal's tender "Master, Speak! Thy Servant Heareth!"

> *Thy Master, speak! Thy servant heareth,*
> *Waiting for Thy gracious word,*
> *Longing for Thy voice that cheereth;*
> *Master! let it now be heard.**

The other biblical prayer is Psalm 119:18: "Open my eyes, that I may see wondrous things from Your law." This verse inspired Clara Scott to compose both the words and the music to "Open My Eyes That I May See" in 1895.

Clara was born in 1841, just outside Chicago. She was drawn toward music at an early age, having the privilege of attending the first musical institute of Chicago, conducted by the famous music publisher, C. M Cady.

Three years later, she became the music teacher of an all-girl's school in Iowa. In 1861, she married Henry Clay Scott and began writing songs. Some of her work came to the attention of Horatio Palmer, author of "Yield Not to Temptation." With his encouragement, she started writing in earnest, and Palmer published a number of her songs in his collections.

In 1882, she published *The Royal Anthem Book*, which holds the distinction of being the first volume of anthems ever published by a woman. In 1895, "Open My Eyes That I May See" was published and became her best-known hymn. The next year she published a book called *Truth in Song for Lovers of Truth*.

The next year, 1897, began with the excitement of another book on the way, Clara's *Short Anthems*. But that summer, as she was visiting in the Mississippi River town of Dubuque, Iowa, she climbed into a horse-drawn carriage. Something spooked the horse, sending it careening down the street at breakneck speed. Clara was thrown from the runaway buggy and killed. She was fifty-five.

---

*There's also a glorious old German hymn by Anna Sophia of Hessen-Darmstadt, published in 1658, titled "Speak, O Lord, Thy Servant Heareth." The final stanza says: *"Precious Jesus, I beseech Thee, / May Thy Words take root in me. / May this gift from heav'n enrich me, / That I may bear fruit for Thee."*

O to Be Like Thee!

Thomas O. Chisholm

William J. Kirkpatrick

1. O to be like Thee! Bless-ed Re-deem-er, This is my con-stant
2. O to be like Thee! Full of com-pas-sion, Lov-ing, for-giv-ing,
3. O to be like Thee! Low-ly in spir-it, Ho-ly and harm-less,
4. O to be like Thee! While I am plead-ing, Pour out Thy Spir-it,

long-ing and prayer; Glad-ly I'll for-feit all of earth's treas-ures,
ten-der and kind. Help-ing the help-less, cheer-ing the faint-ing.
pa-tient and brave; Meek-ly en-dur-ing cru-el re-proach-es,
fill with Thy love. Make me a tem-ple deemed to re-ceive You:

Je-sus, Thy per-fect like-ness to wear.
Seek-ing the wan-dering sin-ner to find!
Will-ing to suf-fer oth-ers to save.
Fit me for life and heav-en a-bove.

O to be like Thee!

O to be like Thee, Bless-ed Re-deem-er, pure as Thou art! Come in Thy

sweet-ness, come in Thy full-ness; Stamp Thine own im-age deep on my heart.

O to Be Like Thee!

<u>1897</u>

As for me, I will see Your face in righteousness; I shall be satisfied when I awake in Your likeness. Psalm 17:15 (NKJV)

This is one of the earliest poems of Thomas Chisholm, author of "Great is Thy Faithfulness" and "Living for Jesus." He was born in a log cabin in Kentucky, and came to Christ at age twenty-seven during a revival meeting conducted by Dr. H. C. Morrison. He later became editor of Morrison's paper, *The Pentecostal Herald.* "O to Be Like Thee" was written shortly after Thomas' conversion, as he yearned for increasing Christlikeness in his experience.*

The words were discovered and set to music by William James Kirkpatrick, who wrote the music to many popular gospel songs and is remembered as one of the finest Christian composers of the late 1800s and early 1900s.

Kirkpatrick was born in Pennsylvania, and was taught music at an early age by his father, a schoolteacher. He took to music naturally, and later his parents provided the best training available. Young William studied under Pasquale Rondinella, Leopold Meignen, and T. Bishop. As a teen, he moved to Philadelphia and joined the Wharton Street Methodist Episcopal Church. By twenty-one, he was editing his first songbook, *Devotional Melodies,* and dreaming of becoming a world-class violinist.

William fell in love and married in 1861, at the onset of the Civil War. He enlisted as a fife-major in the 91st Regiment of the Pennsylvania Volunteers. He served but a short time before returning to Philadelphia, where he worked in a furniture store to support his new wife. All the while, he was devoting his extra time to music.

In 1880, he began editing collections of songbooks, and over the next forty years he published more than one hundred collections of hymns. William's own compositions flowed from his love for Christ, his musical talents, and his bouts of personal sorrow. His wife died in 1878, and in his grief he poured himself into his music. He married again in 1893, and the second Mrs. Kirkpatrick died around 1910. He then married the widow of hymnwriter John Sweney.

William Kirkpatrick is best remembered for his popular hymn tunes, such as:

"Blessed Be the Name" • "The Cradle Song"
"He Hideth My Soul" • "Lead Me to Calvary"
"Lord, I'm Coming Home"
"Redeemed, How I Love to Proclaim It"
"Singing I Go" • "'Tis So Sweet to Trust in Jesus"
"We Have an Anchor"

---

*For more on Thomas Chisholm, see the story behind "Living for Jesus" in this book, and the hymn story for "Great Is Thy Faithfulness" in *Then Sings My Soul,* Volume 1.

Tell Mother I'll Be There

Charles M. Fillmore

Charles M. Fillmore

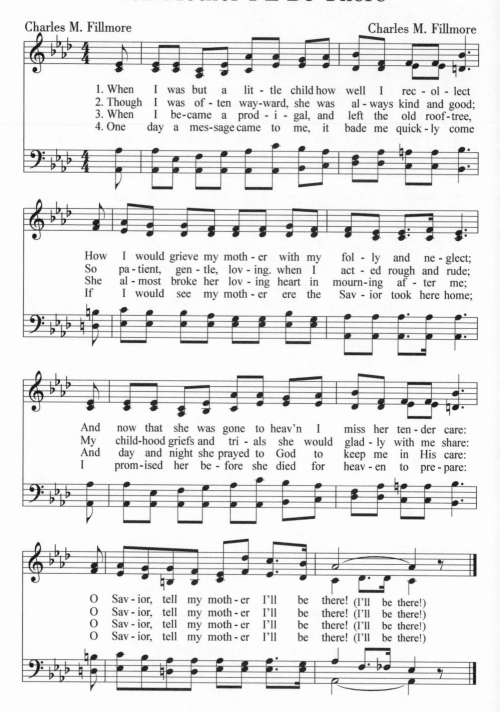

1. When I was but a lit - tle child how well I rec - ol - lect
2. Though I was of - ten way-ward, she was al - ways kind and good;
3. When I be-came a prod - i - gal, and left the old roof-tree,
4. One day a mes-sage came to me, it bade me quick - ly come

How I would grieve my moth - er with my fol - ly and ne - glect;
So pa - tient, gen - tle, lov - ing. when I act - ed rough and rude;
She al - most broke her lov - ing heart in mourn-ing af - ter me;
If I would see my moth - er ere the Sav - ior took here home;

And now that she was gone to heav'n I miss her ten - der care:
My child-hood griefs and tri - als she would glad - ly with me share:
And day and night she prayed to God to keep me in His care:
I prom-ised her be - fore she died for heav - en to pre - pare:

O Sav - ior, tell my moth - er I'll be there! (I'll be there!)
O Sav - ior, tell my moth - er I'll be there! (I'll be there!)
O Sav - ior, tell my moth - er I'll be there! (I'll be there!)
O Sav - ior, tell my moth - er I'll be there! (I'll be there!)

Tell Mother I'll Be There

1898

As one whom his mother comforts, so I will comfort you. Isaiah 66:13 (NKJV)

 cannot subscribe to the idea that luck had very much to do with making me President of the United States," William McKinley once said. "I have never been in doubt since I was old enough to think intelligently that I would sometime be made President."

That may be, but it isn't what his mother had intended.

William was born in 1843, in Ohio, seventh of the nine children of William and Nancy McKinley. His father ran a pig-iron foundry. His mother devoted her time to serving the Lord in her local Methodist church. She taught a Bible class and served as superintendent of the Sunday school. She boasted to friends that her son, William, would one day be a Methodist bishop. (When he became the twenty-fifth President of the United States, she said, "Well, that's all right, too.")

There was always a special bond between William and his mother, and during the winter of 1897, she became seriously ill. President McKinley installed a special telegraph wire connecting the White House to his mother's home in Canton, Ohio. He also kept a special train ready for the trip. One night, the elderly woman called for her son, and the nurses wired, "Mr. President, we think you had better come." He flashed back the answer, TELL MOTHER I'LL BE THERE. He arrived in time, and Mrs. McKinley died in his arms.

When the story was reported in the newspapers, a Midwestern hymnwriter named Charles M. Fillmore was deeply touched. He felt those words expressed the perfect sentiment for wayward children who needed to one day meet their mothers in heaven. "Tell Mother I'll Be There" became one of the most popular invitational hymns of the early twentieth century, and evangelist Charles Alexander once claimed it had "converted more men than any other song."

Four years after his mother's death, President McKinley was attending a reception in Buffalo, New York. At 4:07 P.M., as he reached to shake another hand, two .32 bullets entered his chest at point-blank range, and he fell backwards into the arms of Secret Service agents. As he lay bleeding, he managed to tell his guards not to hurt the assassin and to be very careful how they broke the news to his wife. He died a week later, just six months after his second inauguration.

Higher Ground

Johnson Oatman, Jr.

Charles H. Gabriel

1. I'm press-ing on the up-ward way, New heights I'm gain-ing ev-ery
2. My heart has no de-sire to stay Where doubts a-rise and fears dis-
3. I want to live a-bove the world, Though Sa-tan's darts at me are
4. I want to scale the ut-most height And catch a gleam of glo-ry

day; Still pray-ing as I'm on-ward bound, "Lord, plant my
may; Though some may dwell where these a-bound, My prayer, my
hurled; For faith has caught the joy-ful sound, The song of
bright; But still I'll pray 'til heaven I've found "Lord, lead me

feet on high-er ground."
aim is high-er ground.
saints on high-er ground.
on to high-er ground."

Lord, lift me up and let me

stand By faith on heav-en's ta-ble-land, A high-er

plain than I have found: Lord, plant my feet on high-er ground.

Higher Ground
1898

I press toward the goal for the prize of the upward call of God in Christ Jesus.
Philippians 3:14 (NKJV)

his hymn-prayer, loosely based on Paul's testimony in Philippians 3, was written by Johnson Oatman, author of "Count Your Blessings" and "No, Not One!" Oatman wrote thousands of other hymns, most of which have fallen into the ocean of oblivion.

That's too bad, for Oatman was one of the special gospel songwriters whose hymns focused primarily on Christian growth and personal victory. Behind his hymns was this thought: It isn't enough to know Christ; we need to know Him better and more deeply. This is reflected in "Higher Ground" and in many of Oatman's other songs.

His hymn, "Alone with God," for example, visualizes the sweetness of soul-solitude during one's daily "quiet times" of Bible study and prayer.

> *When storms of life are round me beating,*
> *When rough the path that I have trod,*
> *Within my closet door retreating,*
> *I love to be alone with God.*

Perhaps the song that best expressed Oatman's own experience with Christ was his bright and blithesome hymn, "I'm Living on the Hallelujah Side"—

> *Tho' the world may sweep around me with her dazzle and her dreams,*
> *Yet I envy not her vanities and pride,*
> *For my soul looks up to heaven, where the golden sunlight gleams,*
> *And I'm living on the hallelujah side.*

> *Not for all earth's golden millions would I leave this precious place,*
> *Tho' the tempter to persuade me oft has tried,*
> *For I'm safe in God's pavilion, happy in His love and grace,*
> *And I'm living on the hallelujah side.*

> *Here the sun is always shining, here the sky is always bright;*
> *'Tis no place for gloomy Christians to abide,*
> *For my soul is filled with music and my heart with great delight,*
> *And I'm living on the hallelujah side.*

Nearer, Still Nearer

Lelia N. Morris

Lelia N. Morris

1. Near-er, still near-er, close to Thy heart, Draw me, my Sav-ior, so pre-cious Thou art! Fold me, O fold me close to Thy breast, Shel-ter me safe in that "Ha-ven of Rest," Shel-ter me safe in that "Ha-ven of Rest."

2. Near-er, still near-er, noth-ing I bring, Naught as an of-fering to Je-sus, my King; On-ly my sin-ful, now con-trite heart, Grant me the cleans-ing Thy blood doth im-part, Grant me the cleans-ing Thy blood doth im-part.

3. Near-er, still near-er, Lord, to be Thine! Sin, with its fol-lies I glad-ly re-sign, All of its plea-sures, pomp, and its pride; Give me but Je-sus, my Lord cru-ci-fied, Give me but Je-sus, my Lord cru-ci-fied.

4. Near-er, still near-er, while life shall last, 'Til safe in glo-ry my an-chor is cast; Through end-less a-ges, ev-er to be, Near-er, my Sav-ior, still near-er to Thee, Near-er, my Sav-ior, still near-er to Thee.

Nearer, Still Nearer

1898

Now our salvation is nearer than when we first believed. Romans 13:11 (NKJV)

elia Naylor Morris wrote over one thousand gospel songs, but she shunned the limelight, preferring to be known as Mrs. C. M. Morris, a nondescript homemaker. For forty-seven of her forty-eight years of married life, she lived in the same simple house in McConnelsville, Ohio.

Lelia had been born in the spring of 1862 in the mountains of Ohio near the West Virginia border, just as her father was leaving for the Civil War. When he returned in 1866, the family moved to Malta, Ohio; and when he died, her mother opened a millinery shop in McConnelsville.

As a child, Lelia went forward to the altar several times, seeking salvation. Finally a man came and laid his hand on her head, saying, "Why, little girl, God is here and ready to forgive your sins." That marked her conversion at age ten. Shortly thereafter, she began playing the organ at prayer meetings.

At age nineteen, Lelia married Charles H. Morris, and the young couple joined the Methodist Episcopal Church, becoming active in congregational work, revivals, and camp meetings. Lelia sang in the choir and worked in the Sunday school and women's ministries. The Morris home became a community center of sorts. Charles and Lelia had more books than anyone else in town, and students frequently dropped by to work on school assignments.

In 1892, at a Methodist camp meeting at Mountain Lake Park, Maryland, Lelia had a dramatic Pentecost-like experience. She later said she had read books about the cleansing power of the Holy Spirit, but thought such anointings were only for preachers and bishops. "I did not suppose it was for me. . . . I was so glad when I found that I might have the Holy Spirit in my life. So I opened my heart and let the Holy Spirit come in."

Shortly afterward, back home, she was sitting at her sewing machine when she realized she was composing a hymn of her own. It soon became a pattern. Day after day, as she worked at home, the words and melody of a hymn would compose themselves in her mind. She would go to the piano, work on it, and hide it away. Thus she accumulated a large collection of personal hymns, one of the first of which was "Nearer, Still Nearer."

Let Jesus Come into Your Heart

Lelia N. Morris

Lelia N. Morris

1. If you are tired of the load of your sin, Let Je - sus come
2. If 'tis for pu - ri - ty now that you sigh, Let Je - sus come
3. If there's a tem - pest your voice can - not still, Let Je - sus come
4. If you would join the glad songs of the blest, Let Je - sus come

in - to your heart; If you de - sire a new life to be - gin,
in - to your heart; Foun - tains for cleans-ing are flow - ing near by,
in - to your heart; If there's a void, this world nev - er can fill,
in - to your heart; If you would en - ter the man - sions of rest,

Let Je - sus come in - to your heart. Just now, your

doubt - ings give o'er; Just now, re - ject Him no more; Just now, throw

o - pen the door; Let Je - sus come in - to your heart.

Let Jesus Come into Your Heart

1898

Let not your heart be troubled; you believe in God, believe also in Me. John 14:1
(NKJV)

fter a Pentecost-like experience at the Methodist Camp Meeting at Mountain Lake Park, Maryland, Lelia Morris began writing hymns at her sewing machine. As she devoted more and more time to the Methodist Holiness movement, her hymns became increasingly popular.

One of her finest hymns came early in her songwriting experiences. One Sunday in 1898, while working at the Methodist Camp Meeting at Mountain Lake Park, Maryland, Lelia assisted at the altar of the morning service. The subject of the sermon was repentance, and a large number of people came forward to confess their sins.

One woman was in obvious spiritual anguish. Lelia went to pray with her. So did song leader, Dr. Henry Gilmour, author of "The Haven of Rest." The preacher, L. H. Baker, was also present, and all three converged on the woman.

"Just now your doubting give o'er," said Lelia.

"Just now reject Him no more," added Dr. Gilmour.

"Just now throw open the door," said Rev. Baker.

"Let Jesus come into your heart," concluded Lelia.

After the service had closed, Lelia took those phrases back to her room and worked them into the hymn, "Let Jesus Come into Your Heart," with its popular chorus:

> *Just now, your doubtings give o'er;*
> *Just now, reject Him no more;*
> *Just now, throw open the door;*
> *Let Jesus come into your heart.*

As long as she lived, Lelia served the Lord with tireless zeal. But in 1913, her eyesight began failing. Her son built a huge blackboard with oversized staff lines so she could continue composing, but alas—within a year she was totally blind. Of course, that didn't stop her. Lelia composed hymns in her mind and remembered them until her daughter, Fanny, came for her annual visit. Then she would dictate them all—dozens of them each year—while Fanny wrote down the words and music.

Her life's attitude is best described in another of her popular hymns that reflected her attitude toward growing older, "Sweeter as the Years Go By."

> *Sweeter as the years go by, sweeter as the years go by,*
> *Richer, fuller, deeper, Jesus' love is sweeter,*
> *Sweeter as the years go by.*

Deeper, Deeper

Charles P. Jones

Charles P. Jones

1. Deep-er, deep-er in the love of Je-sus Dai-ly let me go;
2. Deep-er, deep-er bless-ed Ho-ly Spir-it, Take me deep-er still,
3. Deep-er, deep-er tho' it cost hard tri-als, Deep-er let me go!
4. Deep-er, high-er, ev-'ry day in Je-sus, Till all con-flicts past,

High-er, high-er in the school of wis-dom, More of grace to know.
Till my life is whol-ly lost in Je-sus, And His per-fect will.
Root-ed in the ho-ly love of Je-sus, Let me fruit-ful grow.
Finds me con-qu'ror, and in His own im-age Per-fect-ed at last.

O, deep - - - - er yet, I pray,
O deep - er yet, I pray, deep - er yet, I pray, And

And high - - er ev-'ry day, And wis - - - er, bless-ed
high-er ev-'ry day, high-er ev-'ry day, And wis-er, bless-ed Lord,

Lord, In Thy pre-cious, ho-ly Word.
wis - er bless - ed Lord,

Deeper, Deeper

1900

Can you search out the deep things of God? Can you find out the limits of the Almighty? Job 11:7 (NKJV)

O ne of America's first African-American hymnists, Charles Price Jones, was born in Rome, Georgia, at the end of the Civil War. His father died when he was young, but Charles later said, "I love his memory. I had not sense enough when young to appreciate his worth. But the years have taught me his true value."

After his mother's death when he was seventeen, Charles wandered across the South, ending up in Arkansas, where he found Christ as Savior. He immediately began witnessing of his newfound faith, and soon he was formally licensed to preach. He married in 1891, and became a popular preacher. Yet he felt something was missing.

"I was pastor of the Tabernacle Baptist Church, Selma, Alabama, and my ministry with that church . . . seemed to be accepted and much loved. But as I read my Bible and observed conditions, I felt that we were not, as a brother once said to me, 'toting fair with Jesus.' I began then to seek Him with all my heart for that power that would make my life wholly His. . . . I fasted and prayed three days and nights. He then sanctified me sweetly in His love. . . . The earnestness of the Spirit was mine. I was sealed in Him unto the day of Redemption. The blessing of God rested upon me—all on the merits of Christ. . . . For in myself I felt more unworthy and undone than ever. It was the nearness, the eminence, the reality of the presence of God that exalted my spirit and filled me with joy, the joy of the Holy Ghost."

In 1895, Jones became pastor of the Mt. Helm Baptist Church in Jackson, Mississippi, and there his "Holiness" teachings created a storm. "I was looked on as a fanatic by some; by others as weak in the brain," he said. While trying to minister amid a storm of criticism, Charles suffered a personal tragedy when his four-year-old daughter was burned in a fire and died. Soon thereafter, he was dismissed as pastor of Mt. Helm and began holding services in an empty store where he preached from the counter. But his attitude was victorious, as expressed in his great hymn, written during this period: "O deeper yet, I pray, and higher every day."

I Would Not Be Denied

Charles P. Jones

Charles P. Jones

1. When pangs of death seized on my soul, Un - to the Lord I cried,
2. As Ja - cob in the days of old, I wres - tled with the Lord;
3. Old Sa - tan said my Lord was gone And would not hear my prayer,

Till Je - sus came and made me whole, I would not be de - nied.
And in - stant with a cour - age bold, I stood up - on His Word.
But praise the Lord the work is done, And Christ the Lord is here.

I would not be de - nied, I would not be de - nied,
de - nied, de - nied,

Till Je - sus came and made me whole, I would not be de - nied.
de - nied.

I Would Not Be Denied

1901

Then Jacob was left alone; and a Man wrestled with him until the breaking of day. Genesis 32:24 (NKJV)

hen Charles Price Jones was evicted from his church in Jackson, Mississippi, because of his "Holiness" doctrine, many of the members followed him to an old store where Jones preached from the counter. The congregation soon built their own building.

Using his new church as a base, Jones began traveling widely, preaching as far west as Los Angeles. Churches were started in cities like Chicago, St. Louis, Cleveland, and San Diego. When he was dismissed from his Baptist denomination because of his holiness doctrines, Jones (along with C. M. Mason) formed the young churches into a new denomination, "The Church of God in Christ."

It wasn't easy. All his life, Jones faced religious misunderstanding and racial prejudice. In 1905, a gang of white men with dogs burned his church in Jackson to the ground. On two occasions in Mississippi, shots were fired into his congregations as he preached. In Jackson, a mob approached the house where Jones was staying, intending to harm him. They backed down only when the owner of the house met them nose-to-nose on the porch, saying, "You can't come in unless you walk over my dead body." A conflict over speaking in tongues tore his young denomination in two, leading to a painful split with C. M. Mason, and the founding of "The Church of Christ (Holiness), USA."

But out of these backbreaking trials came heart-touching hymns. Jones' secretary said, "In those days of persecution many of those lovely, inspiring, encouraging, and heart-strengthening songs were born in the heart of our pastor. Sometimes when they were given to him in the night, he would have us join him through the hours and sing. Often we remained in the church until midnight."

"I Would Not Be Denied" was written on one such occasion as Jones studied the story of Jacob wrestling with the Lord in Genesis 32. "I prayed in every closet," Jones said, "behind every door; wherever I could hide I went to my knees begging for mercy. But no comfort came. . . . Satan tempted me to despair. (But finally) my mourning became a song. When all the trial was over, thinking of it all one day while alone communing with God and thanking Him for His mercy to me, my soul felt that it must express itself in song; and so was born 'I Would Not Be Denied.'"

God Leads Us Along

G. A. Young

G. A. Young

1. In shad-y green pas-tures, so rich and so sweet, God leads His dear
2. Some-times on the mount where the sun shines so bright, God leads His dear
3. Though sor-rows be-fall us and Sa-tan op-pose, God leads His dear
4. A-way from the mire and a-way from the clay, God leads His dear

chil-dren a-long; Where the wa-ter's cool flow bathes the wea-ry one's feet,
chil-dren a-long; Some - times in the val-ley, in dark-est of night,
chil-dren a-long; Through grace we can con-quer, de - feat all our foes,
chil-dren a-long; A - way up in glo-ry, e - ter-ni-ty's day

God leads His dear chil-dren a - long. Some thru the wa-ters, some thru the

flood, Some thru the fire, but all thru the blood; Some thru great sor-row, but

God gives a song, In the night sea-son, and all the day long.

God Leads Us Along

1903

He leads me beside the still waters. He restores my soul. Psalm 23:2, 3 (NKJV)

G eorge Young, a carpenter, and his wife dedicated their lives to following the Lord, wherever He would lead. "He does the leading," they often said, "and we do the following." God led them to the rural Midwest and they traveled from church to church in revival efforts. Their finances were always tight, but "through the many years we never went hungry!" Mrs. Young said years later. "Oh, sometimes we didn't have too much of this world's goods but . . . we always had so much of Jesus."

Finally they saved enough to buy a small piece of land on which George built a cottage. Though small, it was the fulfillment of a life's dream, and when they moved in they dedicated the house to God and sang the Doxology. But some time later, when the Youngs were away on a ministry trip, a thug who had been offended by George's preaching set the house afire. Returning home, the Youngs found a heap of ashes. All their worldly goods and cherished possessions were gone.

As George gazed at the ruins, he recounted the precious possessions fire could never destroy—his family, his relationship with Christ, his ministry, his eternal home. There and then, the words to "God Leads Us Along" began forming in his mind. Within a few days, he had written all three stanzas.

Years later, Dr. Harold Lillenas, seeking to track down George's widow, drove to the small Kansas town where she resided. Stopping for directions, he was alarmed to hear that Mrs. Young was living in the run-down Country Poor House. Lillenas was deeply troubled that the widow of the author of such a hymn about God's guidance should spend her final days in the Poor House. But when he finally found her, Mrs. Young explained, "One day God took my sweet husband home. Oh, how I missed him for we had always served the Lord together. In my heart, I wondered—where will God now lead me? Dr. Lillenas, God led me here! I'm so glad He did, for you know, about every month someone comes into this place to spend the rest of their days, and, Dr. Lillenas, so many of them don't know my Jesus. I'm having the time of my life introducing them to Jesus! Dr. Lillenas, isn't it wonderful how God leads?"

Jesus Is All the World to Me

Will L. Thompson

Will L. Thompson

1. Je-sus is all the world to me, My life, my joy, my all;
2. Je-sus is all the world to me, My Friend in tri-als sore;
3. Je-sus is all the world to me, And true to Him I'll be;
4. Je-sus is all the world to me, I want no bet-ter friend;

He is my strength from day to day, With-out Him I would fall;
I go to Him for bless-ings, and He gives them o'er and o'er.
Oh, how could I this Friend de-ny, When He's so true to me?
I trust Him now, I'll trust Him when life's fleet-ing days shall end.

When I am sad, to Him I go, No oth-er one can cheer me so;
He sends the sun-shine and the rain, He sends the har-vest's gold-en grain;
Fol-low-ing Him I know I'm right, He watch-es o'er me day and night;
Beau-ti-ful life with such a Friend, Beau-ti-ful life that has no end;

When I am sad, He makes me glad, He's my Friend.
Sun-shine and rain, har-vest of grain, He's my Friend.
Fol-low-ing Him, by day and night, He's my Friend.
E-ter-nal life, e-ter-nal joy, He's my Friend.

Jesus Is All the World to Me

1904

There is one God, the Father, of whom are all things, and we for Him; and one Lord Jesus Christ, through whom are all things, and through whom we live. 1 Corinthians 8:6 (NKJV)

Y ou can take the boy out of the town, but you can't take the town out of the boy. Will L. Thompson grew up in East Liverpool, Ohio, in the mid-1800s. A few hours away by horseback were the grimy steel mills of Pittsburgh, Pennsylvania; but East Liverpool was known for a happier trade—its pottery. Will's parents, Josiah and Sarah Thompson, were local entrepreneurs who had helped transform the area into a pottery manufacturing region.

Will showed early signs of his dad's entrepreneurial spirit; and, being from a financially comfortable family, he was also able to devote time to his other passion—music. By age sixteen, he had already published two songs, "Liverpool Schottische" and "Darling Minnie Gray."

After musical training in Boston and Germany, Will tried to sell his music to major publishers. When they didn't offer him enough money, he published them himself. He printed copies of his most popular song, "Gathering Shells by the Sea," and sent them to minstrel organizations throughout the country. Soon "Gathering Shells" was one of America's most popular songs, just behind Stephen Foster's "Old Folks at Home" in popularity.

With his earnings, Will established his own music publishing business in Chicago, "Will L. Thompson & Co." Having arrived at financial success, Will decided to devote himself exclusively to Christian music. He wrote the great invitational hymn, "Softly and Tenderly Jesus Is Calling," the rousing gospel song "There's a Great Day Coming," and this beautiful hymn, "Jesus Is All the World to Me."

Despite being wealthy, famous, widely traveled, and in great demand, Will never wanted to leave his hometown. He opened a music business in East Liverpool.* He became a prominent land developer and owned property throughout the town. He was a generous philanthropist, supporting heavily the local YMCA and the Emmanuel Presbyterian Church. He served as the first president of the local library. He also donated acreage for a park that bears his name to this day, stipulating that no alcoholic beverages be allowed in the park and no sports permitted there on Sundays.

He regularly hitched up his two-horse wagon on which he placed a portable piano, and he traveled throughout the area singing his hymns in churches and public squares.

Will Thompson died in 1909; but in 2002, the grateful citizens of East Liverpool inducted him into the Lou Holtz/Upper Ohio Valley Hall of Fame.

---

*The store Thompson built still stands at the corner of Fourth and Washington Streets and now houses the Pottery City Galleries Antique Mall.

Nothing Between

Charles A. Tindley

Charles A. Tindley

1. Noth-ing be-tween my soul and the Sav - ior, Naught of this world's de-
2. Noth-ing be-tween, like world - ly plea-sure: Hab - its of life, though
3. Noth-ing be-tween, like pride or sta - tion: Self or friends shall
4. Noth-ing be-tween, e'en man - y hard tri - als, Though the whole world a -

lu - sive dream; I have re - nounced all sin - ful plea-sure,
harm - less they seem, Must not my heart from Him ev - er sev - er,
not in - ter - vene; Though it may cost me much trib - u - la - tion,
gainst me con - vene, Watch - ing with prayer and much self - de - ni - al,

Je - sus is mine! There's noth - ing be - tween.
He is my all! There's noth - ing be - tween.
I am re - solved! There's noth - ing be - tween.
Tri - umph at last, with noth - ing be - tween.

Noth - ing be - tween my

soul and the Sav - ior, So that His bless - ed face may be seen;

Noth-ing pre-ven-ting the least of His fa - vor: Keep the way clear! Let noth-ing be-tween.

Nothing Between

1905

Nor height nor depth, nor any other created thing, shall be able to separate us from the love of God which is in Christ Jesus our Lord. Romans 8:39 (NKJV)

Charles Tindley was born into slavery in 1851. "My father was poor as it relates to this world's goods," Charles wrote, "but was rich in the grace of God. He was unable to send me to school or to keep me with him at his little home. It therefore became my lot to be hired out. . . . The people with whom I lived were not all good. Some of them were very cruel. . . . I used to find bits of newspaper on the roadside . . . in order to study the ABCs from them. During the day I would gather pine knots, and when the people were asleep at night I would light these pine knots, and . . . with fire-coals, mark all the words I could make out. I continued in this way, and without any teacher, until I could read the Bible."

One day Charles slipped into church and sat in the back. When the preacher asked any child who could read the Bible to come forward, Charles went to the front. He later recalled the odd looks people gave him and overheard someone refer to him as "the boy with the bare feet." From that moment, Charles resolved to gain an education.

After emancipation, he moved to Philadelphia, and it was there, in a Methodist church, that he gave his life to Christ. His entrance into "full-time" ministry began humbly—as the church janitor.

"My first plan was to buy every book I could," he explained. "Then I entered by correspondence all the schools to which my limited means would afford . . . Thus while I was unable to go through the schools, I was able to let the schools go through me."

In 1885, he applied for ordination. One of the other candidates asked him, "How do you expect to pass your examination? The other candidates and I have diplomas. What do you hold?"

"Nothing but a broom," was Tindley's reply. But the boy with the broom went on to become a world-famous pastor, preacher, and hymnist.

One evening as he studied, according to most accounts of the story, a piece of paper, caught by the wind, flew across Charles' lamp, causing a shadow to fall over his writing. Pausing, Charles considered the power of a sin to darken his soul, and out of that came his great hymn: "Nothing Between."

Stand by Me

Charles A. Tindley   Charles A. Tindley

Stand by Me

1905

He calms the storm, So that its waves are still. Psalm 107:29 (NKJV)

I n 1902, Charles A. Tindley was elected pastor of the Bainbridge Street Methodist Church in Philadelphia—the church in which he was converted and where he had once served as janitor. There were one hundred thirty members, but under Tindley's powerful preaching, the numbers grew, making it necessary to relocate. The congregation purchased a building from a white Presbyterian church and moved in, changing the name to East Calvary Methodist Episcopal Church.

As large numbers of African-Americans flooded into Philadelphia during World War I to take jobs vacated by whites who had left for the war, East Calvary Church mushroomed in growth. Tindley stood on the street corners, sharing Christ and doing evangelistic work. "Up and down this area, Tindley walked and talked about God's saving grace," wrote one biographer. "Sometimes individually and sometimes in small clusters . . . Counseling and consoling, Tindley moved among the unchurched. Many . . . cabbies . . . were often aroused by Tindley for a shared moment of prayer. He came to be known as 'Our Preacher.'"

He organized benevolence ministries, and started a home-loan program so that his poor parishioners could begin saving for houses. He established soup kitchens and opened the church to the homeless in cold weather.

Charles Tindley was a striking man, standing six-foot-three and possessing a strong, deep voice. Multitudes were attracted to Christ through his preaching, and the church was expanded until it held over three thousand people. Even then, Tindley had to encourage members not to attend all the services so that guests could come.

At the congregation's insistence, the church was renamed "Tindley Temple"; but in the wee hours of the Sunday appointed for the dedication, his wife, Daisy, died suddenly, and Tindley was unable to attend the opening.

Such a prominent ministry also invites attacks, criticism, misunderstanding, and heavy burdens. Tindley once said, "It was when I was overburdened with criticisms, abuse, and hard and many oppositions—some of them from those whom I took to be my best friends—I wrote 'Stand by Me.'"

> *When the storms of life are raging, stand by me;*
> *When the storms of life are raging, stand by me.*
> *When the world is tossing me like a ship upon the sea*
> *Thou Who rulest wind and water, stand by me.*

We'll Understand It Better By and By

Charles A. Tindley   Charles A. Tindley

We'll Understand It Better By and By

1905

Consider what I say, and may the Lord give you understanding in all things.
2 Timothy 2:7 (NKJV)

Y ou are an unlettered ignoramus. You know you are not educationally fit to be a bishop." Those words were spoken by a Methodist minister to Charles Tindley, author of "Stand by Me," "I Will Not Be Denied," "Nothing Between," and "We'll Understand It Better By and By." Charles was being considered for a Methodist bishopric, a position sought by the rival minister. Just before the election, an anonymous letter falsely accused Tindley of immorality.

As a prominent, powerful African-American preacher in Philadelphia, Charles often suffered racially motivated persecution. He once said in a sermon, "Previous conditions of servitude, in the eyes of our enemies, have left its ineffaceable marks of inferiority upon every human being whose veins contain one drop of Negro blood."

His worst heartaches, however, arose within his own family. The deepest blows were the death of his wife, Daisy, on the eve of the dedication of the Tindley Temple Methodist Church, and the death of one of his sons in World War I. Eventually Charles remarried; but several of his grown children, still living at home, didn't get along with their stepmother. Charles finally sent them packing.

Atop those pressures were the financial burdens of a large church made up of poverty-stricken masses. "All of us know we are without jobs," he told his congregation when they were struggling to meet the church's bills. "We don't own big bank accounts. We don't even know what tomorrow will bring. But we do have hope. We do have God. We do have salvation. We do have faith." It was in this spirit that he wrote this great old gospel hymn for his church. One additional stanza says:

We are often destitute of the things that life demands,
Want of food and want of shelter, thirsty hills and barren lands;
We are trusting in the Lord, and according to God's Word,
We will understand it better by and by.

Tindley served Christ faithfully until he was in his eighties. One day in 1933, he showed up at the hospital. "How are you, Reverend?" asked the hospital director. "What can we do for you?"

"I have come to die," said Tindley. He declined rapidly, and passed away on July 26, 1933. All Philadelphia mourned, but he was buried in an unmarked grave, for his church did not have funds for a memorial.

The Way of the Cross Leads Home

Jessie B. Pounds

Charles H. Gabriel

1. I must needs go home by the way of the cross,
2. I must needs go on in the blood-sprin-kled way,
3. Then I bid fare-well to the way of the world,

There's no oth-er way but this; I shall ne'er get sight
The path that the Sav-ior trod, If I ev-er climb
To walk in it nev-er more; For my Lord says, "Come,"

of the gates of light, If the way of the cross I miss.
to the heights sub-lime, Where the soul is at home with God.
and I seek my home, Where He waits at the o-pen door.

The way of the cross leads home, The way of the cross leads home;

leads home,

leads home;

It is sweet to know as I on-ward go, The way of the cross leads home.

The Way of the Cross Leads Home

<u>1906</u>

Go your way, sell whatever you have and give to the poor, and you will have treasure in heaven; and come, take up the cross, and follow Me. Mark 10:21 (NKJV)

I know that My Redeemer Liveth," "Anywhere with Jesus," "The Touch of His Hand on Mine," and "The Way of the Cross Leads Home" were all written by a Midwestern woman named Jessie Brown Pounds.

Jessie was born in 1861 in Hiram, Ohio, outside Cleveland. Her father, Rev. Holland Brown, was a pioneer preacher among the Disciples of Christ. Her mother, Jane Abell Brown, loved children's literature and encouraged Jessie from kindergarten to write poetry.

Jessie began writing poems and articles for Christian magazines when she was fifteen, and for over thirty years she wrote hymns and religious poetry for Charles H. Fillmore, which he set to music. Like Jessie, Fillmore was a member of the Christian Church (Disciples of Christ), and the two became a prolific gospel-songwriting team.

In 1897, Jessie, thirty-eight, married Rev. John E. Pounds, pastor of the Central Christian Church in Indianapolis. One Sunday a few weeks after her wedding, she woke up feeling unwell. Her husband went to church without her, and in the quietness of the morning, Jessie began thinking of heaven. Taking a pen she scribbled out a poem titled "Beautiful Isle of Somewhere." It became a favorite hymn of President William McKinley and was sung at his funeral after he was assassinated in Buffalo, New York.

Somewhere the sun is shining, somewhere the songbirds dwell;
Hush, then, thy sad repining, God lives, and all is well.

Somewhere, somewhere, Beautiful Isle of Somewhere!
Land of the true, where we live anew, Beautiful Isle of Somewhere!

In all, Jessie wrote nine books, fifty cantata librettos, and over four hundred hymns. We don't know the background behind "The Way of the Cross Leads Home," but many have speculated that it was inspired by a popular story and sermon illustration that was circulating during those days.

The geographical heart of London is Charing Cross, which is referred to locally simply as "the Cross." A London police officer came upon a lost child who was unable to tell him where he lived. Finally, amid sobs and tears, the child simply said, "If you will take me to the Cross, I think I can find my way home from there."

"I must needs go home by the way of the cross," wrote Jessie Pounds. "There's no other way but this."

Go, Tell It on the Mountain

John W. Work Jr.

American Folk Song

Go, tell it on the moun-tain, O-ver the hills and ev-ery-where;

Go, tell it on the moun-tain, That Je-sus Christ is born!

1. While shep-herds kept their watch-ing O'er si-lent flocks by night, Be-
2. The shep-herds feared and trem-bled When lo! A-bove the earth Rang
3. Down in a low-ly man-ger The hum-ble Christ was born, And

hold through-out the heav-ens There shone a ho-ly light.
out the an-gel cho-rus That hailed our Sav-ior's birth.
brought us God's sal-va-tion That bless-ed Christ-mas morn.

Go, Tell It on the Mountain
1907

Then the shepherds returned, glorifying and praising God for all the things that they had heard and seen, as it was told them. Luke 2:20 (NKJV)

During the bitter days of slavery, black workers on American plantations, solaced themselves with song and created a unique form of American hymnology—the Negro spiritual. It was the Jubilee Singers of Fisk University in Nashville, Tennessee, that took the plantation songs of the Negro slaves to the entire world. One of the last "spirituals" to be uncovered and published was this unique Christmas carol, "Go, Tell It on the Mountain."

How did it come about?

John Wesley Work Jr. was born in Nashville, on or about August 6, 1871. His father was choir director for a Nashville church who often wrote his own arrangements. John grew up singing in his dad's choirs, and when he enrolled in Fisk University, he became active in its music program, though his primary subjects were history and Latin. Returning to Fisk to work on his master's degree, John was eventually hired as professor of Latin and Greek. But his greatest love was the preservation and performance of the Negro spiritual.

Many of the spirituals had been published, but "Go, Tell It on the Mountain" was largely unknown, though it had been performed by the Jubilee Singers since 1879. Some of the original stanzas were obscure, for spirituals, by definition, were unwritten songs passed from plantation to plantation and from generation to generation. The chorus, however, was crystal clear and highlighted the theme for the whole: "Go, tell it on the mountain / Jesus Christ is born."

Intrigued by the chorus and melody, John wrote two new stanzas for this song, and it became his custom before sunrise on Christmas morning to take students caroling from building to building, singing,"Go, Tell It on the Mountain." It was first published in 1907 in *Work's Folk Songs of the Negro as Sung on the Plantations.*

John Work has been called the first black collector of Negro folk songs, a pursuit continued by his two sons, John Wesley Work II and Frederick J. Work. Both young men served on the faculty of Fisk University, working with the Jubilee Singers and collecting and publishing African-American spirituals and folk music.

"Go Tell It on the Mountain" is classic in that genre. To black slaves in antebellum America, the birth of a liberating Savior was a message to be heralded from the highest mountains.

It still is, for us all.

Will the Circle Be Unbroken?

Ada Ruth Habershon

Charles H. Gabriel

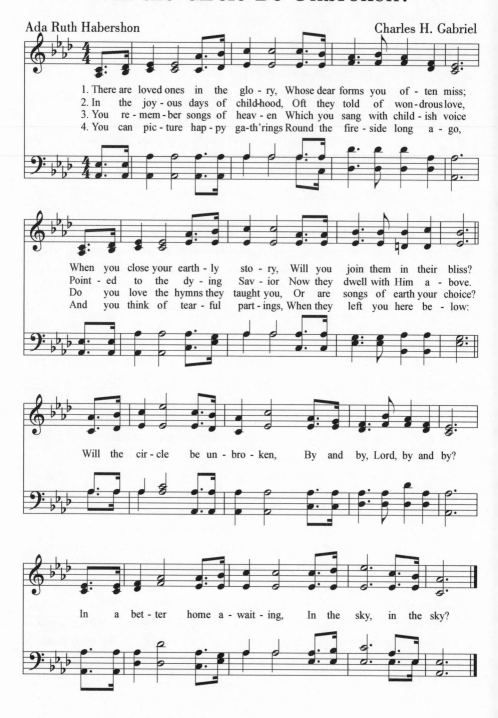

1. There are loved ones in the glo - ry, Whose dear forms you of - ten miss;
2. In the joy - ous days of child-hood, Oft they told of won - drous love,
3. You re - mem - ber songs of heav - en Which you sang with child - ish voice
4. You can pic - ture hap - py ga - th'rings Round the fire - side long a - go,

When you close your earth - ly sto - ry, Will you join them in their bliss?
Point - ed to the dy - ing Sav - ior Now they dwell with Him a - bove.
Do you love the hymns they taught you, Or are songs of earth your choice?
And you think of tear - ful part - ings, When they left you here be - low:

Will the cir - cle be un - bro - ken, By and by, Lord, by and by?

In a bet - ter home a - wait - ing, In the sky, in the sky?

Will the Circle Be Unbroken?

1908

And the heavens will praise Your wonders, O LORD; Your faithfulness also in the assembly of the saints. Psalm 89:5 (NKJV)

O ne of my choice possessions is a little black-and-white photograph taken when I was a toddler in the early 1950s. It's a picture of my father's family, standing by a Christmas tree. My dad is beside his mother, surrounded by his six brothers and sisters. I'm a tiny fellow being held in my Uncle George's arms.

I look at the picture wistfully now, for my dad, my grandmother, and all my uncles and aunts are gone; and I think of that picture whenever I hear this song, because it poses a poignant question. As one of the verses puts it:

> *One by one their seats were emptied,*
> *One by one they went away;*
> *Here the circle has been broken—*
> *Will it be complete one day?*

Many people consider this an Appalachian folk hymn, because the Carter Family, the founding family of country music, popularized it. A. P. Carter wrote the bluegrass version sometime between 1931 and 1939; and the Carter Family's version became so well known that he is sometimes credited with composing the song.

The words, however, were actually written by a brilliant London Bible teacher named Ada Ruth Habershon, the youngest daughter of a godly doctor, S. O. Habershon. Ada was a precocious child and a tender Christian, and even as a teen she was an avid Bible student. When D. L. Moody and Ira Sankey toured England in 1884, they were so impressed with Ada, then twenty-three, they invited her to visit America and teach the Bible at Moody's Conference Center in Northfield, Massachusetts. Her lectures on the Old Testament were later published, along with a number of other books, some of which are still in print. They include *Study of the Types, Study of the Miracles, Study of the Parables, Study of the Tabernacle,* and *Types in the Old Testament.*

In 1901, when Ada was forty and suffering from an illness, she began writing poetry. Four years later, when the powerful evangelistic team of R. A. Torrey and Charles M. Alexander visited England, Alexander asked her to write some gospel songs. Within a year, she had sent him two hundred!

Ada Habershon never married, and she passed away in 1918, at the age of fifty-seven. But her books continue to be studied to this day and her hymns are still sung around the world.

259

One Day

J. Wilbur Chapman

Charles H. Marsh

1. One day when heav - en was filled with His prais - es,
2. One day they led Him up Cal - va - ry's moun - tain,
3. One day they left Him a - lone in the gar - den,
4. One day the grave could con - ceal Him no long - er,
5. One day the trum - pet will sound for His com - ing,

One day when sin was as black as could be,
One day they nailed Him to die on the tree;
One day He rest - ed, from suf - fer - ing free;
One day the stone rolled a - way from the door;
One day the skies with His glo - ry will shine;

Je - sus came forth to be born of a vir - gin,
Suf - fer - ing an - guish, de - spised and re - ject - ed,
An - gels came down o'er His tomb to keep vig - il;
Then He a - rose, o - ver death He had con - quered,
Won - der - ful day, my be - lov - ed one's bring - ing!

Dwelt a - mong men, my Ex - am - ple is He!
Bear - ing our sins, my Re - deem - er is He!
Hope of the hope - less, my Sav - ior is He!
Now is as - cend - ed, my Lord ev - er - more!
Glo - ri - ous Sav - ior, this Je - sus is mine!

One Day

1908

And she will bring forth a Son, and you shall call His name JESUS, for He will save His people from their sins. Matthew 1:21 (NKJV)

his was written by one of America's greatest evangelists, J. Wilbur Chapman. Under D. L. Moody's ministry, Chapman received absolute assurance of his salvation. And it was Moody who encouraged him to enter full-time evangelism.

Chapman wrote a number of books and pastored several churches. His hymn, "Our Great Savior," is one of my favorites.* A leader among American Presbyterians, Chapman was elected Moderator of the Presbyterian General Assembly in 1918, but he passed away on Christmas Day that year. He was only fifty-nine years old.

One of Chapman's young musicians, Charles Marsh, was a gifted pianist who wrote the music for "One Day." He later described the legal wrangling over this song:

> It was about 1908 or 1909 that Dr. Chapman was invited to conduct a Bible Conference at Stony Brook, Long Island, and he took me with him. It was at Stony Brook that he gave me the poem "One Day" and another entitled "All Hail the Power." I set them both [to music] that summer and as I remember, they were copyrighted in my name. Within a year or two Dr. Parley E. Zartmann (Dr. Chapman's assistant) persuaded me to sell my interest in the songs to him. I wanted to go to college, so I left my association with Dr. Chapman, much as I enjoyed it. Soon after that, Dr. Chapman joined forces with Charles M. Alexander and the next time I saw "One Day" in print, it had at the bottom "Charles M. Alexander, owner of the copyright." In the meantime, Dr. Zartmann had sold the two songs to Hope Publishing Company. I don't know who won out in the mess that was raging at the time, but I do think Dr. Zartmann and the Hope Publishing Company were in the right and that Alexander had simply appropriated the song because of Dr. Chapman's having written the words.

Well, nothing can keep a good hymn down—especially one that presents such an all-inclusive view of the Savior's great work for us. As the refrain says:

> *Living, He loved me; dying, He saved me;*
> *Buried, He carried my sins far away;*
> *Rising, He justified, freely forever;*
> *One day He's coming—O glorious day!*

---

*See this story in *Then Sings My Soul*, Volume 1.

Dwelling in Beulah Land

C. Austin Miles   C. Austin Miles

1. Far   a - way the   noise of strife   up - on my ear is   fall - ing,
2. Far   be - low the   storm of doubt   up - on the world is   beat - ing,
3. Let   the storm - y   breez - es blow, their   cry can - not a - larm me;
4. View - ing here the   works of God,   I   sink in   con - tem - pla - tion.

Then   I   know the   sins of earth be - set on ev - ery   hand;
Sons   of men   in   bat - tle   long the   en - e - my with - stand;
I   am safe - ly   shel - tered here, pro - tect - ed by God's   hand;
Hear - ing now His   bless - ed voice, I   see the way He   planned;

Doubt and fear and   things of earth in   vain to   me   are   call - ing,
Safe am I with - in   the   cas - tle   of God's Word re - treat - ing,
Here the sun is   al - ways shin - ing, here there's naught can   harm me,
Dwell - ing in the   Spir - it, here I   learn of   full   sal - va - tion,

None   of these shall   move me   from Beu - lah   Land.
Noth - ing then   can   reach me,   'tis Beu - lah   Land.
I   am safe for - ev - er   in Beu - lah   Land.
Glad - ly will   I   tar - ry   in Beu - lah   Land.

Dwelling in Beulah Land

1911

I will both lie down in peace, and sleep; For You alone, O LORD, make me dwell in safety. Psalm 4:8 (NKJV)

T his peppy song about heaven was written by pharmacist-turned-publisher, C. Austin Miles, born on January 7, 1868, in Lakehurst, New Jersey. He had wanted to train for the ministry, but circumstances forced him to take a job with a pharmacy at age sixteen. Soon Miles found himself attending the Philadelphia College of Pharmacy and the University of Pennsylvania, after which he settled down as a druggist for several years.

It all changed when he wrote his first gospel song, "List 'Tis Jesus' Voice." After Hall-Mack Publishing Company of Philadelphia published it, Miles abandoned drugs for hymns. For nearly four decades, he was employed by the Hall-Mack Publishing Company as music editor, even after it merged with the Rodeheaver Company. In a way, of course, he hadn't changed vocations at all, just venue. He was now filling prescriptions for the soul.

Interestingly, Miles wrote many of his hymns in the darkroom. He was an amateur photographer, and he found he could read his Bible in the glow of the special light in the darkroom. While waiting for photographs to develop, Miles would read the Scriptures and pray them into songs. One day, for example, while waiting for some film to develop, he poured over John 20, the story of Mary coming to Christ's tomb on Easter morning. Out of his meditation came the song, "In the Garden."

Miles also wrote the popular gospel hymn, "If Jesus Goes with Me I'll Go Anywhere," and the exuberant song that says, "There's a new name written down in Glory—and it's mine, O yes, it's mine!"

In his spare time, Miles was in demand as a song leader at conferences, churches, conventions, and camp meetings. He also published some of his compositions as poetry, his best-known work being "The World's Greatest Need."

THE WORLD'S GREATEST NEED

A little more kindness and a little less greed;
A little more giving and a little less need;
A little more smile and a little less frown;
A little less kicking a man when he's down;
A little more "we" and a little less "I"
A little more laughs and a little less cry;
A little more flowers on the pathway of life;
And fewer on graves at the end of the strife.

Rise Up, O Men of God

William P. Merrill

William H. Walter

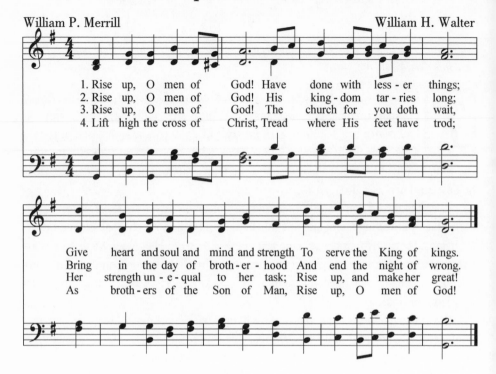

1. Rise up, O men of God! Have done with less - er things;
2. Rise up, O men of God! His king - dom tar - ries long;
3. Rise up, O men of God! The church for you doth wait,
4. Lift high the cross of Christ, Tread where His feet have trod;

Give heart and soul and mind and strength To serve the King of kings.
Bring in the day of broth - er - hood And end the night of wrong.
Her strength un - e - qual to her task; Rise up, and make her great!
As broth - ers of the Son of Man, Rise up, O men of God!

Rise Up, O Men of God

<u>1911</u>

Who will rise up for me against the evildoers? Who will stand up for me against the workers of iniquity? Psalm 94:16 (NKJV)

 his hymn was written somewhere on Lake Michigan, on a steamship heading toward Chicago. Its author was William Merrill, who was nearing the end of his pastorate in Chicago before moving east to assume the leadership of New York's famous Brick Church.

Merrill had come to Christ at age eleven. As a young man, he attended Rutgers College and Union Theological Seminary and was ordained into the Presbyterian ministry in 1890. He pastored churches in Philadelphia, then in Chicago.

In 1911, he became pastor of the Brick Presbyterian Church, where he remained until his retirement in 1938.* He wrote ten books and several hymns, the best known of which was "Rise Up, O Men of God."

He once explained how the hymn was written. While pastoring in Chicago, he was associated with a Presbyterian publication known as *The Continent.* Its editor, Nolan R. Best, approached him, suggesting the need for a strong hymn challenging men to rise up for Christ, especially in light of the Brotherhood Movement within the Presbyterian Church. Shortly afterward, Merrill read an article by Gerald Stanley Lee entitled, "The Church of Strong Men."

"I was on one of the Lake Michigan steamers going back to Chicago for a Sunday at my own church," Merrill later wrote, "when suddenly this hymn came up, almost without conscious thought or effort." It first appeared in *The Continent* on February 16, 1911, and the next year was published in *The Pilgrim Hymnal.*

William Merrill was also instrumental in starting the Church Peace Union, now known as the Carnegie Council on Ethics and International Affairs. In 1914, the steel magnate, Andrew Carnegie, wanted to establish an organization seeking to end war forever. They planned to gather on August 1, 1914, on the shore of Lake Constance in southern Germany. But when Germany invaded Belgium, trains carrying delegates were halted and turned back and other delegates were arrested by German authorities. The arrival of the First World War crushed Carnegie's dreams of banning war; but the Church Peace Union continued its work, and William Merrill served as its first president. Today on Manhattan's Upper East Side, two adjoining townhouses, named for William Merrill, serve as headquarters for the Carnegie Council's popular public speaker series.

---

*Other famous pastor/hymnists of Brick Church include Henry Van Dyke ("Joyful, Joyful, We Adore Thee) and Maltbie Babcock ("This Is My Father's World"). These stories are told in the first volume of *Then Sings My Soul.*

What If It Were Today?

Lelia N. Morris

Lelia N. Morris

1. Je - sus is com - ing to earth a - gain, What if it were to - day?
2. Sa - tan's do - min - ion will then be o'er, O that it were to - day!
3. Faith - ful and true would He find us here If He should come to - day?

Com - ing in pow - er and love to reign, What if it were to - day?
Sor - row and sigh - ing shall be no more, O that it were to - day!
Watch - ing in glad - ness and not in fear, If He should come to - day?

Com - ing to claim His cho - sen bride, All the re - deemed and pu - ri - fied,
Then shall the dead in Christ a - rise, Caught up to meet Him in the skies;
Signs of His com - ing mul - ti - ply, Morn - ing light breaks in east - ern sky,

O - ver this whole earth scat - tered wide, What if it were to - day?
When shall these glo - ries meet our eyes? What if it were to - day?
Watch, for the time is draw - ing nigh, What if it were to - day?

What If It Were Today?

1912

And if I go and prepare a place for you, I will come again and receive you to Myself; that where I am, there you may be also. John 14:3 (NKJV)

Christians of every generation have longed for Christ to return in their lifetime. *The Didache*, one of the earliest documents in church history, says, *Let not your lamps be quenched, nor your loins unloosed; but be ready, for you know not the hour in which our Lord will come.* St. Cyril wrote in the fourth century, *But let us wait and look for the Lord's coming upon the clouds from heaven. Then shall angelic trumpets sound.*

Augustine felt the Lord would return somewhere around the year A.D. 1000. In the 1300s, John Wycliffe, the "Morning Star of the Reformation," studied the "signs of the times" and concluded that the end of the world and the Second Coming of Christ should be expected immediately. In the sixteenth century, John Calvin preached: *We must hunger after Christ until the dawning of that great day when our Lord will fully manifest the glory of His kingdom.* Today His return seems closer than ever.

It's not surprising, then, that the Return of Christ has been the theme of hundreds of hymns through the ages. "What If It Were Today?" was written by Ohio homemaker, Lelia Morris, whose story has already been told in connection with her hymns, "Nearer, Still Nearer" and "Let Jesus Come into Your Heart." It was one of the most popular Second Coming songs of the last hundred years. But look at a much older hymn about the Second Coming.

John Newton, the London pastor who wrote "Amazing Grace," showed the other side of the Lord's return with his hymn "Day of Judgment! Day of Wonders!" It provides an important contrast to Lelia Morris' uplifting strains.

> *Day of judgment! Day of wonders!*
> *Hark! the trumpet's awful sound,*
> *Louder than a thousand thunders,*
> *Shakes the vast creation round!*
> *How the summons shall the sinner's heart confound!*

> *At His call the dead awaken,*
> *Rise to life from earth and sea;*
> *All the powers of nature shaken*
> *By His look, prepares to flee.*
> *Careless sinner, what will then become of thee!*

Love Lifted Me

James Rowe   Howard E. Smith

1. I was sink-ing deep in sin, Far from the peace-ful shore, Ver-y deep-ly
2. All my heart to Him I give; Ev-er to Him I'll cling, In His bless-ed
3. Souls in dan-ger, look a-bove; Je-sus com-plete-ly saves. He will lift you

stained with-in, Sink-ing to rise no more. But the Mas-ter of the sea
pres-ence live, Ev-er His prais-es sing. Love so might-y and so true
by His love Out of the an-gry waves. He's the Mas-ter of the sea,

Heard my de-spair-ing cry, From the wa-ters lift-ed me-Now safe am I.
Mer-its my soul's best songs; Faith-ful, lov-ing ser-vice, too, To Him be-longs.
Bil-lows His will o-bey. He your Sav-ior wants to be, Be saved to-day.

Love lift-ed me! Love lift-ed me!   When noth-ing
    e-ven me,   e-ven me,

else could help, Love lift-ed me;.   Love lift-ed me.

Love Lifted Me

1912

My hands also I will lift up to Your commandments, Which I love, And I will meditate on Your statutes. Psalm 119:48 (NKJV)

T he two huddled together, working line by line, bar by bar, composing this hymn in tandem. The words were jotted down by James Rowe, and the music was hammered out at the piano by his friend, Howard E. Smith, whose hands were so twisted from arthritis that his friends wondered how he could play the piano at all. But there they were, James pacing back and forth while Howard banged away the melody. When they finished, the world had "Love Lifted Me."

James Rowe was a New Year's baby, born in Devonshire, England, on the first day of 1865. His father, John Rowe, was a copper miner. As a young man, James went to work for the Irish government, but when he was in his mid-twenties, he decided to immigrate to the United States. He settled down in Albany, New York, got married, and found a job with the railroad. He later became superintendent of the Hudson River Humane Society in Albany before eventually becoming a full-time writer. He composed hymns and edited music journals for several publishers. His last years were spent in Wells, Vermont, where he supported himself by writing messages for greeting card publishers, working alongside his daughter who was an artist.

During his lifetime, James claimed to have written more than 19,000 song texts. James Rowe and Howard Smith created "Love Lifted Me" in Saugatuck, Connecticut, in 1912, and sold the copyright to Charles Tillman, who transferred it to Robert Coleman in 1915 for one hundred dollars.

Several of James' other hymns are well known, including "I Choose Jesus," "I Would Be Like Jesus," and "Sweeter as the Days Go By." Among his lesser-known songs is one entitled, "God Holds the Future in His Hands."

Dread not the things that are ahead,
The burdens great, the sinking sands,
The thorns that o'er the path are spread,
God holds the future in His hands.

God holds the future in His hands
And every heart He understands.
On Him depend, He is your Friend,
He holds the future in His hands.

To Canaan's Land I'm on My Way

William M. Golden

William M. Golden

1. To Ca-naan's land I'm on my way, Where the soul (of man) nev-er dies;
2. A rose is bloom-ing there for me, Where the soul (of man) nev-er dies;
3. A love-light beams a - cross the foam, Where the soul (of man) nev-er dies;
4. I'm on my way to that fair land, Where the soul (of man) nev-er dies;

My dark-est night will turn to day, Where the soul (of man) nev-er dies.
And I will spend e - ter-ni-ty, Where the soul (of man) nev-er dies.
It shines to light the shores of home, Where the soul (of man) nev-er dies.
Where there will be no part-ing hand, Where the soul (of man) nev-er dies.

No sad fare - wells, no tear - dimmed eyes,
Dear friends, there'll be no sad fare-wells, There'll be no tear-dimmed eyes,

Where all is love, and the soul nev - er dies.
Where all is peace and joy and love, and the soul of man nev - er dies.

To Canaan's Land I'm on My Way
1914

Now may the God of peace Himself sanctify you completely; and may your whole spirit, soul, and body be preserved blameless at the coming of our Lord Jesus Christ.
1 Thessalonians 5:23 (NKJV)

When William Golden wrote this song in 1914, he called it "To Canaan's Land I'm on My Way." Hank Williams later recorded it under the title, "Where the Soul of Man Never Dies," and it became a hit. It's been sung by many gospel groups, but it was Duane Allen, lead singer for the Oak Ridge Boys, who gave me this wonderful story.

"In 1976, the Oak Ridge Boys were invited to Russia," Duane said. "The Communists were still in charge and the Iron Curtain was in place. Before we made the trip, the Soviets demanded the lyrics of all our songs for approval.

"Shortly after the tour began, we realized we needed more songs. At that time we didn't have country music hits. We only had our gospel music, and it was difficult to get those songs approved by the Communists.

"I wanted to use 'Where the Soul of Man Never Dies,' because we'd won a Grammy for it. But fearing it would be rejected by the censors, I submitted it under the original title, 'To Canaan's Land I'm On My Way.' The Soviets took the lyrics into a room, and half an hour later they called me in.

"We could sing the song, they said, if we changed the first line. They didn't know what 'Canaan' was. That word wasn't in their dictionaries. They asked if we would sing: 'To *Disneyland* I'm on my way . . .' They knew all about Disneyland.

"I was appalled, but after thinking a moment, I asked if we could sing, 'To *that fair land* I'm on my way.' That satisfied them, and it became one of our biggest hits of the tour.

"That evening after the concert," Duane added, "they loaded us onto a military bus for departure, and as we were getting ready to leave an old woman ran up and knocked on the glass. When I pulled down the window, she pitched in a note that fell to my feet. I bent over and picked it up, then turned to wave goodbye. To my horror, she was being dragged off and beaten by the authorities. Opening the note, I read her words, which I've never forgotten: 'Keep singing about Jesus,' said the note. 'There are still those over here who love His message.'"

Since Jesus Came Into My Heart

Rufus H. McDaniel

Charles H. Gabriel

1. What a won-der-ful change in my life has been wrought, Since Je - sus came
2. I have ceased from my wan - d'ring and go - ing a - stray, Since Je - sus came
3. I'm pos - sessed of a hope that is stead-fast and sure, Since Je - sus came
4. I shall go there to dwell in that Cit - y, I know, Since Je - sus came

in - to my heart! I have light in my soul, For which long I have sought,
in - to my heart; And my sins, which were man - y, are all washed a - way,
in - to my heart; And no dark clouds of doubt now my path - way ob - scure,
in - to my heart; And I'm hap - py, so hap - py, as on - ward I go,

Since Je - sus came in - to my heart.
Since Je - sus came in, came

heart, Since Je - sus came in - to my heart, Floods of joy o'er my
in - to my heart, Since Je - sus came in, came in - to my heart,

soul Like the sea bil - lows roll, Since Je - sus came in - to my heart.

Since Jesus Came Into My Heart

1914

Let not your heart be troubled; you believe in God, believe also in Me. John 14:1
(NKJV)

Rufus McDaniel, born in rural Ohio in 1850, was licensed to preach when he was only nineteen. He was soon afterward ordained into the Christian Church and married. His blessings were tripled by the births of Clarence, Minnie, and Herschel. Clarence, the firstborn, followed in his father's footsteps and became a minister in the Christian denomination. The daughter, Minnie, married an Ohio boy and lived nearby in Dayton. It was Herschel who broke his dad's heart by his untimely death in 1913.

After Rufus had buried his son, he realized anew that joy and contentment cannot be based on human affection or external gift. They flow from an endless relationship with our Lord Jesus Christ. Out of that experience, he wrote, "Since Jesus Came Into My Heart."

Rufus went on to pastor churches in southern Ohio for many years before retiring to Dayton to be near his daughter. He wrote over a hundred hymns, but this is the only one that has endured. It, too, would have been lost to us but for the great evangelist Billy Sunday, who counted it among his favorites.

This notice appeared among the obituaries in the *Dayton Daily News* on February 13, 1940:

REV. MCDANIEL, NOTED WRITER OF HYMNS, DIES.

The Rev. Rufus H. McDaniel, 90, retired Congregational Christian minister, died at 9 a.m. Tuesday at the home of the daughter, Mrs. Frank R. Liesenhoff . . . He had been ailing for some time, but had been seriously ill about one week. The Rev. McDaniel, who celebrated his ninetieth birthday on Jan. 29, composed and published more than one hundred hymns that have been used by all denominations, yet he received nothing in the way of cash remuneration. He was the guest on Ken Randolph's program over WHIO the day after he had celebrated his eighty-ninth birthday, and sang "Since Jesus Came Into My Heart," a hymn he wrote many years ago and which is now one of the best known of its type in evangelistic circles.

Ivory Palaces

Henry Barraclough   Henry Barraclough

1. My Lord has gar-ments so won-drous fine, And myrrh their tex-ture fills;
2. His life had al-so its sor-rows sore, For al-oes had a part;
3. His gar-ments too were in cas-sia dipped, With heal-ing in a touch;
4. In gar-ments glo-ri-ous He will come, To o-pen wide the door;

Its fra-grance reached to this heart of mine, With joy my be-ing thrills.
And when I think of the cross He bore, My eyes with tear-drops start.
Each time my feet in some sin have slipped, He took me from its clutch.
And I shall en-ter my heav'n-ly home, To dwell for-ev-er-more.

Out of the i-vo-ry pal-a-ces, In-to a world of woe,

On-ly His great, e-ter-nal love Made my Sav-ior go.

Ivory Palaces

1915

All Your garments are scented with myrrh and aloes and cassia, Out of the ivory palaces, by which they have made You glad. Psalm 45:8 (NKJV)

Billy Graham enjoys telling the story behind this hymn which was written near his home. Billy and Ruth Graham live in a rambling log cabin at the end of a steep, winding road outside Asheville, North Carolina. At the bottom of the hill is Montreat Conference Center that, for a hundred years, has served as a major conference grounds for the Presbyterian Church (USA).

In the summer of 1915, evangelist J. Wilbur Chapman was preaching at Montreat Conference Center. He brought his famous song leader, Charles M. Alexander, and his young pianist, Henry Barraclough.

Barraclough, twenty-four, had begun studying organ and piano at age five in his native England. As a young man, he worked in insurance, and then became secretary for a Member of Parliament. When Chapman met him and recognized his musical talents, he invited him to join his team as pianist. With great excitement, Barraclough traveled to Montreat as part of an evangelistic tour.

One evening, Chapman spoke of Psalm 45, and the eighth verse of the psalm was Dr. Chapman's text: "All thy garments shall smell of myrrh, and aloes, and cassia, out of the ivory palaces . . ." Chapman was speaking on one of his favorite themes, having previously written a book entitled *Ivory Palaces of the King*. On this evening in Montreat, he spoke with such tender passion that the young pianist was deeply moved.

After the service, some of Chapman's team took a drive through the mountains and stopped at a country store. Sitting in the front seat of the car, Barraclough scribbled down the words to "Ivory Palaces." Returning to the conference hotel, he developed his hymn through the night, and the next morning it was sung as a duet at the conference by Mrs. Alexander and Albert Brown.

Mr. Graham adds an additional link in the story, as well. It was Albert Brown, one of the original singers, who, years later, introduced Graham to song leader Cliff Barrows at the Ben Lippen Conference Center in Asheville. Thus began another great evangelistic partnership that has lasted over fifty years.*

---

*Some of the information for this story came from "Ivory Palaces: A Hymn Story by Billy Graham," in *Crusader Hymns and Hymn Stories* (Minneapolis: The Billy Graham Evangelistic Association, 1967), pp. 25–26.

Living for Jesus

Thomas O. Chisholm

C. Harold Lowden

1. Liv-ing for Je - sus, a life that is true.
2. Liv-ing for Je - sus Who died in my place,
3. Liv-ing for Je - sus, wher - ev - er I am.
4. Liv-ing for Je - sus, through earth's lit - tle while,

Striv - ing to please Him in all that I do.
Bear - ing on Cal - v'ry, my sin and dis - grace.
Do - ing each du - ty in His ho - ly name.
My dear - est trea - sure, the light of His smile.

Yield - ing al - le - giance, glad heart - ed and free.
Such love con - strains me, to an - swer His call,
Will - ing to suf - fer af - flic - tion or loss.
Seek - ing the lost ones, He died to re - deem.

This is the path - way of bless - ing for me.
Fol - low His lead - ing and give Him my all.
Deem - ing each tri - al a part of my cross.
Bring - ing the wea - ry to find rest in Him.

Living for Jesus
1917

And I give them eternal life, and they shall never perish; neither shall anyone snatch them out of My hand. John 10:28 (NKJV)

I n the 1950s, a frail figure would be seen on the boardwalks of Ocean Park, New Jersey. Though modest and shy, he was warmly greeted as he ducked in and out of shops and cafés. Behind his back people would whisper. "See that man? He's the author of 'Great Is Thy Faithfulness,' 'Living for Jesus,' and 'O to Be Like Thee.'"

His name was Thomas Obadiah Chisholm, and he had settled into the Methodist Home for the Aged in Ocean Park to enjoy his sunset years.

Thomas was born in 1866, in a log cabin in Franklin, Kentucky. His education was sparse, yet at age sixteen he began teaching in the same one-room schoolhouse he had attended as a child. Four years later, the local newspaper, *The Franklin Advocate*, offered him a job.

When Thomas was twenty-seven, the founder and president of Asbury College, Dr. H. C. Morrison, came to Franklin to preach. During that revival, Thomas found Christ as his Savior, and Dr. Morrison soon asked him to become office editor and business manager for the *Pentecostal Herald*, headquartered in Louisville.

In 1903, Thomas applied for ordination in the Methodist church and accepted the pastorate of a church in Scottsville, Kentucky. He labored there a single year before his health collapsed, forcing him to move to Winona Lake, Indiana, where his family had property. There he supported himself by selling insurance.

Thomas wrote poems for personal therapy, some of which were published and came to the attention of pastor/musician C. Harold Lowden of New Jersey. One day in 1915, Lowden composed a song for the children in his church. He called it the "Sunshine Song," and used it during a Children's Day service. Two years later, as Lowden prepared to publish a songbook, he wanted to use his tune but felt the words were lacking. He contacted Thomas, asking him to compose new words.

"[Thomas] returned it to me," Lowden later wrote, "saying he didn't have the slightest idea as to the method used in writing words to music. Immediately, I sent the material back to him, telling him I believed God led me to select him."

Since Thomas couldn't read music, he asked his daughter to hum the melody over and over until he understood it enough to compose suitable words. Thus was born "Living for Jesus." It was published in Lowden's collection of hymns, *Uplifting Songs,* in 1917.

Saved!

Oswald Jeffrey Smith

Roger M. Hickman

1. Saved! Saved! Saved! My sins are all for-giv'n,
2. Saved! Saved! Saved! By grace and grace a-lone.
3. Saved! Saved! Saved! O joy be-yond com-pare!

Christ is mine! I'm on my way to heav'n,
Oh, what won-drous love to me was shown,
Christ my life, and I His con-stant care,

Once a guilt-y sin-ner, lost, un-done,
In my stead Christ Je-sus bled and died.
Yield-ing all and trust-ing Him a-lone,

Now a child of God, Saved thro' His Son.
Bore my sins, for me was cru-ci-fied.
Liv-ing now each mo-ment as His own.

Saved!
1917

And she will bring forth a Son, and you shall call His name JESUS, for He will save His people from their sins. Matthew 1:21 (NKJV)

Canadian Oswald J. Smith came to Christ as a teen during an evangelistic campaign by R. A. Torrey and Charles Alexander. He enrolled in Bible College at eighteeen to be a missionary, but was later turned down for service due to poor health. So he began preaching and writing hymns.

In his autobiography, he wrote, "Never will I forget the thrill that was mine when I saw the first printed copies of two of my hymns. It was in 1914 when I was twenty-four. The music was by Dr. D. B. Towner, and it was he who sent them to me. My whole being was electrified as I gazed at them. The ecstasy of that moment will never be erased. I was then in South Chicago. But in those early days only a few of my hymns ever really saw the light of day. I wrote scores, but for years it was a struggle with many discouraging experiences."

One of his earliest hymns was "Saved!" published in 1918. "It was born in Toronto in the year 1917," wrote Smith, "when I was twenty-seven. The music was written by Roger M. Hickman. Arthur W. McKee was the first to introduce it. To hear the great Massey Hall audience sing this hymn during the Paul Rader campaign was an experience never to be forgotten. It is known and sung throughout America."

> *Saved! I'm saved thro' Christ, my all in all;*
> *Saved! I'm saved whatever may befall;*
> *He died upon the cross for me,*
> *He bore the awful penalty;*
> *And now I'm saved eternally—*
> *I'm saved! Saved! Saved!*

As a hymn writer, Oswald Smith may have struggled for recognition, but as a pastor he made his mark. Having been rejected for overseas service, he started a church in 1928 in Toronto to send out missionaries. It was known as the Cosmopolitan Tabernacle (now the Peoples Church). It became one of the strongest churches in Canada and one of the greatest missionary churches in the world.

Later in life when his hymns became more widely used (including the popular songs, "Then Jesus Came" and "The Song of the Soul Set Free"), Smith wrote, "I have never written in a mechanical way just for the sake of writing. As I rule I wait until I am passing through some great crisis, and then I cannot help writing. And because they have been born out of personal experiences, they appeal to others."*

---

*Oswald J. Smith, *The Story of My Life* (London: Marshall, Morgan, & Scott, 1962), pp. 109–112.

Lead Me to Calvary

Jennie Evelyn Hussey

William J. Kirkpatrick

1. King of my life, I crown Thee now, Thine shall the glo - ry be;
2. Show me the tomb where Thou wast laid, Ten - der - ly mourned and wept;
3. Let me, like Ma - ry, through the gloom, Come with a gift to Thee;
4. May I be will - ing, Lord, to bear, Dai - ly my cross for Thee;

Lest I for - get Thy thorn crowned brow, Lead me to Cal - va - ry.
An - gels in robes of light ar - rayed, Guard - ed Thee whilst Thou slept.
Show to me now the emp - ty tomb, Lead me to Cal - va - ry.
E - ven Thy cup of grief to share, Thou hast borne all for me.

Lest I for - get Geth - sem - a - ne, Lest I for - get Thine ag - o - ny,

Lest I for - get Thy love for me, Lead me to Cal - va - ry.

Lead Me to Calvary
1921

And when they had come to the place called Calvary, there they crucified Him . . .
Luke 23:33 (NKJV)

J ennie Hussey was born in Henniker, New Hampshire, on February 8, 1874, and lived most of her life in a farmhouse where four generations of her Quaker ancestors had lived. Much of her time was devoted to her helpless, invalid sister, but Jennie wasn't known to complain or grumble. She displayed a cheerful personality. Whenever weary, she would open her Bible and turn to the story of Calvary, finding there fresh strength.

Jennie eventually became disabled with deformative arthritis, but her attitude remained positive. "Please, Lord," she said, "make me willing to bear my cross daily without complaining because you bore yours for me." It was out of that experience that she wrote "Lead Me to Calvary," with its last verse:

May I be willing, Lord, to bear daily my cross for Thee;
Even Thy cup of grief to share—Thou hast borne all for me.

When Jennie was baptized in the First Baptist Church of Concord, New Hampshire, she told the pastor, "I've spent so much of my life hidden away in the country, and I'd like to have the opportunity before God takes me home to tell everybody (that) I love Jesus." Her request was fulfilled in this famous hymn, along with approximately one hundred fifty others that she wrote.

Jennie spent her last years in the Home for the Aged in Concord, New Hampshire, and passed away in 1958. Her remains were taken the seventeen miles back to Henniker, where she was buried in the Quaker Cemetery.

There's an interesting P.S. to her story. Civil War buffs know Jennie Hussey as the author of a famous poem called "The War Dog." It's the true story of a stray mutt named Sallie who became attached to one of the soldiers from Pennsylvania and followed him into battle. When her master fell in battle, the dog refused to leave his body. Sallie was "adopted" as the mascot of the 11th Regiment of Pennsylvania Volunteers, and she stayed with her soldiers until she was shot and killed at the Battle of Hatcher's Run, Virginia, in 1864. A cast bronze replica of Sallie stands today in Gettysburg National Military Park.

Sallie was a lady; she was a soldier too—
She marched beside the colors, our own red, white, and blue.
It was in the days of our Civil War that she lived her life so true. . . .

Only Believe

Paul Rader

Paul Rader

1. Fear not, lit - tle flock, from the cross to the throne, From death in - to
2. Fear not, lit - tle flock, He go - eth a - head, Your Shep - herd se -
3. Fear not, lit - tle flock, what - ev - er your lot; He en - ters all

life He went for His own; All pow - er in earth, all pow - er a -
lect - eth the path you must tread; The wa - ters of Ma - rah, He'll sweet - en for
rooms, "the doors be - ing shut." He nev - er for - sakes, He nev - er is

bove, Is giv - en to Him for the flock of His love.
thee, He drank all the bit - ter in Geth - sem - a - ne. On - ly be - lieve,
gone, So count on His presence in dark - ness and dawn.

on - ly be - lieve; All things are pos - si - ble, on - ly be - lieve;

On - ly be - lieve, on - ly be - lieve; All things are pos - si - ble, on - ly be - lieve.

Only Believe

As soon as Jesus heard the word that was spoken, He said to the ruler of the synagogue, "Do not be afraid; only believe." Mark 5:36 (NKJV)

W ritten very clearly upon my mind is the memory of the night I was converted when a boy of nine years," testified evangelist Paul Rader in a 1930s-era sermon at Chicago's Moody Memorial Church. Paul was traveling with his preacher-dad in Cheyenne, Wyoming, and a revival was in progress. "A few soldiers from a nearby fort were at the altar, and more grown folks, but no children," said Paul. But God was dealing mightily with the boy, and that evening back at their lodgings his father led him to Christ.

"The days I spent with my father as we traveled together while he preached to the men of the plains, hundreds of miles from any railroad, gave my soul a firm grasp of the simple gospel as he saw it," said Paul. "There came to me a great desire in those days to preach the gospel . . . ."

Paul enrolled in a university in Colorado. During class one day, a professor questioned the reliability of the Bible. "I stayed at the close of the class," Paul later said, "and with cutting sarcasm he gave me to understand that my simple faith in the Bible came from my ignorance."

Paul's crisis of faith eventually soured him to Scripture. "I then gave up and quit preaching . . . I vowed I would never preach again." Leaving school, Paul, who was a splendid athlete, became a boxer, then a boxing promoter, then the public relations agent for an oil company—but God wasn't through with him.

Sometime about 1912, "I was walking the streets of New York when God spoke to my heart in a tender pleading way, just as He used to do when I was a boy. I almost ran to my room and dropped on my knees beside the bed. . . . Three days and nights the fight with self lasted. At four on the third morning I took the splendid Bible given me . . . and threw it in the air above the bed, letting it light and settle into stillness. I had promised God that when the old Book became still on the bed I would give up and obey Him at any cost."

Paul Rader went on to become one of the most visionary, progressive, effective, and influential evangelists of the early twentieth century—and, appropriately, the author of:

Only believe, only believe;
All things are possible, only believe.

Turn Your Eyes Upon Jesus

Helen H. Lemmel   Helen H. Lemmel

1. O soul, are you wea-ry and trou - bled? No light in the
2. Thro' death in - to life ev - er - last - ing He passed, and we
3. His word shall not fail you He prom - ised; Be - lieve Him, and

dark-ness you see? There's light for a look at the Sav - ior, And
fol - low Him there; O - ver us sin no more hath do - min - ion For
all will be well; Then go to a world that is dy - ing, His

life more a - bun - dant and free!
more than con - qu'rors we are!   Turn your eyes up-on Je - sus,
per - fect sal - va - tion to tell!

Look full in His won - der - ful face,   And the things of

earth will grow strange-ly dim In the light of His glo - ry and grace.

Turn Your Eyes Upon Jesus

1922

Let us fix our eyes on Jesus, the author and perfecter of our faith, who for the joy set before him endured the cross, scorning its shame, and sat down at the right hand of the throne of God. Hebrews 12:2 (NIV)

 he Bible is full of verses about keeping our eyes on the Lord, but two are especially dear to me. I found them once during a difficult period, and I've kept them in my prayer journal ever since: Matthew 17:8 and Psalm 34:5.*

When they looked up, they saw no one except Jesus.
Those who look to Him are radiant.

That's the theme of this beloved hymn by Helen Lemmel. Helen was born in England in 1863, and came to America with her family when she was a child. Her father, a Wesleyan Methodist preacher, settled in Wisconsin. There Helen spent her teen years, growing in musical interest and ability. Her parents provided the best training possible, including a stint in Germany, studying with the masters.

After returning to America, Helen found herself in demand, traveling widely and giving concerts in auditoriums and churches across the Midwest. She could have been a popular singer in the secular world, but Helen's greatest desire was to serve Christ with her voice. Accordingly, she joined the Moody Bible Institute and trained young people in music and song.

In 1918, Helen, fifty-four, was visiting a friend who showed her a gospel tract by Lillias Trotter, missionary to North Africa, entitled, "Focused." There Helen read these words: "So then, turn your eyes upon Him, look full into His face and you will find that the things of earth will acquire a strange new dimness."

Helen later described how she turned that simple sentence into a famous hymn: "Suddenly, as if commanded to stop and listen, I stood still, and singing in my soul and spirit was the chorus, with not one conscious moment of putting word to work to make rhyme, or note to note to make melody. The verses were written the same week, after the usual manner of composition, but nonetheless dictated by the Holy Spirit."

The song was published in Britain in 1922, and two years later in the United States.

After her retirement, Helen moved to Seattle where she passed away at the age of ninety-seven, in 1961. She had written over five hundred hymns, as well as many children's songs. She also composed and published several volumes of poetry and a popular book for children entitled *Story of the Bible.*

Her long life was spent looking up, seeing Jesus only, and reflecting His radiance to others.

---

*New International Version

In My Heart There Rings a Melody

Elton M. Roth

Elton M. Roth

1. I have a song that Je - sus gave me, It was sent from
2. I love the Christ who died on Cal - v'ry, For He washed my
3. 'Twill be my end - less theme in glo - ry, With the an - gels

heav'n a - bove; There nev - er was a sweet - er mel - o - dy, 'Tis a
sins a - way; He put with - in my heart a mel - o - dy, And I
I will sing; 'Twill be a song with glo - rious har - mo - ny, When the

mel - o - dy of love.
know it's there to stay.
courts of heav - en ring.

In my heart there rings a mel - o - dy, There

rings a mel - o - dy with heav - en's har - mo - ny; In my heart there

rings a mel - o - dy, There rings a mel - o - dy of love.

Words & Music: Elton M. Roth. © Copyright 1924. Renewal 1951 Hope Publishing Co.,
Carol Stream, IL 60188. All rights reserved. Used by permission.

In My Heart There Rings a Melody

1923

Let the word of Christ dwell in you richly in all wisdom, teaching and admonishing one another in psalms and hymns and spiritual songs, singing with grace in your hearts to the Lord. Colossians 3:16 (NKJV)

T he great evidence of being "Spirit-filled" is singing, according to Ephesians 5:18, 19: "Be filled with the Spirit, speaking to one another in psalms and hymns and spiritual songs, singing and making melody in your heart to the Lord." That's the theme of this happy little gospel chorus with its irresistible melody. It's been a favorite for many years around the world.

Its author, Elton Menno Roth, was born during the Thanksgiving season of 1891. He led his first church choir when he was only fourteen. After attending Moody Bible Institute and Fort Wayne Bible School in his native state of Indiana, he studied music in Europe. Elton became a singing evangelist and song leader for evangelistic meetings. In the 1930s, he formed a popular singing group called the Ecclesia Choir that performed across the country. He was also a noted instructor of music at a number of Christian schools and colleges. Los Angeles became his home in his latter years, and he passed away there at age sixty on the last day of 1951.

"I Have a Song That Jesus Gave Me" was one of the first of the one hundred or so hymns written by Elton Roth. He composed this hymn in 1923 while conducting evangelistic meetings in Texas. "One hot summer afternoon," he wrote, "I took a little walk to the cotton mill just outside of town. On my way back through the burning streets . . . I became weary with the oppressive heat, and paused at a church on the corner. The door being open, I went in. There were no people in the pews, no minister in the pulpit. Everything was quiet, with a lingering of the sacred presence. I walked up and down the aisle and began singing, 'In My Heart There Rings a Melody,' then hurried into the pastor's study to find some paper. I drew a staff and sketched the melody, remaining there for an hour or more to finish the song, both words and music. That evening I introduced it by having over two hundred boys and girls sing it at the open-air meeting, after which the audience joined in the singing. I was thrilled as it seemed my whole being was transformed by the song."

Jesus Is the Sweetest Name I Know

Lela B. Long

Lela B. Long

1. There have been names that I have loved to hear, But never has there
2. There is no name in earth or heav'n above, That we should give such
3. And some day I shall see Him face to face To thank and praise Him

been a name so dear To this heart of mine as the name divine, The
honor and such love As the blessed name; let us all acclaim That
for His wondrous grace Which He gave to me when He made me free; The

precious, precious name of Jesus.
wondrous, glorious name of Jesus. Jesus is the sweetest name I
blessed Son of God called Jesus.

know, And He's just the same as His lovely name, And that's the reason

why I love Him so; O Jesus is the sweetest name I know.

Jesus Is the Sweetest Name I Know

1924

Repent, and let every one of you be baptized in the name of Jesus Christ for the remission of sins; and you shall receive the gift of the Holy Spirit. Acts 2:38 (NKJV)

We're indebted to gospel songwriter and historian, Al Smith, for the story of this hymn by Lela B. Long. Smith collected it firsthand from Dr. P. W. Philpot, who told him:

"While I was pastor of Moody Church in Chicago, I received a frantic phone call about 2 o'clock in the morning from the Stephens Hotel. The voice on the line pleaded with me to come, for a young lady was very ill and very disturbed. At the hotel I found a very sick young lady who from outward appearances did not have long to live. I spent some time talking with her and was eventually able to lead her to the Lord. As I left, her family thanked me and assured me they would keep me informed as to her progress. Late the next day, having not heard from them and anxious to know how she was, I phoned the hotel and was informed that they had checked out and were en route to California, which was their home. For the remaining years of my stay in Chicago, I did not again receive any communication from them. I then moved to California where I became pastor of the Church of the Open Door in Los Angeles.

"One Sunday afternoon after the service, who should come to see me but the three people I had met at the hotel in Chicago those many years before. They told me that their leaving Chicago had been so sudden they had forgotten to advise me. That past week they had seen a church ad in the paper and had come to thank me for my help and to apologize for not advising me sooner of what had transpired. The young lady especially thanked me for leading her to Christ and testified to the fact that her life had been wonderfully changed and that now she was using a special talent the Lord had given her in music, for Him. The talent was writing gospel songs. With that she handed me a manuscript of a new song saying, 'I have written this especially for you in remembrance of the day that you introduced me to the most wonderful person I have ever known.' As I opened the manuscript I saw a beautifully written song she had titled, 'Jesus Is the Sweetest Name I Know.'"*

---

*Condensed from Alfred B. Smith's *Treasury of Hymn Histories.*

I'll Fly Away

Albert E. Brumley

Albert E. Brumley

© Copyright 1932 in "Wonderful Message" by Hartford Music Co. Renewed 1960 by Alfred E. Brumley & Sons/SESAC (admin. by ICG). All rights reserved. Used by permission.

I'll Fly Away
1932

Therefore you now have sorrow; but I will see you again and your heart will rejoice, and your joy no one will take from you. John 16:22 (NKJV)

I *could* tell you this old Southern hymn was written by a sacred soul on his knees with Psalm 90 open before him: "The days of our lives are seventy years; and if by reason of strength they are eighty years, yet their boast is only labor and sorrow; for it is soon cut off, and we fly away."

The truth, however, is a little plainer.

Albert E. Brumley was born on a cotton farm near Spiro, Oklahoma, in 1905. The medium of radio was gaining popularity as he grew up, and one of the most requested songs was a sad ballad called "If I Had the Wings of an Angel" which said:

> *Now if I had the wings of an angel,*
> *Over these prison walls I would fly,*
> *I'd fly to the arms of my poor darling,*
> *And there I'd be willing to die.*

One hot Oklahoma day, Albert was in the fields picking cotton and singing this song. The thought of flying away suddenly seemed quite appealing to him, and he began composing "I'll Fly Away" on the spot. "I was dreaming of flying away from that cotton field when I wrote 'I'll Fly Away,'" he later said. The middle verse of Albert's song echoes the old prison ballad when it says:

> *When the shadows of this life have grown, I'll fly away;*
> *Like a bird from prison bars has flown, I'll fly away.*

Of course, "I'll Fly Away" is about far more than escaping cotton fields. It expressed Brumley's personal hope of eternal life through Jesus Christ. It was one of a number of gospel songs he wrote during those days, but all of them were stashed away in drawers and boxes, unpublished.

Two years later, Albert married Goldie Schell, whom he met while teaching a singing school in Powell, Missouri. With her encouragement, Albert mailed "I'll Fly Away" to the Hartford Music Company. It was published in 1932, and shortly afterward, Albert was hired by Hartford for $12.50 a month. He spent thirty-four years writing for the Hartford and Stamps/Baxter companies before forming the Albert E. Brumley & Sons Music Company. In all, Albert wrote over eight hundred songs and became one of the most respected names in the development of twentieth-century Southern gospel music.

Wherever He Leads, I'll Go

B. B. McKinney

B. B. McKinney

1. "Take up Thy cross and fol-low Me," I heard my Mas-ter say; "I
2. He drew me clos-er to His side, I sought His will to know, And
3. It may be through the shad-ows dim, Or o'er the storm-y sea, I
4. My heart, my life, my all I bring To Christ who loves me so; He

gave my life to ran-som Thee, Sur-ren-der your all to-day." Wher-
in that will I now a-bide; Wher-ev-er He leads, I'll go.
take my cross and fol-low Him Wher-ev-er He lead-eth me.
is my Mas-ter, Lord, and King, Wher-ev-er He leads I'll go.

ev-er He leads, I'll go, Wher-ev-er He leads, I'll go, I'll

fol-low my Christ who loves me so; Wher-ev-er He leads, I'll go.

Words & Music: B. B. McKinney. © Copyright 1936. Published by Broadman Press. Used by permission.

Wherever He Leads, I'll Go

1936

Then he said to them all: "If anyone would come after me, he must deny himself and take up his cross daily and follow me." Luke 9:23 (NIV)

T he twentieth century produced no greater hymnist than Baylus Benjamin Mc-Kinney, who wrote such classics as: "Breathe on Me," "Have Faith in God," "Send a Great Revival," "Satisfied with Jesus," "Lord, Lay Some Soul Upon My Heart," "Let Others See Jesus in You," and "The Nail-Scarred Hand."

McKinney was born in Heflin, Louisiana during the summer of 1886. He attended Southwestern Baptist Theological Seminary and after further training in music, he returned to the seminary as a member of the music faculty. When the Great Depression sent the seminary into financial crisis, McKinney resigned to serve as assistant pastor of the Travis Avenue Baptist Church in Fort Worth.

In 1935, McKinney was named music editor for the Baptist Sunday School Board of the Southern Baptist Convention. In January of the following year, he traveled to Clanton, Alabama, to participate in the Alabama Sunday School Convention, where he led the music. The featured speaker at the meetings was his good friend, R. S. Jones, missionary to Brazil. Late one afternoon as the two men had supper together, Jones told McKinney that the doctors were forbidding him from returning to Brazil. His health wouldn't allow it.

McKinney's heart went out to his friend, and he asked if Jones had any idea what he'd do now. "I don't know," said Jones, "but wherever He leads I'll go." It was a sentence that lingered in McKinney's mind. Returning to his hotel, McKinney sat down and wrote the words and music of this hymn before leaving for the convention session that night. After Jones had preached, McKinney told the audience of their earlier conversation, and handing a copy of the music to the organist, he sang it as a solo for the first time.

> *Wherever He leads, I'll go,*
> *Wherever He leads I'll go;*
> *I'll follow my Christ who loves me so;*
> *Wherever He leads I'll go.*

For the next several years, McKinney traveled widely among Southern Baptists, promoting the ministry of Christian music and leading singing in churches and conventions. On Sunday, September 7, 1952, McKinney left a conference in Ridgecrest, North Carolina, heading for Gatlinburg, Tennessee. Near Bryson City, North Carolina, he was killed in a car wreck.

He left behind a wife, two sons, several brothers, and a legacy of hundreds of hymns.

It Took a Miracle

John W. Peterson   John W. Peterson

1. My Father is om-nip-o-tent, And that you can't de-ny;
2. Though here His glo-ry has been shown, We still can't ful-ly see
3. The Bi-ble tells us of His pow'r And wis-dom all way through,

A God of might and mir-a-cles; 'Tis writ-ten in the sky.
The won-ders of His might, His throne; 'Twill take e-ter-ni-ty.
And ev-ery lit-tle bird and flow'r Are tes-ti-mo-nies, too.

It took a mir-a-cle to put the stars in place; It took a

mir-a-cle to hang the world in space. But when He saved my soul,

Cleansed and made me whole, It took a mir-a-cle of love and grace.

© Copyright 1948, renewed 1976 by John W. Peterson Music Company. All rights reserved.
Used by permission.

It Took a Miracle

1948

He is the Maker of the Bear and Orion, the Pleiades and the constellations of the south. He performs wonders that cannot be fathomed, miracles that cannot be counted. Job 9:9, 10 (NIV)

John W. Peterson's life reads like a novel. He was born in Kansas, where his brothers, Bill and Bob, lived a wild and dangerous life of "boozing, gambling, fast driving, and sheriff-baiting."

Then one night Bill came home, took his mother in his arms, kissed her, and said, "Mother, I have found your Christ as my Savior." The change in him was immediate and dramatic. Soon Bob, too, was saved along with other members of the family. Then John, twelve, gave his heart to Christ as well. The brothers became traveling evangelists, and John often joined them on their trips, singing at the meetings.

When World War II began, John joined the Air Force and became a pilot, who repeatedly risked his life while transporting men and materials over the fabled "China Hump." In his spare time he studied the Bible and wrote gospel songs. When the war ended, John enrolled in the Moody Bible Institute of Chicago.

"I sat in a classroom at Moody one day when the lecturer said something that started me thinking in a concentrated way about the grace and love of God. . . . Soon I lost contact with the lecture, and my mind turned back to my childhood when I had seen the radical change in the lives of my brothers Bob and Bill through the power of the gospel. I relived my own conversion—to me such a miraculous thing. . . .

"My thoughts raced on to the flights over the Himalayas, the spectacular power of God revealed in those electrical storms, the majesty of the mountains themselves, the incredible variety of the jungle, and the star-filled nights of dazzling beauty high in the air.

"As these scenes flashed through my memory, I began to focus on the element of the miraculous in all of God's work, creation, and redemption. The words of a song were forming in my mind, and before the class period was over the chorus was all thought out. I hurried over to the music building, found a vacant studio, and started to write:

> *It took a miracle to put the stars in place;*
> *It took a miracle to hang the world in space;*
> *But when he saved my soul,*
> *Cleansed and made me whole,*
> *It took a miracle of love and grace!"**

---

*Adapted from *The Miracle Goes On* by John W. Peterson with Richard Engquist (Grand Rapids: Zondervan, 1976), pp. 54–62 and 143–144.

Heaven Came Down

John W. Peterson   John W. Peterson

© Copyright 1961, renewed 1989 by John W. Peterson Music Company. All rights reserved.
Used by permission.

Heaven Came Down
1961

The heavens declare His righteousness, And all the peoples see His glory. Psalm 97:6 (NKJV)

As a teenager, John W. Peterson dreamed of being a singer and soloist. He often sang on local radio programs and in churches. "Only in singing did I feel competent and confident," he wrote. "Here was at least one place where I could excel. I knew it, and I made the most of it."

One summer John got a job in a factory, earning fifteen cents an hour at a machine making canvas for wheat binders. The machines were so noisy he sang at the top of his lungs, hours on end, making up melodies and imagining he was on stage.

John realized too late that he was ruining his voice. "I put such a terrific strain on my faltering voice," he wrote, "through overuse and inexperience that I damaged it beyond repair. When I realized fully what had happened, that my voice would never again be beautiful, I suffered such an emotional shock that it took months before I recovered."

Looking back now, John is grateful. "If that had not happened, I might never have developed as a writer," he wrote. "With my voice damaged, I turned more and more to writing and that talent was allowed to emerge and develop. What at first seemed a tragedy was used for good, and the course of my life began to take shape."

Today John W. Peterson is called the "Dean of Modern Hymn Writers." He's the author of such favorites as "So Send I You," "It Took a Miracle," "Surely Goodness and Mercy," "Jesus Led Me All the Way," "No One Understands Like Jesus," and "I Believe in Miracles."

"Heaven Came Down," one of John's most popular compositions, was written during the summer of 1961. He was ministering at Montrose Bible Conference Grounds in Montrose, Pennsylvania. During one of the sessions, an opportunity was given for people to share a word of testimony. A man known as "Old Jim" rose to his feet and told of how he had come to Christ. "It seemed like Heaven came down and glory filled my soul," he said.

"Right away I sensed that it would be a fine title for a song," John wrote, "so I wrote it down and later in the week completed the song. It became a favorite almost immediately."*

CHORUS:

Heaven came down and glory filled my soul (filled my soul),
When at the cross the Savior made me whole (made me whole);
My sins were washed away and my night turned to day,
Heaven came down and glory filled my soul (filled my soul)!

---

*Adapted from *The Miracle Goes On* by John W. Peterson with Richard Engquist (Grand Rapids: Zondervan, 1976), pp. 71–72.

Because He Lives

Gloria Gaither and William J. Gaither

William J. Gaither

1. God sent His Son, they called Him Je-sus; He came to love, heal and for-give. He lived and died, to buy my par-don. An emp-ty grave is there to prove my Sav-ior lives!

2. How sweet to hold a new-born ba-by, And feel the pride, and joy he gives; But great-er still the calm as-sur-ance, This child can face un-cer-tain days be-cause He lives.

3. And then one day I'll cross that riv-er, I'll fight life's fi-nal war with pain; And then as death gives way to vic-tory, I'll see the lights of glo-ry and I'll know He reigns.

Be-cause He lives, I can face to-mor-row. Be-cause He lives, all fear is gone; Be-cause I know He holds the fu-ture, And life is worth the liv-ing, Just be-cause He lives!

Copyright © 1971 by William J. Gaither. All rights reserved. Used by permission of Gaither Music Company.

Because He Lives

1971

There is hope in your future, says the LORD. Jeremiah 31:17 (NKJV)

As I prepared this volume of hymn stories, Gloria Gaither graciously shared with me the background for this beloved song:

When Bill and I started our family in the sixties, racial tensions were tearing the country apart. Civil rights activists had suffered and some had been killed. The Vietnam conflict was claiming thousands of lives, and tensions boiled over on university campuses. Many young people were growing disillusioned and "dropping out."

In this climate, Bill and I sought to write songs with lasting answers to the turmoil of the human spirit. But in the fall of 1969, several things happened to test the reality of our own convictions. We realized we were expecting another baby. Though we had always intended to have another child, we weren't planning on a baby so soon. My body hadn't quite recovered from the last pregnancy. Making matters worse, Bill contracted mononucleosis, which left him exhausted and depressed.

This combination of national turmoil and personal trouble discouraged us, and we occasionally asked each other, "If the world is like this now, what will it be in fifteen or sixteen years for our baby? What will this child face?"

While pondering and praying about these things, we came to realize anew that our courage doesn't come from a stable world, for the world has never been stable. Jesus Himself was born in the cruelest of times. No, we have babies, raise families, and risk living because the Resurrection is true!

Our baby arrived safe and sound, and we named him Benjamin, which means "most beloved son." A few weeks later "Because He Lives" was born in our hearts and poured from our souls:

> *How sweet to hold our newborn baby*
> *And feel the pride and joy he gives;*
> *But greater still, the calm assurance—*
> *This child can face uncertain days because He lives.*

Over the years this song has reassured us that our Lord's Resurrection is the central truth of life. Because He lives, we can face tomorrow. Many times since, as our children grew, our business-life changed, our fortunes shifted, or our direction clouded, our family has found assurance in this very personal song.

It's "our song," but we're grateful others have loved it, too.

Join All the Glorious Names

Isaac Watts, stanzas 2 and 3 Robert J. Morgan

John Darwall

1. Join all the glo - rious names, Of wis - dom, love and pow'r, That ev - er mor - tals knew, That an - gels ev - er bore: All are too mean to speak His worth, Too poor to set my Sav - ior forth.

2. The Babe of Beth - le - hem, the Faith - ful Wit - ness, He Is first and last, was dead, now lives to set us free. He washed our sins. He is the King, the Lord, the Word, to Him we sing.

3. Al - pha, O - me - ga He, One like the Son of Man, Ar - rayed in light, He reigned be - fore the world be - gan. He was, and is, and is to come our Glo - rious Lord, God's on - ly Son.

Join All the Glorious Names (Revisited)

2004

Thus says the LORD, the King of Israel, And his Redeemer, the LORD of hosts: "I am the First and I am the Last; Besides Me there is no God." Isaiah 44:6 (NKJV)

I want to plant an idea in your head, especially if you're a pastor. In researching our great hymns, I noticed that some of the richest were written by pastors for their weekly sermons. John Newton, author of "Amazing Grace" is a great example. He often ended his message with a hymn summarizing the truths he had just preached and it provided us with some of our richest hymnology.

I've occasionally tried this myself. After speaking from a passage, we'll sing a stanza from a well-known hymn, and then add one or two new stanzas I've composed for the occasion. The congregation doesn't know it has just sung a "new" hymn; and though some realize the words seem strangely appropriate to the message, most worshipers don't know their pastor is the culprit. But if my theology, rhyme, and rhythm are reasonably good, the hymn brings the service to an inspiring finish.

Recently I preached on the names of Christ found in the first chapter of Revelation. For the closing hymn, we chose Isaac Watts's great hymn, "Join All the Glorious Names." With apologies to Watts, I added these two stanzas:

> *The Babe of Bethlehem, the Faithful Witness, He*
> *Is first and last, was dead, now lives to set us free.*
> *He washed our sins. He is the King, the Lord, the Word, to Him we sing.*

> *Alpha, Omega He, One like the Son of Man,*
> *Arrayed in light, He reigned before the world began.*
> *He was, and is, and is to come our Glorious Lord, God's only Son.*

On another occasion, I preached a Father's Day sermon from the book of Proverbs. We closed with the moving Irish hymn "Be Thou My Vision," and I wrote a second verse that expressed the truth of the sermon:

> *Bless thou our children that they may believe.*
> *Help us to guide them Thy Son to receive.*
> *Give us righteous garments, wise souls richly dressed,*
> *That our dear children may forever be blessed.*

One couple requested a copy of the words and created an engraving for their child's bedroom. It became their prayer of dedication as parents.

You, too, can write hymns to bless your church. Why not try it soon, before you forget?

301

Alphabetical by Title

Author/Songwriter

305

First Line of Hymn

A wonderful Savior is Jesus my Lord, 208
All for Jesus, all for Jesus!, 130
All people that on earth do dwell, 6
All things bright and beautiful, 74
Almost persuaded now to believe, 134
Angels we have heard on high, 92
Away in a manger, no crib for a bed, 198

Be still, my soul; the Lord is on thy side, 44
Beneath the cross of Jesus, 116
Break Thou the bread of life, 170

Children of the heavenly Father, 82
Christ for the world we sing, 122
Come, Christians, join to sing, 66
Come, Thou long expected Jesus, 40
Come, we that love the Lord, 18
Come, ye sinners, poor and needy, 46
Come, ye thankful people, come, 68

Deeper, deeper in the love of Jesus, 240
Down in the valley, with my Savior I would go, 176
Dying with Jesus, by death reckoned mine, 220

Encamped along the hills of light, 216

Faith of our fathers, living still, 78
Fall on your knees! O hear the angel voices!, 72
Far away the noise of strife, 262
Fear not, little flock, 282
For all the saints who from their labors rest, 98
From heav'n above to earth I come, 4

Give to the winds Thy fears, 30
Glorious things of Thee are spoken, 50
Go, tell it on the mountain, 256
God of our fathers, whose Almighty hand, 164
God sent His Son, they called Him Jesus, 298

Have you been to Jesus for the cleansing power?, 178
Holy Spirit, breathe on me, 180

I am Thine O Lord; I have heard Thy voice, 148
I have a song that Jesus gave me, 286
I have found a friend in Jesus, 186
I heard the bells on Christmas day, 96
I know not why God's wondrous grace, 190
I love Thy kingdom Lord, 56
I love to tell the story of unseen things above, 108
I must needs go home, 254
I was sinking deep in sin, 268
I will sing the wondrous story, 196
If thou but suffer God to guide thee, 10
If you are tired of the load of your sin, 238
I'll praise my Maker while I've breath, 26
I'm pressing on the upward way, 234
Immortal, invisible, God only wise, 166
In shady green pastures, so rich and so sweet, 244
In some way or other the Lord will provide, 222
I've a message from the Lord, 204
I've reached the land of joy divine, 156
I've wandered far away from God, 218

Jesu, joy of man's desiring, 14
Jesus is all the world to me, 246
Jesus is coming to earth again, 266
Jesus, keep me near the cross, 120
Jesus, Savior, pilot me, 132
Jesus, Thy blood and righteousness, 28
Join all the glorious names, 22
Join all the glorious names, 300
Joy to the world! The Lord is come, 24

King of my life, I crown Thee now, 280

Lead on, O King eternal, 202
Living for Jesus, a life that is true, 276
Look ye saints! The sight is glorious, 58

306